DE QUINCEY'S WORKS.

VOLUME II.

RECOLLECTIONS OF THE LAKES

AND THE

LAKE POETS

COLERIDGE, WORDSWORTH, AND SOUTHEY

BY

THOMAS DE QUINCEY

EDINBURGH
ADAM AND CHARLES BLACK
MDCCCLXII.

[*Reprinted 1881*]

PRINTED BY NEILL AND COMPANY, EDINBURGH.

RYDAL MOUNT

TO THE READER.

THE following brief extract from the life of De Quincey, in the "English Cyclopædia," edited by Charles Knight, may be appropriately placed here in connection with this volume :—

"It was in the year 1807 that De Quincey first made the acquaintance of Coleridge, Wordsworth, and Southey; and on quitting college in 1808 he took up his abode at the Lakes, and became one of the intellectual brotherhood there constituted by these men. Wilson was a resident at the Lakes about the same time. The difference between De Quincey and the Lakists was—that his element was exclusively Prose. Like Coleridge, but with peculiarities sufficient to distinguish him from that thinker, he philosophised, and analysed, and speculated in sympathy with the new literary movement of which the Lake party was a manifestation. He resided ten or eleven years at the Lakes; and during these ten or eleven years we are to suppose him increasing his knowledge of Greek, of German, and of Universal History and Literature.

"In point of time De Quincey preceded Carlyle as a literary medium between Germany and this country; and some of his earliest literary efforts were translations from Lessing, Richter, and other German authors.

"These literary efforts, begun while he was still a student at the Lakes, were continued with growing abundance after he left them in 1819."

CONTENTS.

RECOLLECTIONS OF THE LAKES.

EARLY MEMORIALS OF GRASMERE.

Soon after my return to Oxford in 1807-8, I received a letter from Miss Wordsworth, asking for any subscriptions I might succeed in obtaining, amongst my college friends, in aid of the funds then raising on behalf of an orphan family, who had become such by an affecting tragedy that had occurred within a few weeks from my visit to Grasmere.

Miss Wordsworth's simple but fervid memoir not being within my reach at this moment, I must trust to my own recollections and my own impressions to retrace the story; which, after all, is not much of a story to excite or to impress, unless for those who can find a sufficient interest in the trials and calamities of hard-working peasants, and can reverence the fortitude which, being lodged in so frail a tenement as the person of a little girl, not much, if anything, above nine years old, could face an occasion of sudden mysterious abandonment, and could tower up, during one night, into the perfect energies of womanhood, under the mere pressure of difficulty, and under the sense of new-born responsibilities awfully bequeathed to her, and in the most lonely, perhaps, of English habitations.

The little valley of Easedale, which, and the neighbourhood of which, were the scenes of these interesting events.

II.—A

is, on its own account, one of the most impressive solitudes amongst the mountains of the Lake district; and I
must pause to describe it. Easedale is impressive *as* a
solitude; for the depth of the seclusion is brought out and
forced more pointedly upon the feelings by the thin scattering of houses over its sides, and over the surface of what
may be called its floor. These are not above six at the
most; and one, the remotest of the whole, was untenanted
for all the thirty years of my acquaintance with the place.
Secondly, it is impressive from the excessive loveliness
which adorns its little area. This is broken up into small
fields and miniature meadows, separated, not—as too often
happens, with sad injury to the beauty of the Lake country—by stone walls, but sometimes by little hedgerows,
sometimes by little sparkling, pebbly " becks," lustrous to
the very bottom, and not too broad for a child's flying leap;
and sometimes by wild self-sown woodlands of birch, alder,
holly, mountain ash, and hazel, that meander through the
valley, intervening the different estates with natural sylvan
marches, and giving cheerfulness in winter by the bright
scarlet of their berries. It is the character of all the
northern English valleys, as I have already remarked—and
it is a character first noticed by Wordsworth—that they
assume, in their bottom areas, the level, floor-like shape,
making everywhere a direct angle with the surrounding
hills, and definitely marking out the margin of their out-
lines : whereas the Welsh valleys have too often the glaring
imperfection of the basin shape, which allows no sense of any
flat area or valley surface : the hills are already commencing at the very centre of what is called the level area. The
little valley of Easedale is, in this respect, as highly finished
as in every other; and in the Westmoreland spring, which
may be considered May and the earlier half of June, whilst

the grass in the meadows is yet short from the habit of
keeping the sheep on it until a much later period than
elsewhere (viz., until the mountains are so far cleared of
snow and the probability of storms, as to make it safe
to send them out on their summer migration), it follows naturally that the little fields in Easedale have the
most lawny appearance, and, from the humidity of the
Westmoreland * climate, the most verdant that it is
possible to imagine. But there is a third advantage
possessed by this Easedale, above other rival valleys, in
the sublimity of its mountain barriers. In one of its
many rocky recesses is seen a " force " (such is the local
name for a cataract), white with foam, descending at all
seasons with considerable strength, and, after the melting
of snows, with an Alpine violence. Follow the leading of
this " force " for three quarters of a mile, and you come to
a little mountain lake, locally termed a " tarn," † the very
finest and most gloomily sublime of its class. From this
tarn it was, I doubt not, though applying it to another,
that Wordsworth drew the circumstances of his general

* It is pretty generally known, perhaps, that Westmoreland and
Devonshire are the two rainiest counties in England. At Kirkby
Lonsdale, lying just on the outer margin of the Lake district, one-
fifth more rain is computed to fall than in the adjacent counties on
the same western side of England. But it is also notorious, that the
western side of the island universally is more rainy than the east.
Collins called it the showery west.

† A tarn is a lake, generally (perhaps always) a small one : and
always, as I think (but this I have heard disputed), lying above the
level of the inhabited valleys and the large lakes; and subject to this
farther restriction, first noticed by Wordsworth, that it has no main
feeder. Now, this latter accident of the *thing* at once explains and
authenticates my account of the *word*, viz., that it is the Danish word
taaren (*a trickling of tears*), a deposit of waters from the weeping of
rain down the smooth faces of the rocks.

description.   And far beyond this " enormous barrier,"
that thus imprisons the very winds, tower upwards the
aspiring heads (usually enveloped in cloud and mist) of
Glaramara, Bow Fell, and the other fells of Langdale
Head and Borrowdale.   Easedale, in its relation to Grasmere, is a chamber within a chamber, or rather a closet
within a chamber—a chapel within a cathedral—a little
private oratory within a chapel.   The sole approach, as I
have mentioned, is from Grasmere ; and some *one* outlet
there must inevitably be in every vale that can be interesting to a human occupant, since without water it would
not be habitable ; and running water must force an egress
for itself, and, consequently, an ingress for the reader and
myself : but, properly speaking, there is no other.   For,
when you explore the remoter end of the vale, at which
you suspect some communication with the world outside,
you find before you a most formidable amount of climbing,
the extent of which can hardly be measured where there is
no solitary object of human workmanship or vestige of
animal life, not a sheep-track, not a shepherd's hovel, but
rock and heath, heath and rock, tossed about in monotonous confusion.   And, after the ascent is mastered, you
descend into a second vale—long, narrow, sterile—known
by the name of " Far Easedale : " from which point, if you
could drive a tunnel *under* the everlasting hills, perhaps
six or seven miles might bring you to the nearest habita-
tion of man, in Borrowdale ; but, going *over* the mountains,
the road cannot be less than twelve or fourteen, and, in
point of fatigue, at the least twenty.   This long valley,
which is really terrific at noonday, from its utter loneliness
and desolation, completes the defences of little sylvan Easedale.   There is one door into it from the Grasmere side :
but that door is obscure : and on every other quarter there

is no door at all ; not any, the roughest, access, but such as would demand a day's walking.

Such is the solitude—so deep and so rich in miniature beauty—of Easedale ; and in this solitude it was that George and Sarah Green, two poor and hard-working peasants, dwelt, with a numerous family of small children. Poor as they were, they had won the general respect of the neighbourhood, from the uncomplaining firmness with which they bore the hardships of their lot, and from the decent attire in which the good mother of the family contrived to send out her children to the Grasmere parish-school. It is a custom, and a very ancient one, in Westmoreland— the same custom (resting on the same causes) I have witnessed also in southern Scotland—that any sale by auction of household furniture (and seldom a month passes without something of the sort) forms an excuse for the good women, throughout the whole circumference of perhaps four or five valleys, to assemble at the place of sale, with the nominal purpose of buying something they may happen to want. A sale, except it were of the sort exclusively interesting to farming *men*, is a kind of general intimation to the country, from the owner of the property, that he will, on that afternoon, be "at home" to all comers, and hopes to see as large an attendance as possible. Accordingly, it was the almost invariable custom—and often, too, when the parties were far too poor for such an effort of hospitality —to make ample provision, not of eatables, but of liquor, for all who came. Even a gentleman, who should happen to present himself on such a festal occasion, by way of seeing the "humours" of the scene, was certain of meeting the most cordial welcome. The good woman of the house more particularly testified her sense of the honour done to her, and was sure to seek out some cherished and solitary

article of china—a wreck from a century back—in order
that he, being a porcelain man among so many delf men
and women, might have a porcelain cup to drink from.

The main secret of attraction at these sales—many of
which I have attended—was the social rendezvous thus
effected between parties so remote from each other (either
by real distance, or by virtual distance, resulting from the
separation effected by mountains 3000 feet high), that, in
fact, without some such common object, they would not be
likely to hear of each other for months, or actually to meet
for years.   This principal charm of the " gathering," sea-
soned, doubtless, to many by the certain anticipation that
the whole budget of rural gossip would then and there be
opened, was not assuredly diminished to the men by the
anticipation of excellent ale (usually brewed six or seven
weeks before, in preparation for the event), and possibly of
still more excellent *pow-sowdy* (a combination of ale, spirits,
and spices) ; nor to the women by some prospect, not so
inevitably fulfilled, but pretty certain in a liberal house, of
communicating their news over excellent tea.   Even the
auctioneer was always a character in the drama : he was
always a rustic old humorist, and a jovial drunkard, privileged in certain good-humoured liberties and jokes with
all bidders, gentle or simple, and furnished with an ancient
inheritance of jests appropriate to the articles offered for
sale—jests that had, doubtless, done their office from Elizabeth's golden days ; but no more, on that account, failing
of their expected effect, with either man or woman of this
nineteenth century, than the sun fails to gladden the heart,
because it is that same old superannuated sun that has
gladdened it for thousands of years.

One thing, however, in mere justice to the Dalesmen of
Westmoreland and Cumberland, I am bound in this place

to record : Often as I have been at these sales, and years before even a scattering of gentry began to attend, yet so true to the natural standard of politeness was the decorum uniformly maintained, that even the old buffoon of an auctioneer never forgot himself so far as to found upon any article of furniture a jest fitted to call up a painful blush in any woman's face. He might, perhaps, go so far as to awaken a little rosy confusion upon some young bride's countenance, when pressing a cradle upon her attention ; but never did I hear him utter, nor would he have been tolerated in uttering, a scurrilous or disgusting jest, such as might easily have been suggested by something offered at a household sale. Such jests as these I heard, for the first time, at a sale in Grasmere in 1814 ; and, I am ashamed to say it, from some " gentlemen" of a great city. And it grieved me to see the effect, as it expressed itself upon the manly faces of the grave Dalesmen—a sense of insult offered to their women, who met in confiding reliance upon the forbearance of the men, and upon their regard for the dignity of the female sex, this feeling struggling with the habitual respect they are inclined to show towards what they suppose gentle blood and superior education. Taken generally, however, these were the most picturesque and festal meetings which the manners of the country produced. There you saw all ages and both sexes assembled ; there you saw old men whose heads would have been studies for Guido ; there you saw the most colossal and stately figures amongst the young men that England has to show ; there the most beautiful young women. There it was that the social benevolence, the innocent mirth, and the neighbourly kindness of the people, most delightfully expanded, and expressed themselves with the least reserve.

To such a scene it was, to a sale of domestic furniture

at the house of some proprietor in Langdale, that George
and Sarah Green set forward in the forenoon of a day fated
to be their last on earth. The sale was to take place in
Langdalehead ; to which, from their own cottage in Easedale, it was possible in daylight, and supposing no mist
upon the hills, to find out a short cut of not more than five
or six miles. By this route they went ; and, notwithstand-
ing the snow lay on the ground, they reached their destina-
tion in safety. The attendance at the sale must have been
diminished by the rigorous state of the weather ; but still
the scene was a gay one as usual. Sarah Green, though a
good and worthy woman in her maturer years, had been
imprudent, and—as the merciful judgment of the country
is apt to express it—" unfortunate" in her youth. She
had an elder daughter, who was illegitimate ; and I believe
the father of this girl was dead. The girl herself was
grown up ; and the peculiar solicitude of poor Sarah's maternal heart was at this time called forth on *her* behalf :
she wished to see her placed in a very respectable house,
where the mistress was distinguished for her notable qualities, and for success in forming good servants. This object,
as important to Sarah Green in the narrow range of her
cares, as, in a more exalted family, it might be to obtain a
ship for a lieutenant that had passed as master and com-
mander, or to get him " posted"—occupied her almost
throughout the sale. A doubtful answer had been given
to her application ; and Sarah was going about the crowd,
and weaving her person in and out, in order to lay hold of
this or that intercessor who might have, or might seem to
have, some weight with the principal person concerned.

This I think it interesting to notice, as the last occupation which is known to have stirred the pulses of her heart.
An illegitimate child is everywhere, even in the indulgent

society of Westmoreland Dalesmen, under some cloud of discountenance ;* so that Sarah Green might consider her duty to be the stronger towards this child of her " misfortune." And she probably had another reason for her anxiety —as some words dropped by her on this evening led people to presume—in her conscientious desire to introduce her daughter into a situation less perilous than that which had compassed her own youthful steps with snares. If so, it is painful to know that the virtuous wish, whose

> " Vital warmth
> Gave the last human motion to her heart,"

should not have been fulfilled. She was a woman of ardent and affectionate spirit, of which Miss Wordsworth gave me some circumstantial and affecting instances. This ardour it was, and her impassioned manner, that drew attention to what she did ; for, otherwise, she was too poor a person to be important in the estimation of strangers, and, of all possible situations, to be important at a sale, where the public attention was naturally fixed upon the chief purchasers, and the attention of the purchasers fixed upon the chief competitors. Hence it happened that, after she ceased to challenge notice by the emphasis of her solicitations for her daughter, she ceased to be noticed at all ; and nothing was recollected of her subsequent behaviour until the time arrived for general separation. This time was considerably after sunset ; and the final recollections of the crowd with

---

* But still nothing at all in England by comparison with its gloomy excess in Scotland. In the present generation, the rancorous bigotry of this feeling has been considerably mitigated. But, if the reader wishes to view it in its ancient strength, I advise him to look into the " Life of Alexander Alexander" (2 vols. 1830). He was a poor outcast, whose latter days were sheltered from ruin by the munificence of the late Mr. Blackwood, senior.

respect to George and Sarah Green were, that, upon their intention being understood to retrace their morning path, and to attempt the perilous task of dropping down into Easedale from the mountains above Langdalehead, a sound of remonstrance arose from many quarters. However, at such a moment, when everybody was in the hurry of departure, and to such persons (persons, I mean, so mature in years and in local knowledge), the opposition could not be very obstinate ; party after party rode off ; the meeting melted away, or, as the northern phrase is, *scaled ;** and at length nobody was left of any weight that could pretend to influence the decision of elderly people. They quitted the scene, professing to obey some advice or other upon the choice of roads ; but, at as early a point as they could do so unobserved, began to ascend the hills, everywhere open from the rude carriage-way. After this they were seen no more. They had disappeared into the cloud of death. Voices were heard, some hours afterwards, from the mountains—voices, as some thought, of alarm ; others said, No, that it was only the voices of jovial people, car· ried by the wind into uncertain regions. The result was, that no attention was paid to the sounds.

    .   .   .   .   .   .

That night, in little peaceful Easedale, six children sat by a peat-fire, expecting the return of their parents, upon whom they depended for their daily bread. Let a day pass, and they were starving. Every sound was heard

---

* *Scaled :*— *Scale* is a verb both active and neuter. I use it here as a neuter verb, in the sense (a Cumberland sense) of separating to all the points of the compass. But by Shakspere it is used in an active or transitive sense. Speaking of some secret news, he says, " We'll scale it a little more"—*i. e.,* spread it in all directions, and disentangle its complexities.

with anxiety; for all this was reported many hundred times to Miss Wordsworth, and to those who, like myself, were never wearied of hearing the details. Every sound, every echo amongst the hills, was listened to for five hours, from seven to twelve. At length the eldest girl of the family—about nine years old—told her little brothers and sisters to go to bed. They had been trained to obedience; and all of them, at the voice of their eldest sister, went off fearfully to their beds. What could be *their* fears, it is difficult to say; they had no knowledge to instruct them in the dangers of the hills; but the eldest sister always averred that they had as deep a solicitude as she herself had about their parents. Doubtless she had communicated her fears to *them.* Some time in the course of the evening—but it was late, and after midnight—the moon arose, and shed a torrent of light upon the Langdale fells, which had already, long hours before, witnessed in darkness the death of their parents.

That night, and the following morning, came a further and a heavier fall of snow; in consequence of which the poor children were completely imprisoned, and cut off from all possibility of communicating with their next neighbours. The brook was too much for them to leap; and the little, crazy wooden bridge could not be crossed, or even approached with safety, from the drifting of the snow having made it impossible to ascertain the exact situation of some treacherous hole in its timbers, which, if trod upon, would have let a small child drop through into the rapid waters. Their parents did not return. For some hours of the morning, the children clung to the hope that the extreme severity of the night had tempted them to sleep in Langdale; but this hope forsook them as the day wore away. Their father, George Green, had served as a

soldier, and was an active man, of ready resources, who
would not, under any circumstances, have failed to force
a road back to his family, had he been still living; and
this reflection, or rather semi-conscious feeling, which the
awfulness of their situation forced upon the minds of all
but the mere infants, awakened them to the whole extent
of their calamity.   Wonderful it is to see the effect of
sudden misery, sudden grief, or sudden fear, in sharpening
(where they do not utterly upset) the intellectual perceptions.   Instances must have fallen in the way of most of
us.   And I have noticed frequently that even sudden and
intense bodily pain forms part of the machinery employed
by nature for quickening the development of the mind.
The perceptions of infants are not, in fact, excited by gra-
duated steps and continuously, but *per saltum*, and by un-
equal starts.   At least, within the whole range of my own
experience, I have remarked, that, after any very severe fit
of those peculiar pains to which the delicate digestive organs
of most infants are liable, there always became apparent
on the following day a very considerable increase of vital
energy and of quickened attention to the objects around
them.   The poor desolate children of Blentarn Ghyll,*
hourly becoming more pathetically convinced that they
were orphans, gave many evidences of this awaking power

---

* Wordsworth's conjecture as to the origin of the name is probably
the true one.   There is, at a little elevation above the place, a small
concave tract of ground, shaped like the bed of a tarn.   Some causes
having diverted the supplies of water, at some remote period, from
the little reservoir, the tarn has probably disappeared; but the bed,
and other indications of a tarn (particularly a little ghyll, or steep
rocky cleft for discharging the water), having remained as memorials
that it once existed, the country people have called it the Blind Tarn
—the tarn which wants its eye—in wanting the luminous sparkle of
the waters of right belonging to it.

as lodged, by a providential arrangement, in situations of trial that most require it. They huddled together, in the evening, round their hearth-fire of peats, and held their little family councils upon what was to be done towards any chance—if chance remained—of yet *giving aid to their parents*; for a slender hope had sprung up that some hovel or sheep-fold might have furnished them a screen (or, in Westmoreland phrase, a *bield*) against the weather quarter of the storm, in which hovel they might even now be lying snowed up; and, secondly, as regarded themselves, in what way they were to make known their situation, in case the snow should continue or should increase; for starvation stared them in the face, if they should be confined for many days to their house.

Meantime, the eldest sister, little Agnes, though sadly alarmed, and feeling the sensation of *eeriness* as twilight came on, and she looked out from the cottage-door to the dreadful fells on which, too probably, her parents were lying corpses (and possibly not many hundred yards from their own threshold), yet exerted herself to take all the measures which their own prospects made prudent. And she told Miss Wordsworth, that, in the midst of the oppression on her little spirit, from vague ghostly terrors, she did not fail, however, to draw some comfort from the consideration, that the very same causes which produced their danger in one direction, sheltered them from danger of another kind—such dangers as she knew, from books that she had read, would have threatened a little desolate flock of children in other parts of England; for she considered thankfully, that, if *they* could not get out into Grasmere, on the other hand, bad men, and wild seafaring foreigners, who sometimes passed along the high road even in that vale, could not get to *them ;* and that, as to their neighbours, so far from having anything to fear in that quarter, their greatest apprehension was, lest they might not be able to acquaint them with their situation ; but that, if this could be accomplished, the very sternest amongst them were kind-hearted people, that would contend with each other for the privilege of assisting them. Somewhat cheered with these thoughts, and having caused all her brothers and sisters—except the two little things, not yet of a fit age—to kneel down and say the prayers which they had been taught, this admirable little maiden turned herself to every household task that could have proved useful to them in a long captivity. First of all, upon some recollection that the clock was nearly going down, she wound it up. Next, she took all the milk which remained from what her mother had provided for the children's consumption during her absence, and for the breakfast of the following morning—this luckily was still in sufficient plenty for two days' consumption (skimmed or "blue" milk being only one halfpenny a quart, and the quart a most redundant one, in Grasmere)—this she took and scalded, so as to save it from turning sour. That done, she next examined the meal chest ; made the common oatmeal porridge of the country (the "burgoo" of the Royal Navy); but put all of the children, except the two youngest, on short allowance ; and, by way of reconciling them in some measure to this stinted meal, she found out a little hoard of flour, part of which she baked for them upon the hearth into little cakes ; and this unusual delicacy persuaded them to think that they had been celebrating a feast. Next, before night coming on should make it too trying to her own feelings, or before fresh snow coming on might make it impossible, she issued out of doors. There her first task was, with the assistance of two younger brothers, to carry in from the peat-stack as many peats as might serve them for a week's consumption. That done, in the second place she examined the potatoes, buried in "brackens" (that is, withered fern): these were not many, and she thought it better to leave them where they were, excepting as many as would make a single meal, under a fear that the heat of their cottage would spoil them, if removed.

Having thus made all the provision in her power for supporting their own lives, she turned her attention to the cow. Her she milked; but, unfortunately, the milk she gave, either from being badly fed, or from some other cause, was too trifling to be of much consideration towards the wants of a large family. Here, however, her chief anxiety was to get down the hay for the cow's food from a loft above the outhouse : and in this she succeeded but imperfectly, from want of strength and size to cope with the difficulties of the case ; besides, that the increasing darkness by this time, together with the gloom of the place, made it a matter of great self-conquest for her to work at all ; but, as respected one night at any rate, she placed the cow in a situation of luxurious warmth and comfort. Then retreating into the warm house, and "barring" the door, she sat down to undress the two youngest of the children ; them she laid carefully and cosily in their little nests up-stairs, and sang them to sleep. The rest she kept up to bear her company until the clock should tell them it was midnight ; up to which time she had still a lingering hope that some welcome shout from the hills above, which they were all to strain their ears to catch, might yet assure them that they were not wholly orphans, even though one parent should have perished. No shout, it may be supposed, was ever heard ; nor could a shout, in any case, have been heard, for the night was one of tumultuous wind. And though.

amidst its ravings, sometimes they fancied a sound of voices, still, in the dead lulls that now and then succeeded, they heard nothing to confirm their hopes. As last services to what she might now have called her own little family, Agnes took precautions against the drifting of the snow *within* the door and *within* the imperfect window, which had caused them some discomfort on the preceding day; and finally, she adopted the most systematic and elaborate plans for preventing the possibility of their fire being extinguished, which, in the event of their being thrown upon the ultimate resource of their potatoes, would be absolutely indispensable to their existence ; and in any case a main element of their comfort.

The night slipped away, and morning came, bringing with it no better hopes of any kind. Change there had been none, but for the worse. The snow had greatly increased in quantity ; and the drifts seemed far more formidable. A second day passed like the first ; little Agnes still keeping her young flock quiet, and tolerably comfortable ; and still calling on all the elders in succession to say their prayers, morning and night.

A third day came ; and whether on that or on the fourth, I do not now recollect, but on one or other there came a welcome gleam of hope. The arrangement of the snow-drifts had shifted during the night ; and, though the wooden bridge was still impracticable, a low wall had been exposed, over which, by a circuit which evaded the brook, it seemed possible that a road might be found into Grasmere. In some walls it was necessary to force gaps ; but this was effected without much difficulty, even by children ; for the Westmoreland field walls are " open," that is, uncemented with mortar ; and the push of a stick will generally detach so much from the upper part of any old crazy fence, as to lower it sufficiently for female or even for childish steps to pass. The little boys accompanied their sister until she came to the other side of the hill, which, lying more sheltered from the weather, offered a path onwards comparatively easy. Here they parted ; and little Agnes pursued her solitary mission to the nearest house she could find accessible in Grasmere.

No house could have proved a wrong one in such a case. Miss Wordsworth and I often heard the description renewed, of the horror which, in an instant, displaced the smile of hospitable greeting, when little weeping Agnes told her sad tale. No tongue can express the fervid sympathy which travelled through the vale, like fire in an American forest, when it was learned that neither George nor Sarah Green had been seen by their children since the day of the Langdale sale. Within half an hour, or little more, from the remotest parts of the valley—some of them distant nearly two miles from the point of rendezvous —all the men of Grasmere had assembled at the little cluster of cottages called "Kirktown," from its adjacency to the venerable parish Church of St. Oswald. There were at the time I settled in Grasmere—viz., in the spring of 1809, and, therefore, I suppose, in 1807-8, fifteen months previously—about sixty-three households in the vale ; and the total number of souls was about 265 to 270 ; so that the number of fighting men would be about sixty or sixty-six, according to the common way of computing the proportion ; and the majority were athletic and powerfully built. Sixty, at least, after a short consultation as to the plan of operations, and for arranging the kind of signals by which they were to communicate from great distances, and in the perilous events of mists or snow-storms, set off with the speed of Alpine hunters to the hills. The dangers of the undertaking were considerable, under the uneasy and agitated

state of the weather ; and all the women of the vale were
in the greatest anxiety, until night brought them back, in a
body, unsuccessful.   Three days at the least, and I rather
think five, the search was ineffectual : which arose partly
from the great extent of the ground to be examined, and
partly from the natural mistake made of ranging almost
exclusively during the earlier days on that part of the hills
over which the path of Easedale might be presumed to have
been selected under any reasonable latitude of circuitousness.
But the fact is, when the fatal accident (for such it has
often proved) of a permanent mist surprises a man on the
hills, if he turns and loses his direction, he is a lost man ;
and without doing this so as to lose the power of *s'orienter*
all at once, it is yet well known how difficult it is to avoid
losing it insensibly and by degrees.   Baffling snow-showers
are the worst kinds of mists.   And the poor Greens had,
under that kind of confusion, wandered many a mile out
of their proper track ; so that to search for them upon any
line indicated by the ordinary probabilities, would perhaps
offer the slenderest chance for finding them.

The zeal of the people, meantime, was not in the least
abated, but rather quickened, by the wearisome disappointments ; every hour of daylight was turned to account ; no
man of the valley ever came home to meals ; and the reply
of a young shoemaker, on the fourth night's return, speaks
sufficiently for the unabated spirit of the vale.   Miss Wordsworth asked what he would do on the next morning.   " Go
up again, of course," was his answer.   But what if to-
morrow also should turn out like all the rest.   " Why, go
up in stronger force on the day after."   Yet this man was
sacrificing his own daily earnings without a chance of re-
compense.   At length, sagacious dogs were taken up ; and,
about noonday, a shout from an aërial height, amongst thick

volumes of cloudy vapour, propagated through repeating bands of men from a distance of many miles, conveyed as by telegraph into Grasmere the news that the bodies were found. George Green was lying at the bottom of a precipice, from which he had fallen. Sarah Green was found on the summit of the precipice ; and, by laying together all the indications of what had passed, and reading into coherency the sad hieroglyphics of their last agonies, it was conjectured that the husband had desired his wife to pause for a few minutes, wrapping her, meantime, in his own greatcoat, whilst he should go forward and reconnoitre the ground, in order to catch a sight of some object (rocky peak, or tarn, or peat-field) which might ascertain their real situation. Either the snow above, already lying in drifts, or the blinding snow-storms driving into his eyes, must have misled him as to the nature of the circumjacent ground ; for the precipice over which he had fallen was but a few yards from the spot in which he had quitted his wife. The depth of the descent and the fury of the wind (almost always violent on these cloudy altitudes) would prevent any distinct communication between the dying husband below and his despairing wife above, but it was believed by the shepherds, best acquainted with the ground and the range of sound, as regarded the capacities of the human ear under the probable circumstances of the storm, that Sarah might have caught, at intervals, the groans of her unhappy partner, supposing that his death were at all a lingering one. Others, on the contrary, supposed her to have gathered this catastrophe rather from the *want* of any sounds, and from his continued absence, than from any one distinct or positive expression of it ; both because the smooth and unruffled surface of the snow where he lay seemed to argue that he had died without a struggle, perhaps without a groan ; and because that tremendous sound of " hurtling" in the upper chambers of the air, which often accompanies a snow-storm, when combined with heavy gales of wind, would utterly suppress and stifle (as they conceived) any sound so feeble as those from a dying man. In any case, and by whatever sad language of sounds or signs, positive or negative, she might have learned or guessed her loss, it was generally agreed that the wild shrieks heard towards midnight in Langdalehead* announced the agonizing moment which brought to her now widowed heart the conviction of utter desolation and of final abandonment to her own solitary and fast-fleeting energies.   It seemed probable that the *sudden* disappearance of her husband from her pursuing eyes would teach her to understand his fate ; and that the consequent indefinite apprehension of instant death lying all around the point on which she sat, had kept her stationary to the very attitude in which her husband left her, until her failing powers, and the increasing bitterness of the cold, to one no longer in motion, would soon make those changes of place impossible, which too awfully had made themselves known as dangerous.   The footsteps

---

* I once heard, also, in talking with a Langdale family upon this tragic tale, that the sounds had penetrated into the valley of Little Langdale ; which is possible enough.   For, although this interesting recess of the entire Langdale basin (which bears somewhat of the same relation to Great Langdale that Easedale bears to Grasmere) does, in fact, lie beyond Langdalehead by the entire breadth of that dale, yet, from the singular accident of having its area raised far above the level of the adjacent vales, one most solitary section of Little Langdale (in which lies a tiny lake, and on the banks of that lake dwells one solitary family) being exactly at right angles both to Langdalehead and to the other complementary section of the Lesser Langdale, is brought into a position and an elevation virtually much nearer to objects (especially to audible objects) on the Easedale Fells.

in some places, wherever drifting had not obliterated them, yet traceable as to the outline, though partially filled up with later falls of snow, satisfactorily showed that, however much they might have rambled, after crossing and doubling upon their own tracks, and many a mile astray from their right path, so they must have kept together to the very plateau or shelf of rock at which (*i.e., on* which, and *below* which) their wanderings had terminated; for there were evidently no steps from this plateau in the retrograde order.

By the time they had reached this final stage of their erroneous course, all possibility of escape must have been long over for both alike; because their exhaustion must have been excessive before they could have reached a point so remote and high; and, unfortunately, the direct result of all this exhaustion had been to throw them farther off their home, or from " *any* dwelling-place of man," than they were at starting. Here, therefore, at this rocky pinnacle, hope was extinct for the wedded couple, but not perhaps for the husband. It was the impression of the vale, that, perhaps, within half-an-hour before reaching this fatal point, George Green might, had his conscience or his heart allowed him in so base a desertion, have saved himself singly, without any very great difficulty. It is to be hoped, however—and, for my part, I think too well of human nature to hesitate in believing—that not many, even amongst the meaner-minded and the least generous of men, could have reconciled themselves to the abandonment of a poor fainting female companion in such circumstances. Still, though not more than a most imperative duty, it was such a duty as most of his associates believed to have cost him (perhaps consciously) his life. It is an impressive truth—that sometimes in the very lowest forms of duty, less than which would rank a man as a villain, there is, nevertheless, the sublimest ascent of self-sacrifice. To do *less*, would class you as an object of eternal scorn : to do so much, presumes the grandeur of heroism. For his wife not only must have disabled him greatly by clinging to his arm for support ; but it was known, from her peculiar character and manner, that she would be likely to rob him of his coolness and presence of mind, by too painfully fixing his thoughts, where her own would be busiest, upon their helpless little family. " *Stung* with the thoughts of home "—to borrow the fine expression of Thomson, in describing a similar case —alternately thinking of the blessedness of that warm fireside at Blentarn Ghyll, which was not again to spread its genial glow through her freezing limbs, and of those darling little faces which, in this world, she was to see no more ; unintentionally, and without being aware even of that result, she would rob the brave man (for such he was) of his fortitude, and the strong man of his *animal* resources. And yet (such, in the very opposite direction, was equally the impression universally through Grasmere), had Sarah Green foreseen, could her affectionate heart have guessed, even the tenth part of that love and neighbourly respect for herself which soon afterwards expressed themselves in showers of bounty to her children ; could she have looked behind the curtain of destiny sufficiently to learn that the very desolation of these poor children, which wrung her maternal heart, and doubtless constituted to her the sting of death, would prove the signal and the pledge of such anxious guardianship as not many rich men's children receive, and that this overflowing offering to her own memory would not be a hasty or decaying tribute of the first sorrowing sensibilities, but would pursue her children steadily until their hopeful settlement in life,—anything approaching this, known or guessed, would have caused her (so said all who knew her) to welcome the bitter end by which such privileges were to be purchased, and solemnly to breathe out into the ear of that holy angel who gathers the whispers of dying mothers torn asunder from their infants, a thankful *Nunc dimittis* (Lord, now lettest thou thy servant depart in peace), as the farewell ejaculation rightfully belonging to the occasion.

The funeral of the ill-fated Greens was, it may be supposed, attended by all the vale : it took place about eight days after they were found ; and the day happened to be in the most perfect contrast to the sort of weather which prevailed at the time of their misfortune : some snow still remained here and there upon the ground; but the azure of the sky was unstained by a cloud ; and a golden sunlight seemed to sleep, so balmy and tranquil was the season, upon the very hills where the pair had wandered—then a howling wilderness, but now a green pastoral lawn, in its lower ranges, and a glittering expanse of virgin snow, in its higher. George Green had, I believe, an elder family by a former wife ; and it was for some of these children, who lived at a distance, and who wished to give their attendance at the grave, that the funeral was delayed. At this point, because really suggested by the contrast of the funeral tranquillity with the howling tempest of the fatal night, it may be proper to remind the reader of Wordsworth's memorial stanzas :—

> " Who weeps for strangers? Many wept
> For George and Sarah Green;
> Wept for that pair's unhappy fate,
> Whose graves may here be seen

> " By night upon these stormy fells.
> Did wife and husband roam ;
> Six little ones at home had left,
> And could not find that home.

" For *any* dwelling-place of man
   As vainly did they seek
He perish'd; and a voice was heard—
   The widow's lonely shriek.

" Not many steps, and she was left
   A body without life—
A few short steps were the chain that bound
   The husband to the wife.

" *Now* do these sternly-featured hills
   Look gently on this grave;
And quiet *now* are the depths of air.
   As a sea without a wave.

" But deeper lies the heart of peace
   In quiet more profound;
The heart of quietness is here
   Within this churchyard bound.

" And from all agony of mind
   It keeps them safe, and far
From fear and grief, and from all need
   Of sun or guiding star.

" O darkness of the grave! how deep,
   After that living night—
That last and dreary living one
   Of sorrow and affright!

" O sacred marriage-bed of death!
   That keeps them side by side
In bond of peace, in bond of love,
   That may not be untied!"

After this solemn ceremony of the funeral was over — at
which, by the way, I heard Miss Wordsworth declare that
the grief of Sarah's illegitimate daughter was the most over-
whelming she had ever witnessed—a regular distribution of
the children was made amongst the wealthier families of the
vale. There had already, and before the funeral, been a perfect struggle to obtain one of the children, amongst all who
had any facilities for discharging the duties of such a trust;
and even the poorest had put in their claim to bear some

LANGDALE PIKES, FROM WINDERMERE.

part in the expenses of the case. But it was judiciously decided, that none of the children should be intrusted to any persons who seemed likely, either from old age or from slender means, or from nearer and more personal responsibilities, to be under the necessity of devolving the trust, sooner or later, upon strangers, who might have none of that interest in the children which attached, in the minds of the Grasmere people, to the circumstances that made them orphans. Two twins, who had naturally played together and slept together from their birth, passed into the same family: the others were dispersed; but into such kind-hearted and intelligent families, with continued opportunities of meeting each other on errands, or at church, or at sales, that it was hard to say which had the more comfortable home. And thus, in so brief a period as one fortnight, a household that, by health and strength, by the humility of poverty and by innocence of life, seemed sheltered from all attacks but those of time, came to be utterly broken up. George and Sarah Green slept in Grasmere Churchyard, never more to know the want of " sun or guiding star." Their children were scattered over wealthier houses than those of their poor parents, through the Vales of Grasmere or Rydal; and Blentarn Ghyll, after being shut up for a season, and ceasing for months to send up its little slender column of smoke at morning and evening, finally passed into the hands of a stranger.

The Wordsworths, meantime, acknowledged a peculiar interest in the future fortunes and education of the children. They had taken by much the foremost place in pushing the subscriptions on behalf of the family, feeling, no doubt, that when both parents, in any little sequestered community like that of Grasmere, are suddenly cut off by a tragical death, the children, in such a case, devolve by a sort of natural right and providential bequest on the other members of this community—that they energetically applied themselves to the task of raising funds by subscription; most of which, it is true, might not be wanted until future years should carry one after another of the children successively into different trades or occupations; but they well understood, that more, by tenfold, would be raised under an immediate appeal to the sympathies of men, whilst yet burning fervently towards the sufferers in this calamity, than if the application were delayed until the money should be needed. I have mentioned that the Royal Family were made acquainted with the details of the case; that they were powerfully affected by the story, especially by the account of little Agnes, and her premature assumption of the maternal character; and that they contributed most munificently. Her Majesty, and three, at least, of her august daughters, were amongst the subscribers to the fund. For my part, I could have obtained a good deal from the careless liberality of Oxonian friends towards such a fund. But, knowing previously how little, in such an application, it would aid me to plead the name of Wordsworth as the founder of the subscription (a name that *now* would stand good for some thousands of pounds in that same Oxford—so passes the injustice as well as the glory of this world!)—knowing this, I did not choose to trouble anybody; and the more so, as Miss Wordsworth, upon my proposal to write to various ladies, upon whom I could have relied for their several contributions, wrote back to me, desiring that I would not; and upon this satisfactory reason—that the fund had already swelled under the Royal patronage, and the interest excited by so much of the circumstances as could be reported in hurried letters, to an amount beyond what was likely to be wanted for persons whom there was no good reason for pushing out of the sphere to which their birth had called them. The parish even was liable to give aid ; and, in the midst of Royal bounty, this aid was not declined. Perhaps this was so far a solitary and unique case, that it might be the only one, in which some parochial Mr. Bumble found himself pulling in joint harness with the denizens of Windsor Castle, and a coadjutor of " Majesties " and " Royal Highnesses." Finally, to complete their own large share in the charity, the Wordsworths took into their own family one of the children, a girl ; the least amiable, I believe, of the whole ; slothful and sensual ; so, at least, I imagined ; for this girl it was, that in years to come caused by her criminal negligence the death of little Kate Wordsworth.

From a gathering of years, far ahead of the events, looking back by accident to this whole little cottage romance of Blentarn Ghyll, with its ups and downs, its lights and shadows, and its fitful alternations, of grandeur derived from mountain solitude, and of humility derived from the very lowliest poverty, its little faithful Agnes keeping up her records of time in harmony with the mighty world outside, and feeding the single cow—the total " estate " of the new-made orphans—I thought of that beautiful Persian apologue, where some slender drop, or crystallizing filament, within the shell of an oyster, fancies itself called upon to bewail its own obscure lot—consigned apparently and irretrievably to the gloomiest depths of the Persian Gulf. But changes happen, good and bad luck will fall out, even in the darkest depths of the Persian Gulf ; and messages of joy can reach those that wait in silence, even where no post-horn has ever sounded. Behold ! the slender filament has ripened into the most glorious of pearls. In a happy hour for himself, some diver from the blossoming

forests of Ceylon brings up to heavenly light the matchless
pearl ; and very soon that solitary crystal drop, that had
bemoaned its own obscure lot, finds itself glorifying the
central cluster in the tiara bound upon the brow of him
who signed himself " King of kings," the Shah of Persia,
and that shook all Asia from the Indus to the Euphrates.
Not otherwise was the lot of little Agnes—faithful to
duties so suddenly revealed amidst terrors ghostly as well
as earthly—paying down her first tribute of tears to an
affliction that seemed past all relief, and such, that at first
she with her brothers and sisters seemed foundering simultaneously with her parents in one mighty darkness.   And
yet, because, under the strange responsibilities which had
suddenly surprised her, she sought counsel and strength
from God, teaching her brothers and sisters to do the
same, and seemed (when alone at midnight) to hear her
mother's voice calling to her from the hills above, one moon
had scarcely finished its circuit, before the most august
ladies on our planet were reading, with sympathizing tears,
of Agnes Green ; and from the towers of Windsor Castle
came gracious messages of inquiry to little, lowly Blentarn
Ghyll.

In taking leave of this subject, I may mention, by the
way, that accidents of this nature are not by any means so
uncommon in the mountainous districts of Cumberland and
Westmoreland, as the reader might infer from the intensity
of the excitement which waited on the catastrophe of the
Greens.   In that instance, it was not the simple death by
cold upon the hills, but the surrounding circumstances,
which invested the case with its agitating power : the fellowship in death of a wife and husband ; the general impression that the husband had perished in his generous
devotion to his wife (a duty, certainly, and no more than a

duty, but still, under the instincts of self-preservation, a generous duty) ; sympathy with their long agony, as expressed by their long ramblings, and the earnestness of their efforts to recover their home ; awe for the long concealment which rested upon their fate ; and pity for the helpless condition of the children, so young, and so instantaneously made desolate, and so nearly perishing through the loneliness of their situation, co-operating with stress of weather, had they not been saved by the prudence and timely exertions of a little girl not much above eight years old ;—these were the circumstances and necessary adjuncts of the story which pointed and sharpened the public feelings on that occasion. Else the mere general case of perishing upon the mountains is not, unfortunately, so rare, in *any* season of the year, as for itself alone to command a powerful tribute of sorrow from the public mind. Natives as well as strangers, shepherds as well as tourists, have fallen victims, even in summer, to the misleading and confounding effects of deep mists. Sometimes they have continued to wander unconsciously in a small circle of two or three miles ; never coming within hail of a human dwelling, until exhaustion has forced them into a sleep which has proved their last. Sometimes a sprain or injury, that disabled a foot or leg, has destined them to die by the shocking death of hunger.* Sometimes a fall from the summit

---

* The case of Mr. Gough, who perished in the bosom of Helvellyn, and was supposed by some to have been disabled by a sprain of the ankle, whilst others believed him to have received that injury and his death simultaneously in a fall from the lower shelf of a precipice, became well known to the public, in all its details, through the accident of having been recorded in verse by two writers nearly at the same time, viz., Sir Walter Scott and Wordsworth. But here, again, as in the case of the Greens, it was not the naked fact of his death amongst the solitudes of the mountains that would have won the public atten-

of awful precipices has dismissed them from the anguish of
perplexity in the extreme, from the conflicts of hope and
fear, by dismissing them at once from life.   Sometimes

---

tion, or have obtained the honour of a metrical commemoration.   Indeed, to say the truth, the general sympathy with this tragic event
was not derived chiefly from the unhappy tourist's melancholy end,
for that was too shocking to be even hinted at by either of the two
writers (in fact, there was too much reason to fear that it had been
the lingering death of famine)—not the personal sufferings of the
principal figure in the little drama—but the sublime and mysterious
fidelity of the secondary figure, his dog; this it was which won the
imperishable remembrance of the vales, and which accounted for the
profound interest that immediately gathered round the incidents—an
interest that still continues to hallow the memory of the dog.   Not
the dog of Athens, nor the dog of Pompeii, so well deserve the im-
mortality of history or verse.   Mr. Gough was a young man, belonging to the Society of Friends, who took an interest in the mountain
scenery of the Lake district, both as a lover of the picturesque and as
a man of science.   It was in this latter character, I believe, that he
had ascended Helvellyn at the time when he met his melancholy end.
From his familiarity with the ground—for he had been an annual
visitant to the Lakes—he slighted the usual precaution of taking a
guide.   Mist, unfortunately—impenetrable volumes of mist—came
floating over (as so often they do) from the gloomy fells that compose
a common centre for Easedale, Langdale, Eskdale, Borrowdale, Wast-
dale, Gatesgarthdale (pronounced Keskadale), and Ennerdale.   Ten
or fifteen minutes afford ample time for this aërial navigation: within
that short interval, sunlight, moonlight, starlight, alike disappear; all
paths are lost; vast precipices are concealed, or filled up by treacherous draperies of vapour; the points of the compass are irrecoverably
confounded; and one vast cloud, too often the cloud of death even
to the experienced shepherd, sits like a vast pavilion upon the summits and gloomy coves of Helvellyn.   Mr. Gough ought to have allowed
for this not unfrequent accident, and for its bewildering effects, under
which all local knowledge (even that of shepherds) becomes in an
instant unavailing.   What was the course and succession of his
dismal adventures, after he became hidden from the world by the
vapoury screen, could not be fully deciphered even by the most sagacious of mountaineers, although, in most cases, they manifest an Indian truth of eye, together with an Indian felicity of weaving all the

also, the mountainous solitudes have been made the scenes of remarkable suicides : In particular, there was a case, a little before I came into the country, of a studious and

---

signs that the eye can gather into a significant tale, by connecting links of judgment and natural inference, especially where the whole case ranges within certain known limits of time and of space. But in this case two accidents forbade the application of their customary skill to the circumstances. One was, the want of snow at the time, to receive the impression of his feet; the other, the unusual length of time through which his remains lay undiscovered. He had made the ascent at the latter end of October, a season when the final garment of snow, which clothes Helvellyn from the setting in of winter to the sunny days of June, has frequently not made its appearance. He was not discovered until the following spring, when a shepherd, traversing the coves of Helvellyn or of Fairfield in quest of a stray sheep, was struck by the unusual sound (and its echo from the neighbouring rocks) of a short quick bark, or cry of distress, as if from a dog or young fox. Mr. Gough had not been missed; for those who saw or knew of his ascent from the Wyburn side of the mountain, took it for granted that he had fulfilled his intention of descending in the opposite direction into the valley of Patterdale, or into the Duke of Norfolk's deer-park on Ullswater, or possibly into Matterdale; and that he had finally quitted the country by way of Penrith. Having no reason, therefore, to expect a domestic animal in a region so far from human habitations, the shepherd was the more surprised at the sound, and its continued iteration. He followed its guiding, and came to a deep hollow, near the awful curtain of rock called *Striding-Edge*. There, at the foot of a tremendous precipice, lay the body of the unfortunate tourist; and, watching by his side, a meagre shadow, literally reduced to a skin and to bones that could be counted (for it is a matter of absolute demonstration that he never could have obtained either food or shelter through his long winter's imprisonment), sat this most faithful of servants—mounting guard upon his master's honoured body, and protecting it (as he *had* done effectually) from all violation by the birds of prey which haunt the central solitudes of Helvellyn :—

> " How nourish'd through that length of time.
> *He* knows, who gave that love sublime,
> And sense of loyal duty—great
> Beyond all human estimate."

meditative young boy, who found no pleasure but in books and the search after knowledge. He languished with a sort of despairing nympholepsy after intellectual pleasures— for which he felt too well assured that *his* term of allotted time, the short period of years through which his relatives had been willing to support him at St. Bees, was rapidly drawing to an end. In fact, it was just at hand ; and he was sternly required to take a long farewell of the poets and geometricians, for whose sublime contemplations he hungered and thirsted. One week was to have trans- ferred him to some huxtering concern, which not in any spirit of pride he ever affected to despise, but which in utter alienation of heart he loathed ; as one whom nature, and his own diligent cultivation of the opportunities re- cently opened to him for a brief season, had dedicated to a far different service. He mused—revolved his situation in his own mind—computed his power to liberate himself from the bondage of dependency—calculated the chances of his ever obtaining this liberation, from change in the position of his family, or revolution in his own fortunes— and, finally, attempted conjecturally to determine the amount of effect which his new and illiberal employments might have upon his own mind in weaning him from his present elevated tasks, and unfitting him for their enjoy- ment in distant years, when circumstances might again place it in his power to indulge them.

These meditations were in part communicated to a friend ; and in part, also, the result to which they brought him. That this result was gloomy, his friend knew ; but not, as in the end it appeared, that it was despairing. Such, however, it was ; and, accordingly, having satisfied himself that the chances of a happier destiny were for him slight or none, and having, by a last fruitless effort, ascertained that there was no hope whatever of mollifying his relatives, or of obtaining a year's delay of his sentence, he walked quietly up to the cloudy wildernesses within Blencathara ; read his Æschylus (read, perhaps, those very scenes of the " Prometheus" that pass amidst the wild valleys of the Caucasus, and below the awful summits, untrod by man, of the ancient Elborus) ; read him for the last time ; for the last time fathomed the abyss-like subtleties of his favourite geometrician, the mighty Apollonius ; for the last time retraced some parts of the narrative, so simple in its natural grandeur, composed by that imperial captain, the most majestic man of ancient history—

" The foremost man of all this world "—

Julius the Dictator, the eldest of the Cæsars. These three authors—Æschylus, Apollonius, and Cæsar—he studied until the daylight waned, and the stars began to appear. Then he made a little pile of the three volumes, that served him for a pillow ; took a dose, such as he had heard would be sufficient, of laudanum ; laid his head upon the monuments which he himself seemed in fancy to have raised to the three mighty spirits ; and, with his face upturned to the heavens and the stars, slipped quietly away into a sleep upon which no morning ever dawned. The laudanum—whether it were from the effect of the open air, or from some peculiarity of temperament—had not produced sickness in the first stage of its action, nor convulsions in the last. But, from the serenity of his countenance, and from the tranquil maintenance of his original supine position—for his head was still pillowed upon the three intellectual Titans, Greek and Roman, and his eyes were still directed towards the stars—it would appear that he had died placidly, and without a struggle.

II.—C

In this way the imprudent boy, who, like Chatterton, would
not wait for the change that a day might bring, obtained
the liberty he sought.   I describe him as doing whatsoever
he had described himself in his last conversations as wishing to do ; for whatsoever, in his last scene of life, was not
explained by the objects and the arrangement of the objects
about him, found a sufficient solution in the confidential
explanations of his purposes, which he had communicated,
so far as he felt it safe, to his only friend.*

From this little special episode, where the danger was
of a more exceptional kind, let us fall back on the more
ordinary case of shepherds, whose duties, in searching after
missing sheep, or after sheep surprised by sudden snow-
drifts, are too likely, in all seasons of severity, to force them
upon facing dangers which, in relation to their natural
causes, must for ever remain the same.   This uniformity
it is, this monotony of the danger, which authorizes our
surprise and our indignation, that long ago the resources
of art and human contrivance, in any one of many possible
modes, should not have been applied to the relief of an evil
so constantly recurrent.   A danger, that has no fixed root
in our social system, suggests its own natural excuse, when
it happens to be neglected.   But this evil is one of frightful
ruin when it *does* take effect, and of eternal menace when it
does *not*.   In some years it has gone near to the depopulation
of a whole pastoral hamlet, as respects the most vigorous
and hopeful part of its male population ; and annually it
causes, by its mere contemplation, the heartache to many

---

* This story has been made the subject of a separate poem, entitled
" The Student of St. Bees," by my friend Mr. James Payn of Cambridge.   The volume is published by Macmillan, Cambridge, and
contains thoughts of great beauty, too likely to escape the vapid and
irreflectve reader.

a young wife and many an anxious mother.   In reality,
amongst all pastoral districts, where the field of their labour
lies in mountainous tracts, an allowance is as regularly made
for the loss of human life, by mists or storms suddenly en-
veloping the hills, and surprising the shepherds, as for the
loss of sheep ; some proportion out of each class—shepherds
and sheep—is considered as a kind of tithe-offering to the
stern Goddess of Calamity, and in the light of a ransom for
those who escape.   Grahame, the author of " The Sabbath,"
says, that (confining himself to Scotland) he has known
winters in which a single parish lost as many as ten shepherds.   And this mention of Grahame reminds me of a useful
and feasible plan proposed by him for obviating the main
pressure of such sudden perils, amidst snow, and solitude,
and night.   I call it feasible with good reason ; for Grahame.
who doubtless had made the calculations, declares that, for
so trifling a sum as a few hundred pounds, every square
mile in the southern counties of Scotland (that is, I presume,
throughout the Lowlands) might be fitted up with his appa-
ratus.   He prefaces his plan by one general remark, to
which I believe that every mountaineer will assent—viz.,
that the vast majority of deaths in such cases is owing to
the waste of animal power in trying to recover the right
direction ; and, probably, it *would* be recovered in a far
greater number of instances, were the advance persisted in
according to any unity of plan.   But, partly, the distraction
of mind and irresolution, under such circumstances, cause
the wanderer frequently to change his direction voluntarily,
according to any new fancy that starts up to beguile him ;
and, partly, he changes it often insensibly and unconsciously, from the same cause which originally led him astray.
Obviously, therefore, the primary object should be to com-
pensate the loss of distinct vision—which, for the present,

is irreparable in that form—by substituting an appeal to
another sense.   That error, which has been caused by the
obstruction of the eye, may be corrected by the sounder
information of the ear.   Let crosses, such as are raised for
other purposes in Catholic lands, be planted at intervals—
suppose of one mile—in every direction.   " Snow-storms,"
says Grahame, " are almost always accompanied with wind.
Suppose, then, a pole, fifteen feet high, well fixed in the
ground, with two cross spars placed near the bottom, to
denote the ' airts' (or points of the compass) ; a bell hung
at the top of this pole, with a piece of flat wood (attached
to it) projecting upwards, would ring with the slightest
breeze.   As they would be purposely made to have different tones, the shepherd would soon be able to distinguish
one from another.   He could never be more than a mile
from one or other of them.   On coming to the spot, he
would at once know the points of the compass, and, of
course, the direction in which his home lay."

Another protecting circumstance would rise out of the
simplicity of manners, which is pretty sure to prevail in a
mountainous region, and the pious tenderness universally
felt towards those situations of peril which are incident to
all alike—men and women, parents and children, the strong
and the weak.   The crosses, I would answer for it, whenever they are erected, will be protected by a superstition,
such as that which in Holland protects the stork.   But it
would be right to strengthen this feeling, by instilling it as
a principle of duty in the catechisms of mountainous regions ;
and perhaps, also, in order to invest this duty with a religious sanctity, at the approach of every winter, there
might be read from the altar a solemn commination, such
as that which the English Church appoints for Ash-Wed-
nesday—" Cursed is he that removeth his neighbour's land-

mark," &c. ; to which might now be added,—" Cursed is
he that causeth the steps of the wayfarer to go astray, and
layeth snares for the wanderer on the hills : cursed is he
that removeth the bell from the snow-cross."   And every
child might learn to fear a judgment of retribution upon its
own steps in case of any such wicked action, by reading
the tale of that Scottish sea-rover, who, in order

 " To plague the Abbot of Aberbrothock,"

removed the bell from the Inchcape Rock ; which same
rock, in after days, and for want of this very warning bell,
inflicted miserable ruin upon himself, his ship, and his crew.
Once made sacred from violation, these crosses might afterwards be made subjects of suitable ornament ; that is to
say, they might be made as picturesque in form, and colour,
and material, as the crosses of Alpine countries or the guide-
posts of England often are.   The associated circumstances
of storm and solitude, of winter, of night, and wayfaring,
would give dignity to almost any form which had become
familiar to the eye as the one appropriated to this purpose ;
and the particular form of a cross or crucifix, besides its
own beauty, would suggest to the mind a pensive allegoric
memorial of that spiritual asylum offered by the same em-
blem to the poor erring roamer in our human pilgrimage,
whose steps are beset with other snares, and whose heart
is bewildered by another darkness and another storm—by
the darkness of guilt, or by the storm of affliction.

SAMUEL TAYLOR COLERIDGE.

It was, I think, in the month of August, but certainly in the summer season, and certainly in the year 1807, that I first saw this illustrious man. My knowledge of him as a man of most original genius began about the year 1799. A little before that time Wordsworth had published the first edition (in a single volume) of the " Lyrical Ballads ;" and into this had been introduced Mr. Coleridge's poem of the " Ancient Mariner," as the contribution of an anonymous friend. It would be directing the reader's attention too much to myself, if I were to linger upon this, the greatest event in the unfolding of my own mind. Let me say, in one word, that, at a period when neither the one nor the other writer was valued by the public—both having a long warfare to accomplish of contumely and ridicule, before they could rise into their present estimation—I found in these poems " the ray of a new morning," and an absolute revelation of untrodden worlds, teeming with power and beauty as yet unsuspected amongst men. I may here mention, that, precisely at the same time, Professor Wilson, entirely unconnected with myself, and not even known to me until ten years later, received the same startling and profound impressions from the same volume. With feelings of reverential interest, so early and so deep, pointing towards two contemporaries, it may be supposed that I inquired eagerly after their names. But these inquiries were self-baffled ; the same deep feelings which prompted my curiosity causing me to recoil from all casual opportunities of pushing the inquiry, as too generally lying amongst those who gave no sign of participating in my feelings ; and, extravagant as this may seem, I revolted with as much hatred from coupling my question with any occasion of insult to the persons whom it respected, as a primitive Christian from throwing frankincense upon the altars of Cæsar, or a lover from giving up the name of his beloved to the coarse license of a Bacchanalian party. It is laughable to record for how long a period my curiosity in this particular was thus self-defeated. Two years passed before I ascertained the two names. Mr. Wordsworth published *his* in the second and enlarged edition of the poems ; and for Mr. Coleridge's I was " indebted " to a private source ; but I discharged that debt ill, for I quarrelled with my informant for what I considered his profane way of dealing with a subject so hallowed in my own thoughts. After this I searched east and west, north and south, for all known works or fragments of the same authors. I had read, therefore, as respects Mr. Coleridge, the Allegory which he contributed to Mr. Southey's " Joan of Arc." I had read his fine Ode, entitled " France ; " his Ode to the Duchess of Devonshire ; and various other contributions, more or less interesting, to the two volumes of the " Anthology," published at Bristol about 1799-1800, by Mr. Southey; and, finally, I had, of course, read the small volume of poems published under his own name · these, however, as a juvenile and immature collection, made expressly with a view to pecuniary profit, and therefore courting expansion at any cost of critical discretion, had in general greatly disappointed me.

Meantime, it had crowned the interest which to me invested his name, that about the year 1804 or 1805 I had been informed by a gentleman from the English Lakes, who knew him as a neighbour, that he had for some time applied his whole mind to metaphysics and psychology—which happened to be my own absorbing pursuit. From 1803 to 1808, I was a student at Oxford; and on the first occasion when I could conveniently have sought for a personal knowledge of one whom I contemplated with so much admiration, I was met by a painful assurance that he had quitted England, and was then residing at Malta, in the quality of secretary to the governor. I began to inquire about the best route to Malta; but, as any route at that time promised an inside place in a French prison, I reconciled myself to waiting; and at last, happening to visit the Bristol Hot-wells in the summer of 1807, I had the pleasure to hear that Coleridge was not only once more upon English ground, but within forty and odd miles of my own station. In that same hour I bent my way to the south; and before evening reaching a ferry on the river Bridgewater, at a village called, I think, Stogursey (i. e., Stoke de Courcy, by way of distinction from some other Stoke), I crossed it, and a few miles farther attained my object—viz., the little town of Nether Stowey, amongst the Quantock Hills. Here I had been assured that I should find Mr. Coleridge, at the house of his old friend Mr. Poole. On presenting myself, however, to that gentlemen, I found that Coleridge was absent at Lord

Egmont's, an elder brother (by the father's side) of Mr. Percival, the Prime Minister, assassinated five years later; and, as it was doubtful whether he might not then be on the wing to another friend's in the town of Bridgewater, I consented willingly, until his motions should be ascertained, to stay a day or two with this Mr. Poole—a man on his own account well deserving a separate notice; for, as Coleridge afterwards remarked to me, he was almost an ideal model for a useful member of Parliament. I found him a stout, plain-looking farmer, leading a bachelor life, in a rustic, old-fashioned house, the house, however, upon further acquaintance, proving to be amply furnished with modern luxuries, and especially with a good library, superbly mounted in all departments bearing at all upon political philosophy; and the farmer turning out a polished and liberal Englishman, who had travelled extensively, and had so entirely dedicated himself to the service of his humble fellow-countrymen—the hewers of wood and drawers of water in this southern part of Somersetshire—that for many miles round he was the general arbiter of their disputes, the guide and counsellor of their difficulties; besides being appointed executor and guardian to his children by every third man who died in or about the town of Nether Stowey.

The first morning of my visit, Mr. Poole was so kind as to propose, knowing my admiration of Wordsworth, that we should ride over to Alfoxton—a place of singular interest to myself, as having been occupied in his unmarried days by that poet, during the minority of Mr. St. Aubyn, its present youthful proprietor. At this delightful spot, the ancient residence of an ancient English family, and surrounded by those ferny Quantock Hills which are so beautifully glanced at in the poem of "Ruth," Wordsworth, accompanied by his sister, had passed a good deal of the interval between leaving the university (Cambridge), and the period of his final settlement amongst his native lakes of Westmoreland : some allowance, however, must be made—but how much I do not accurately know—for a long residence in France, for a short one in North Germany, for an intermitting one in London, and for a regular domestication with his sister at Race Down, in Dorsetshire.

Returning late from this interesting survey, we found ourselves without company at dinner ; and, being thus seated *tête-à-tête*, Mr. Poole propounded the following question to me, which I mention, because it furnished me with the first hint of a singular infirmity besetting Coleridge's mind :—" Pray, my young friend, did you ever form any opinion, or, rather, did it ever happen to you to meet with any rational opinion or conjecture of others, upon that most revolting dogma of Pythagoras about beans ? You know what I mean : that monstrous doctrine in which he asserts that a man might as well, for the wickedness of the thing, eat his own grandmother, as meddle with beans."

" Yes," I replied ; " the line is, I believe, in the Golden Verses. I remember it well."

P.—" True : now our dear excellent friend Coleridge, than whom God never made a creature more divinely endowed, yet strange it is to say, sometimes steals from other people, just as you or I might do ; I beg your pardon— just as a poor creature like myself might do, that sometimes have not wherewithal to make a figure from my own exchequer : and the other day, at a dinner party, this question arising about Pythagoras and his beans, Coleridge gave us an interpretation, which, from his manner, I suspect to have been not original. Think, therefore, if you have anywhere read a plausible solution."

" I have : and it was a German author. This German, understand, is a poor stick of a man, not to be named on the same day with Coleridge : so that, if Coleridge should appear to have robbed him, be assured that he has done the scamp too much honour."

P.—" Well : what says the German ?'

" Why, you know the use made in Greece of beans in voting and balloting ? Well : the German says that Pythagoras speaks symbolically ; meaning that electioneering, or more generally, all interference with political intrigues, is fatal to a philosopher's pursuits, and their appropriate serenity. Therefore, says he, follower of mine, abstain from public affairs as you would from parricide."

P.—" Well, then, Coleridge *has* done the scamp too much honour : for, by Jove, that is the very explanation he gave us ! "

Here was a trait of Coleridge's mind, to be first made known to me by his best friend, and first published to the world by me, the foremost of his admirers ! But both of us had sufficient reasons :—Mr. Poole knew that, stumbled on by accident, such a discovery would be likely to impress upon a man as yet unacquainted with Coleridge a most injurious jealousy with regard to all he might write : whereas, frankly avowed by one who knew him best, the fact was disarmed of its sting ; since it thus became evident that, where the case had been best known and most investigated, it had not operated to his serious disadvantage. On the same argument, to forestall, that is to say, other discoverers who would make a more unfriendly use of the discovery, and also as matters of literary curiosity, I shall here point out a few others of Coleridge's unacknowledged obligations, noticed by myself in a very wide course of reading.*

---

* With respect to all these cases of apparent plagiarism, see an explanatory Note at the end of this volume.

1. The Hymn to Chamouni is an expansion of a short poem in stanzas, upon the same subject, by Frederica Brun, a female poet of Germany, previously known to the world under her maiden name of Münter. The mere framework of the poem is exactly the same—an appeal to the most impressive features of the regal mountain (Mont Blanc), adjuring them to proclaim their author : the torrent, for instance, is required to say by whom it had been arrested in its headlong raving, and stiffened, as by the petrific touch of Death, into everlasting pillars of ice ; and the answer to these impassioned apostrophes is made by the same choral burst of rapture. In mere logic, therefore, and even as to the choice of circumstances, Coleridge's poem is a translation. On the other hand, by a judicious amplification of some topics, and by its far deeper tone of lyrical enthusiasm, the dry bones of the German outline have been awakened by Coleridge into the fulness of life. It is not, therefore, a paraphrase, but a re-cast of the original. And how was this calculated, if frankly avowed, to do Coleridge any injury with the judicious ?

2. A more singular case of Coleridge's infirmity is this : —In a very noble passage of " France," a fine expression or two occur from " Samson Agonistes." Now, to take a phrase or an inspiriting line from the great fathers of poetry, even though no marks of quotation should be added, carries with it no charge of plagiarism. Milton is justly presumed to be as familiar to the ear as nature to the eye ; and to steal from him as impossible as to appropriate, or sequester to a private use, some " bright particular star." And there is a good reason for rejecting the typographical marks of quotation : they break the continuity of the passion, by reminding the reader of a printed book ; on which account Milton himself (to give an instance) has

not marked the sublime words, "tormented all the air," as borrowed ; nor has Wordsworth, in applying to an un-principled woman of commanding beauty the memorable expression, " a weed of glorious feature," thought it neces-sary to acknowledge it as originally belonging to Spenser. Some dozens of similar cases might be adduced from Milton. But Coleridge, when saying of republican France that,

> "*Insupportably advancing,*
> Her arm made mockery of the warrior's tramp,"

not satisfied with omitting the marks of acknowledgment, thought fit positively to deny that he was indebted to Milton. Yet who could forget that semi-chorus in the " Samson," where the " bold Ascalonite " is described as having " fled from his lion ramp " ? Or who, that was not in this point liable to some hallucination of judgment, would have ventured on a public challenge (for virtually it was that) to produce from the " Samson " words so impossible to be overlooked as those of " insupportably advancing the foot " ? The result was, that one of the critical journals placed the two passages in juxtaposition, and left the reader to his own conclusions with regard to the poet's veracity. But, in this instance, it was common sense rather than veracity which the facts impeach.

3. In the year 1810, I happened to be amusing myself, by reading, in their chronological order, the great classical circumnavigations of the earth ; and, coming to Shelvocke, I met with a passage to this effect :—That Hatley, his second captain (*i. e.*, lieutenant), being a melancholy man, was possessed by a fancy that some long season of foul weather, in the solitary sea which they were then tra-versing, was due to an albatross which had steadily pur-sued the ship ; upon which he shot the bird, but without

mending their condition.   There at once I saw the germ
of the "Ancient Mariner;" and I put a question to Coleridge accordingly.   Could it have been imagined that he
would see cause utterly to disown so slight an obligation
to Shelvocke?   Wordsworth, a man of stern veracity, on
hearing of this, professed his inability to understand Coleridge's meaning; the fact being notorious, as he told me,
that Coleridge had derived, from the very passage I had
cited, the original hint for the action of the poem; though
it is very possible, from something which Coleridge said,
on another occasion, that, before meeting a fable in which
to embody his ideas, he had meditated a poem on delirium,
confounding its own dream-scenery with external things,
and connected with the imagery of high latitudes.

4.   All these cases amount to nothing at all, as cases of
plagiarism, and for this reason expose the more conspi-
cuously that obliquity of feeling which could seek to
decline the very slight acknowledgments required.   But
now I come to a case of real and palpable plagiarism; yet
that, too, of a nature to be quite unaccountable in a man
of Coleridge's attainments.   It is not very likely that this
particular case will soon be detected; but others will.   Yet
who knows?   Eight hundred or a thousand years hence,
some reviewer may arise, who, having read the "Biographia
Literaria" of Coleridge, will afterwards read the "Philosophical ——" * of Schelling, the great Bavarian professor—a
man in some respects worthy to be Coleridge's assessor; and
he will then make a singular discovery.   In the "Biographia
Literaria" occurs a dissertation upon the reciprocal relations of the *Esse* and the *Cogitare*, that is, of the *objective*

---

* I forget the exact title, not having seen the book since 1823,
and then only for one day; but I believe it was Schelling's "Kleine
Philosophische Werke."

and the *subjective:* and an attempt is made, by inverting the postulates from which the argument starts, to show how each might arise as a product, by an intelligible genesis, from the other. It is a subject which, since the time of Fichte, has much occupied the German metaphysicians; and many thousands of essays have been written on it, or indirectly so, of which many hundreds have been read by many tens of persons. Coleridge's essay, in particular, is prefaced by a few words, in which, aware of his coincidence with Schelling, he declares his willingness to acknowledge himself indebted to so great a man, in any case where the truth would allow him to do so; but, in this particular case, insisting on the impossibility that he could have borrowed arguments which he had first seen some years after he had thought out the whole hypothesis *proprio marte.* After this, what was my astonishment to find that the entire essay, from the first word to the last, is a *verbatim* translation from Schelling, with no attempt in a single instance to appropriate the paper, by developing the arguments or by diversifying the illustrations? Some other obligations to Schelling, of a slighter kind, I have met with in the "Biographia Literaria," but this was a barefaced plagiarism, which could in prudence have been risked only by relying too much upon the slight knowledge of German literature in this country, and especially of that section of the German literature. Had then Coleridge any need to borrow from Schelling? Did he borrow *in forma pauperis?* Not at all: there lay the wonder. He spun daily, and at all hours, for mere amusement of his own activities, and from the loom of his own magical brain, theories more gorgeous by far, and supported by a pomp and luxury of images, such as Schelling—no, nor any German that ever breathed, not John Paul—could have emulated in his dreams. With the riches of El Dorado lying about him, he would condescend to filch a handful of gold from any man whose purse he fancied ; and in fact reproduced in a new form, applying itself to intellectual wealth, that maniacal propensity which is sometimes well-known to attack enormous proprietors and millionaires for acts of petty larceny. The last Duke of Anc—— could not abstain from exercising his furtive mania upon articles so humble as silver-spoons ; and it was the nightly care of a pious daughter, watching over the aberrations of her father, to have his pockets searched by a confidential valet, and the claimants of the purloined articles traced out.

Many cases have crossed me in life of people, otherwise not wanting in principle, who had habits, or at least hankerings, of the same kind. And the phrenologists, I believe, are well acquainted with the case, its signs, its progress, and its history. Dismissing, however, this subject, which I have at all noticed only that I might anticipate, and (in old English) that I might *prevent*, the uncandid interpreter of its meaning, I will assert finally, that, after having read for thirty years in the same track as Coleridge— that track in which few of any age will ever follow us, such as German metaphysicians, Latin schoolmen, thaumaturgic Platonists, religious Mystics—and having thus discovered a large variety of trivial thefts, I do, nevertheless, most heartily believe him to have been as entirely original in all his capital pretensions as any one man that ever has existed ; as Archimedes in ancient days, or as Shakspere in modern. Did the reader ever see Milton's account of the rubbish contained in the Greek and Latin Fathers ? Or did he ever read a statement of the monstrous chaos with which an African Obeah man stuffs his enchanted scarecrows ? Or, take a more common illustration, did he ever amuse himself by searching the pockets of a child—three years old, suppose—when buried in slumber after a long summer's day of out-o'-door's intense activity? I have done this; and, for the amusement of the child's mother, have analyzed the contents, and drawn up a formal register of the whole. Philosophy is puzzled, conjecture and hypothesis are confounded, in the attempt to explain the law of selection which *can* have presided in the child's labours : stones remarkable only for weight, old rusty hinges, nails, crooked skewers, stolen when the cook had turned her back, rags, broken glass, tea-cups having the bottom knocked out, and loads of similar jewels, were the prevailing articles in this *procès-verbal*. Yet, doubtless, much labour had been incurred, some sense of danger, perhaps, had been faced, and the anxieties of a conscious robber endured, in order to amass this splendid treasure. Such in value were the robberies of Coleridge ; such their usefulness to himself or anybody else ; and such the circumstances of uneasiness under which he had committed them. I return to my narrative.

Two or three days had slipped away in waiting for Coleridge's re-appearance at Nether Stowey, when suddenly Lord Egmont called upon Mr. Poole, with a present for Coleridge : it was a canister of peculiarly fine snuff, which Coleridge now took profusely. Lord Egmont, on this occasion, spoke of Coleridge in the terms of excessive admiration, and urged Mr. Poole to put him upon undertaking some great monumental work, that might furnish a sufficient arena for the display of his various and rare accomplishments ; for his multiform erudition on the one hand, for his splendid power of theorizing and combining large and remote notices of facts on the other. And he suggested, judiciously enough, as one theme which offered a field at once large enough and indefinite enough to suit a mind that could not show its full compass of power, unless upon very plastic materials—a History of Christianity, in its progress and in its chief divarications into Church and Sect, with a continual reference to the relations subsisting between Christianity and the current philosophy ; their occasional connexions or approaches, and their constant mutual repulsions. " But, at any rate, let him do something," said Lord Egmont ; " for at present he talks very much like an angel, and does nothing at all." Lord Egmont I understood, from everybody, to be a truly good and benevolent man ; and on this occasion he spoke with an earnestness which agreed with my previous impression. Coleridge, he said, was now in the prime of his powers— uniting something of youthful vigour with sufficient experience of life ; having the benefit, beside, of vast meditation, and of reading unusually discursive. No man had ever been better qualified to revive the heroic period of literature in England, and to give a character of weight to the philosophic erudition of the country upon the Continent. " And what a pity," he added, " if this man were, after all, to vanish like an apparition ; and you, I, and a few others, who have witnessed his grand *bravuras* of display, were to have the usual fortune of ghost-seers, in meeting no credit for any statements that we might vouch on his behalf !"

On this occasion we learned, for the first time, that Lord Egmont's carriage had, some days before, conveyed Coleridge to Bridgewater, with a purpose of staying one single day at that place, and then returning to Mr. Poole's. From the sort of laugh with which Lord Egmont taxed his own simplicity, in having confided at all in the stability of any Coleridgian plan, I now gathered that procrastination in excess was, or had become, a marking feature in Coleridge's daily life. Nobody who knew him ever thought of depending on any appointment he might make : spite of his uniformly honourable intentions, nobody attached any weight to his assurances *in re futura:* those who asked him to dinner or any other party, as a matter of course, sent a carriage for him, and went personally or by proxy to fetch him ; and, as to letters, unless the address were in some female hand that commanded his affectionate esteem, he tossed them all into one general *dead-letter bureau,* and rarely, I believe, opened them at all. Bourrienne mentions a mode of abridging the trouble attached to a very extensive correspondence, by which infinite labour was saved to himself, and to Napoleon, when First Consul. Nine out of ten letters, supposing them letters of business with official applications of a special kind, he contends, answer themselves : in other words, time alone must soon produce events which virtually contain the answer. On this principle the letters were opened periodically, after intervals, suppose, of six weeks; and, at the end of that time, it was found that not many remained to require any further more particular answer. Coleridge's plan, however, was shorter: he opened none, I understood, and answered none. At least such was his habit at that time. But on that same day, all this, which I heard now for the first time, and with much concern, was fully explained; for already he was under the full dominion of opium, as he himself revealed to me, and with a deep expression of horror at the hideous bondage, in a private walk of some length, which I took with him about sunset.

Lord Egmont's information, and the knowledge now gained of Coleridge's habits, making it very uncertain when I might see him in my present hospitable quarters, I im-

mediately took my leave of Mr. Poole, and went over to
Bridgewater. I had received directions for finding out the
house where Coleridge was visiting; and, in riding down a
main street of Bridgewater, I noticed a gateway corresponding to the description given me. Under this was standing, and gazing about him, a man whom I will describe.
In height he might seem to be about five feet eight (he
was, in reality, about an inch and a-half taller, but his
figure was of an order which drowns the height); his person was broad and full, and tended even to corpulence; his
complexion was fair, though not what painters technically
style fair, because it was associated with black hair; his
eyes were large, and soft in their expression; and it was
from the peculiar appearance of haze or dreaminess which
mixed with their light that I recognised my object. This
was Coleridge. I examined him steadfastly for a minute
or more; and it struck me that he saw neither myself nor
any other object in the street. He was in a deep reverie;
for I had dismounted, made two or three trifling arrangements at an inn-door, and advanced close to him, before he
had apparently become conscious of my presence. The
sound of my voice, announcing my own name, first awoke
him; he started, and for a moment seemed at a loss to
understand my purpose or his own situation; for he repeated rapidly a number of words which had no relation to
either of us. There was no *mauvaise honte* in his manner,
but simple perplexity, and an apparent difficulty in re-
covering his position amongst daylight realities. This
little scene over, he received me with a kindness of manner
so marked, that it might be called gracious. The hospitable family with whom he was domesticated were distinguished for their amiable manners and enlightened under-
standings : they were descendants from Chubb, the philo-

sophic writer, and bore the same name. For Coleridge
they all testified deep affection and esteem—sentiments in
which the whole town of Bridgewater seemed to share; for
in the evening, when the heat of the day had declined, I
walked out with him; and rarely, perhaps never, have I
seen a person so much interrupted in one hour's space as
Coleridge, on this occasion, by the courteous attentions of
young and old.

All the people of station and weight in the place, and
apparently all the ladies, were abroad to enjoy the lovely
summer evening; and not a party passed without some
mark of smiling recognition; and the majority stopping
to make personal inquiries about his health, and to express their anxiety that he should make a lengthened stay
amongst them.   Certain I am, from the lively esteem
expressed towards Coleridge, at this time, by the people
of Bridgewater, that a very large subscription might, in
that town, have been raised to support him amongst them,
in the character of a lecturer, or philosophical professor.
Especially, I remarked, that the young men of the place
manifested the most liberal interest in all that concerned
him; and I can add my attestation to that of Mr. Coleridge himself, when describing an evening spent amongst
the enlightened tradesmen of Birmingham, that nowhere
is more unaffected good sense exhibited, and particularly
nowhere more elasticity and *freshness* of mind, than in
the conversation of the reading men in manufacturing
towns.   In Kendal, especially, in Bridgewater, and in
Manchester, I have witnessed more interesting conversations, as much information, and more natural eloquence
in conveying it, than usually in literary cities, or in places
professedly learned.   One reason for this is, that in trading towns the time is more happily distributed; the day

given to business and active duties—the evening to relaxation ; on which account, books, conversation, and literary leisure are more cordially enjoyed : the same satiation
never can take place, which too frequently deadens the
genial enjoyment of those who have a surfeit of books
and a monotony of leisure. Another reason is, that more
simplicity of manner may be expected, and more natural
picturesqueness of conversation, more open expression of
character, in places where people have no previous name
to support. Men in trading towns are not afraid to open
their lips, for fear they should disappoint your expectations, nor do they strain for showy sentiments, that they
may meet them. But elsewhere, many are the men who
stand in awe of their own reputation : not a word which
is unstudied, not a movement in the spirit of natural freedom dare they give way to ; because it might happen that
on review something would be seen to retract or to qualify
—something not properly planed and chiselled, to build
into the general architecture of an artificial reputation.
But to return :—

Coleridge led me to a drawing-room, rang the bell for
refreshments, and omitted no point of a courteous reception. He told me that there would be a very large dinner
party on that day, which, perhaps, might be disagreeable
to a perfect stranger ; but, if not, he could assure me of
a most hospitable welcome from the family. I was too
anxious to see him under all aspects, to think of declining
this invitation. That point being settled, Coleridge, like
some great river, the Orellana, or the St. Lawrence, that,
having been checked and fretted by rocks or thwarting
islands, suddenly recovers its volume of waters and its
mighty music, swept at once, as if returning to his natural
business, into a continuous strain of eloquent dissertation,

certainly the most novel, the most finely illustrated, and traversing the most spacious fields of thought, by transitions the most just and logical that it was possible to conceive. What I mean by saying that his transitions were " just," is by way of contradistinction to that mode of conversation which courts variety through links of *verbal* connexions. Coleridge, to many people, and often I have heard the complaint, seemed to wander ; and he seemed then to wander the most when, in fact, his resistance to the wandering instinct was greatest—viz., when the compass and huge circuit, by which his illustrations moved, travelled farthest into remote regions before they began to revolve. Long before this coming round commenced, most people had lost him, and naturally enough supposed that he had lost himself. They continued to admire the separate beauty of the thoughts, but did not see their relations to the dominant theme. Had the conversation been thrown upon paper, it might have been easy to trace the continuity of the links ; just as in Bishop Berkeley's " Siris," * from a pedestal so low and abject, so culinary, as Tar Water, the method of preparing it, and its medicinal effects, the dissertation ascends, like Jacob's ladder, by just gradations, into the Heaven of Heavens, and the thrones of the Trinity. But Heaven is there connected with earth by the Homeric chain of gold ; and, being subject to steady examination, it is easy to trace the links. Whereas, in conversation, the loss of a single word may cause the whole cohesion to disappear from view. However, I can assert, upon my long and intimate knowledge of

---

* *Seiris* ought to have been the title—*i.e.*, Σειρις, a chain. From this defect in the orthography, I did not in my boyish days perceive, nor could obtain any light upon its meaning.

Coleridge's mind, that logic the most severe was as in-
alienable from his modes of thinking, as grammar from his
language.

On the present occasion, the original theme started by
myself, was Hartley, and the Hartleian theory. I had
carried, as a little present to Coleridge, a scarce Latin pamphlet, " De Ideis," written by Hartley about 1746, that
is, about three years earlier than the publication of his
great work. He had also preluded to this great work,
in a little English medical tract upon Joanna Stephens's
medicine for the stone ; for indeed Hartley was the person
upon whose evidence the House of Commons had mainly
relied in giving to that same Joanna a reward of £5000
for her idle medicines—an application of public money not
without its use, in so far as it engaged men by selfish
motives to cultivate the public service, and to attempt
public problems of very difficult solution ; but else, in that
particular instance, perfectly idle, as the groans of three
generations since Joanna's era have too feelingly established. It is known to most literary people that Coleridge
was, in early life, so passionate an admirer of the Hartleian philosophy, that " Hartley" was the sole baptismal
name which he gave to his eldest child ; and in an early
poem, entitled " Religious Musings,' he has characterized
Hartley as

> " Him of mortal kind
> Wisest, him first who mark'd the ideal tribes
> Up the fine fibres through the sentient brain
> Pass in fine surges."

But at present (August 1807) all this was a forgotten
thing. Coleridge was so profoundly ashamed of the
shallow Unitarianism of Hartley, and so disgusted to think
that he could at any time have countenanced that creed,

that he would scarcely allow to Hartley the reverence which is undoubtedly his due ; for I must contend, that, waving all question of the extent to which Hartley would have pushed it (as though the law of association accounted not only for our complex pleasures and pains, but also might be made to explain the act of ratiocination), waving also the physical substratum of nervous vibrations and miniature vibrations, to which he has chosen to marry his theory of association ;—all this apart, I must contend that the " Essay on Man, his Frame, his Duty, and his Expectations," stands forward as a specimen almost unique of elaborate theorizing, and a monument of absolute beauty, in the impression left of its architectural grace. In this respect it has, to my mind, the spotless beauty and the ideal proportions of some Grecian statue. However, I confess, that being myself, from my earliest years, a reverential believer in the doctrine of the Trinity, simply because I never attempted to bring all things within the mechanic understanding, and because, like Sir Thomas Brown, my mind almost demanded mysteries, in so mysterious a system of relations as those which connect us with another world ; and also, because the farther my understanding opened, the more I perceived of dim analogies to strengthen my creed ; and because nature herself, mere physical nature, has mysteries no less profound ; for these, and for many other " *becauses*," I could not reconcile, with my general reverence for Mr. Coleridge, the fact, so often reported to me, that he was a Unitarian. But, said some Bristol people to me, not only is he a Unitarian—he is also a Socinian. In that case, I replied, I cannot hold him a Christian. I am a liberal man, and have no bigotry or hostile feelings towards a Socinian ; but I can never think that man a Christian who has blotted out of his scheme the very powers by which only the great offices and functions of Christianity can be sustained ; neither can I think that any man, though he make himself a marvellously clever disputant, ever could tower upwards into a very great philosopher, unless he should begin or should end with Christianity. Kant is a dubious exception. Not that I mean to question his august pretensions, so far as they went, and in his proper line. Within his own circle none durst tread but he. But that circle was limited. He was called, by one who weighed him well, the *alles-zermalmender*, the world-shattering Kant. He could destroy—his intellect was essentially destructive. He was the Gog and he was the Magog of Hunnish desolation to the existing schemes of philosophy. He probed them ; he showed the vanity of vanities which besieged their foundations—the rottenness below, the hollowness above. But he had no instincts of creation or restoration within his Apollyon mind ; for he had no love, no faith, no self-distrust, no humility, no childlike docility ; all which qualities belonged essentially to Coleridge's mind, and waited only for manhood and for sorrow to bring them forward.

Who can read without indignation of Kant, that, at his own table, in social sincerity and confidential talk, let him say what he would in his books, he exulted in the prospect of absolute and ultimate annihilation ; that he planted his glory in the grave, and was ambitious of rotting for ever ? The King of Prussia, though a personal friend of Kant's, found himself obliged to level his state thunders at some of his doctrines, and terrified him in his advance ; else I am persuaded that Kant would have formally delivered Atheism from the professor's chair, and would have enthroned the horrid Goulish creed (which privately he

professed) 'in the University of Königsberg.   It required
the artillery of a great king to make him pause : his me-
nacing or warning letter to Kant is extant.   The general
notion is, that the royal logic applied so austerely to the
public conduct of Kant, in his professor's chair, was of
that kind which rests its strength " upon thirty legions."
My own belief is, that the king had private information
of Kant's ultimate tendencies as revealed in his table-talk.
The fact is, that as the stomach has been known, by means
of its own potent acid secretion, to attack not only whatsoever alien body is introduced within it, but also (as John
Hunter first showed) sometimes to attack itself and its
own organic structure ; so, and with the same preternatural extension of instinct, did Kant carry forward his
destroying functions, until he turned them upon his own
hopes and the pledges of his own superiority to the dog—
the ape—the worm.   But " *exoriare aliquis* "—and some
philosopher, I am persuaded, *will* arise ; and " one sling
of some victorious arm " (" Paradise Lost," B. x.) will yet
destroy the destroyer, in so far as he has applied himself
to the destruction of Christian hope.   For my faith is,
that, though a great man may, by a rare possibility, be
an infidel, an intellect of the highest order must build
upon Christianity.   A very clever architect may choose to
show his power by building with insufficient materials ;
but the supreme architect must require the very best ;
because the perfection of the forms cannot be shown but
in the perfection of the matter.

On these accounts I took the liberty of doubting, as
often as I heard the reports I have mentioned of Coleridge ;
and I now found that he disowned most solemnly (and I
may say penitentially) whatever had been true in these
reports.   Coleridge told me that it had cost him a painful

effort, but not a moment's hesitation, to abjure his Unitarianism, from the circumstance that he had amongst the
Unitarians many friends, to some of whom he was greatly
indebted for great kindness.   In particular, he mentioned
Mr. Estlin of Bristol, a distinguished Dissenting clergyman, as one whom it grieved him to grieve.   But he
would not dissemble his altered views.   I will add, at the
risk of appearing to dwell too long on religious topics,
that, on this my first introduction to Coleridge, he reverted
with strong compunction to a sentiment which he had
expressed in earlier days upon prayer.   In one of his
youthful poems, speaking of God, he had said—

> " Of whose omniscient and all-spreading love
> Aught to implore were impotence of mind."

This sentiment he now so utterly condemned, that, on the
contrary, he told me, as his own peculiar opinion, that the
act of praying was the very highest energy of which the
human heart was capable ; praying, that is, with the total
concentration of the faculties ; and the great mass of
worldly men, and of learned men, he pronounced absolutely
incapable of prayer.

For about three hours he had continued to talk, and in
the course of this performance he had delivered many most
striking aphorisms, embalming more weight of truth, and
separately more deserving to be themselves embalmed,
than would easily be found in a month's course of select
reading.   In the midst of our conversation, if that can be
called conversation which I so seldom sought to interrupt,
and which did not often leave openings for contribution,
the door opened, and a lady entered.   She was in person
full and rather below the common height ; whilst her face
showed to my eye some prettiness of rather a commonplace order.   Coleridge paused upon her entrance ; his

features, however, announced no particular complacency, and did not relax into a smile. In a frigid tone he said, whilst turning to me, "Mrs. Coleridge;" in some slight way he then presented me to her : I bowed ; and the lady almost immediately retired. From this short but ungenial scene, I gathered, what I afterward learned redundantly, that Coleridge's marriage had not been a very happy one. But let not the reader misunderstand me. Never was there a baser insinuation, viler in the motive, or more ignoble in the manner, than that passage in some lampoon of Lord Byron's, where, by way of vengeance on Mr. Southey (who was the sole delinquent), he described both him and Coleridge as having married "two milliners from Bath." Everybody knows what is *meant* to be conveyed in that expression, though it would be hard, indeed, if, even at Bath, there should be any class under such a fatal curse, condemned so irretrievably, and so hopelessly prejudged, that ignominy must, at any rate, attach in virtue of a mere name or designation, to the mode by which they gained their daily bread, or possibly supported the declining years of a parent. However, in this case, the whole sting of the libel was a pure falsehood of Lord Byron's. Bath was not the native city, nor at any time the residence, of the ladies in question, but Bristol. As to the other word, "*milliners*," that is not worth inquiring about. Whether they, or any one of their family, ever *did* exercise this profession, I do not know ; they were, at all events, too young, when removed by marriage from Bristol, to have been much tainted by the worldly feelings which may beset such a mode of life. But what is more to the purpose, I heard, at this time, in Bristol, from Mr. Cottle, the author, a man of high principle, as also from his accomplished sisters, from the ladies, again, who had

succeeded Mrs. Hannah More in her school, and who enjoyed her entire confidence, that the whole family of four
or five sisters had maintained an irreproachable character,
though naturally exposed, by their personal attractions, to
some peri., and to the malevolence of envy. This declara-
tion, which I could strengthen by other testimony equally
disinterested, if it were at all necessary, I owe to truth ;
and I must also add, upon a knowledge more personal,
that Mrs. Coleridge was, in all circumstances of her married life, a virtuous wife and a conscientious mother ; and,
as a mother, she showed at times a most meritorious
energy. In particular, I remember that, wishing her
daughter to acquire the Italian language, and having
in her retirement at Keswick, no means of obtaining a
master, she set to work resolutely, under Mr. Southey's
guidance, to learn the language herself, at a time of life
when such attainments are not made with ease or pleasure.
She became mistress of the language in a very respectable
extent, and then communicated her new accomplishment to
her most interesting daughter.

I go on, therefore, to say, that Coleridge afterwards
made me, as doubtless some others, a confidant in this
particular. What he had to complain of was simply
incompatibility of temper and disposition. Wanting all
cordial admiration, or indeed comprehension of her husband's intellectual powers, Mrs. Coleridge wanted the
original basis for affectionate patience and candour. Hearing from everybody that Coleridge was a man of most
extraordinary endowments, and attaching little weight,
perhaps, to the distinction between popular talents and
such as by their very nature are doomed to a slower progress in the public esteem, she naturally looked to see, at
least, an ordinary measure of worldly consequence attend

upon their exercise. Now, had Coleridge been as persevering and punctual as the great mass of professional men, and had he given no reason to throw the *onus* of the different result upon his own different habits, in that case this result might, possibly and eventually, have been set down to the peculiar constitution of his powers, and their essential mal-adaptation to the English market. But this trial having never fairly been made, it was natural to impute his non-success exclusively to his own irregular application, and to his carelessness in forming judicious connexions. In circumstances such as these, however, no matter how caused or how palliated, was laid a sure ground of discontent and fretfulness in any woman's mind, not unusually indulgent or unusually magnanimous. Coleridge, besides, assured me that his marriage was not his own deliberate act, but was in a manner forced upon his sense of honour by the scrupulous Southey, who insisted that he had gone too far in his attentions to Miss Fricker, for any honourable retreat. On the other hand, a neutral spectator of the parties protested to me, that, if ever in his life he had seen a man under deep fascination, and what he would have called desperately in love, Coleridge, in relation to Miss F., was that man. Be that as it might, circumstances occurred soon after the marriage which placed all the parties in a trying situation for their candour and good temper. I had a full outline of the situation from two of those who were chiefly interested, and a partial one from a third : nor can it be denied that all the parties offended in point of prudence. A young lady became a neighbour, and a daily companion of Coleridge's walks, whom I will not describe more particularly, than by saying, that intellectually she was very much superior to Mrs. Coleridge. That superiority alone, when made

conspicuous by its effects in winning Coleridge's regard
and society, could not but be deeply mortifying to a young
wife.   However, it was moderated to her feelings by two
considerations :—1. That the young lady was much too
kind-hearted to have designed any annoyance in this
triumph, or to express any exultation ; 2. That no shadow
of suspicion settled upon the moral conduct or motives of
either party : the young lady was always attended by her
brother; she had no personal charms ; and it was manifest
that mere intellectual sympathies, in reference to literature and natural scenery, had associated them in their
daily walks.

Still, it is a bitter trial to a young married woman to
sustain any sort of competition with a female of her own
age for any part of her husband's regard, or any share of
his company.   Mrs. Coleridge, not having the same relish
for long walks or rural scenery, and their residence being,
at this time, in a very sequestered village, was condemned
to a daily renewal of this trial.   Accidents of another kind
embittered it still further : often it would happen that the
walking party returned drenched with rain ; in which case,
the young lady, with a laughing gaiety, and evidently unconscious of any liberty that she was taking, or any wound
that she was inflicting, would run up to Mrs. Coleridge's
wardrobe, array herself, without leave asked, in Mrs. Coleridge's dresses, and make herself merry with her own un-
ceremoniousness and Mrs. Coleridge's gravity.   In all this,
she took no liberty that she would not most readily have
granted in return ; she confided too unthinkingly in what
she regarded as the natural privileges of friendship ; and
as little thought that she had been receiving or exacting a
favour, as, under an exchange of their relative positions,
she would have claimed to confer one.   But Mrs. Cole-

ridge viewed her freedoms with a far different eye : she felt herself no longer the entire mistress of her own house ; she held a divided empire ; and it barbed the arrow to her womanly feelings, that Coleridge treated any sallies of resentment which might sometimes escape her as narrow-mindedness ; whilst, on the other hand, her own female servant, and others in the same rank of life, began to drop expressions, which alternately implied pity for her as an injured woman, or contempt for her as a very tame one.

The reader will easily apprehend the situation, and the unfortunate results which it boded to the harmony of a young married couple, without further illustration. Whether Coleridge would not, under any circumstances, have become indifferent to a wife not eminently capable of enlightened sympathy with his own ruling pursuits, I do not undertake to pronounce. My own impression is, that neither Coleridge nor Lord Byron could have failed, eventually, to quarrel with *any* wife, though a Pandora sent down from heaven to bless him. But, doubtless, this consummation must have been hastened by a situation which exposed Mrs. Coleridge to an invidious comparison with a more intellectual person ; as, on the other hand, it was most unfortunate for Coleridge himself, to be continually compared with one so ideally correct and regular in his habits as Mr. Southey. Thus was their domestic peace prematurely soured : embarrassments of a pecuniary nature would be likely to demand continual sacrifices ; no depth of affection existing, these would create disgust or dissension ; and at length each would believe that their union had originated in circumstances overruling their own deliberate choice.

The gloom, however, and the weight of dejection which sat upon Coleridge's countenance and deportment at this

time could not be accounted for by a disappointment (if
such it were), to which time must, long ago, have reconciled him.   Mrs. Coleridge, if not turning to him the more
amiable aspects of her character, was at any rate a respectable partner.   And the season of youth was now passed.
They had been married about ten years; had had four
children, of whom three survived; and the interests of a
father were now replacing those of a husband.   Yet never
had I beheld so profound an expression of cheerless despondency.   And the restless activity of Coleridge's mind,
in chasing abstract truths, and burying himself in the dark
places of human speculation, seemed to me, in a great
measure, an attempt to escape out of his own personal
wretchedness.   I was right.   In this instance, at least, I
had hit the mark; and Coleridge bore witness himself at
an after period to the truth of my divination by some impressive verses.   At dinner, when a very numerous party
had assembled, he knew that he was expected to talk, and
exerted himself to meet the expectation.   But he was evidently struggling with gloomy thoughts that prompted him
to silence, and perhaps to solitude: he talked with effort,
and passively resigned himself to the repeated misrepresentations of several amongst his hearers.   The subject
chiefly discussed was Arthur Young, not for his Rural
Economy, but for his Politics.   It must be to this period of
Coleridge's life that Wordsworth refers in those exquisite
" Lines written in my pocket copy of the ' Castle of Indolence.' "   The passage which I mean comes after a description of Coleridge's countenance, and begins in some such
terms as these :—

> " A piteous sight it was to see this man,
>   When he came back to us, a wither'd flow'r," &c.

Withered he was, indeed, and to all appearance blighted.

At night he entered into a spontaneous explanation of this unhappy overclouding of his life, on occasion of my saying accidentally that a toothache had obliged me to take a few drops of laudanum. At what time or on what motive he had commenced the use of opium, he did not say; but the peculiar emphasis of horror with which he warned me against forming a habit of the same kind, impressed upon my mind a feeling that he never hoped to liberate himself from the bondage. My belief is that he never *did*. About ten o'clock at night I took leave of him; and feeling that I could not easily go to sleep after the excitement of the day, and fresh from the sad spectacle of powers so majestic already besieged by decay, I determined to return to Bristol through the coolness of the night. The roads, thoug., in fact, a section of the great highway between seaports so turbulent as Bristol and Plymouth, were as quiet as garden-walks. Once only I passed through the expiring fires of a village fair or wake: that interruption excepted, through the whole stretch of forty miles from Bridgewater to the Hot-wells, I saw no living creature but a surly dog, who followed me for a mile along a park-wall, and a man, who was moving about in the half-way town of Cross. The turnpike-gates were all opened by a mechanical contrivance from a bedroom window; I seemed to myself in solitary possession of the whole sleeping country. The summer night was divinely calm; no sound, except once or twice the cry of a child as I was passing the windows of cottages, ever broke upon the utter silence; and all things conspired to throw back my thoughts upon that extraordinary man whom I had just quitted.

The fine saying of Addison is familiar to most readers—that Babylon in ruins is not so affecting a spectacle, or so solemn, as a human mind overthrown by lunacy. How much more awful, then, when a mind so regal as that of Coleridge is overthrown, or threatened with overthrow, not by a visitation of Providence, but by the treachery of its own will, and by the conspiracy, as it were, of himself against himself! Was it possible that this ruin had been caused or hurried forward by the dismal degradations of pecuniary difficulties? That was worth inquiring. I will here mention briefly, that I *did* inquire two days after; and, in consequence of what I heard, I contrived that a particular service should be rendered to Mr. Coleridge, a week after, through the hands of Mr. Cottle of Bristol, which might have the effect of liberating his mind from anxiety for a year or two, and thus rendering his great powers disposable to their natural uses. That service was accepted by Coleridge. To save him any feelings of distress, all names were concealed; but, in a letter written by him about fifteen years after that time, I found that he had become aware of all the circumstances, perhaps through some indiscretion of Mr. Cottle's. A more important question I never ascertained, viz., whether this service had the effect of seriously lightening his mind. For some succeeding years, he did certainly appear to me released from that load of despondency which oppressed him on my first introduction. Grave, indeed, he continued to be, and at times absorbed in gloom; nor did I ever see him in a state of perfectly natural cheerfulness. But, as he strove in vain, for many years, to wean himself from his captivity to opium, a healthy state of spirits could not be much expected. Perhaps, indeed, where the liver and other organs had, for so large a period in life, been subject to a continual morbid stimulation, it might be impossible for the system ever to recover a natural action. Torpor, I suppose, must result from continued artificial excitement; and, perhaps, upon a scale of corresponding duration. Life, in such a case, may not offer a field of sufficient extent for unthreading the fatal links that have been wound about the machinery of health, and have crippled its natural play.

Meantime—to resume the thread of my wandering narrative—on this serene summer night of 1807, as I moved slowly along, with my eyes continually settling upon the northern constellations, which, like all the fixed stars, by their immeasurable and almost spiritual remoteness from human affairs, naturally throw the thoughts upon the perishableness of our earthly troubles, in contrast with their own utter peace and solemnity—I reverted, at intervals, to all I had ever heard of Coleridge, and strove to weave it into some continuous sketch of his life. I hardly remember how much I then knew ; I know but little now—that little I will here jot down upon paper.

Samuel Taylor Coleridge was the son of a learned clergyman—the vicar of Ottery St. Mary, in the southern quarter of Devonshire. It is painful to mention that he was almost an object of persecution to his mother ; why, I could never learn. His father was described to me, by Coleridge himself, as a sort of Parson Adams, being distinguished by his erudition, his inexperience of the world, and his guileless simplicity. I once purchased in London, and, I suppose, still possess, two elementary books on the Latin language by this reverend gentleman ; one of them, as I found, making somewhat higher pretensions than a common school grammar. In particular, an attempt is made to reform the theory of the cases ; and it gives a pleasant specimen of the rustic scholar's *naïveté*, that he seriously proposes to banish such vexatious terms as the *accusative ;* and, by way of simplifying the matter to tender minds, that we should call it, in all time to come, the "*quale-quare-quidditive*" case, upon what incomprehensible principle I never could fathom. He used regularly to delight his village flock, on Sundays, with Hebrew quotations in his sermons, which he always introduced as the " immediate language of the Holy Ghost." This proved unfortunate to his successor : he also was a learned man, and his parishioners admitted it, but generally with a sigh for past times, and a sorrowful complaint that he was still far below Parson Coleridge—for that *he* never gave them any "immediate language of the Holy Ghost." I presume, that, like the reverend gentleman so pleasantly sketched in "St. Ronan's Well," Mr. Coleridge, who resembled that person in his oriental learning, in his absence of mind, and in his simplicity, must also have resembled him in shortsightedness, of which his son used to relate this ludicrous instance. Dining in a large party, one day, the modest divine was suddenly shocked by perceiving some part, as he conceived, of his own snowy shirt emerging from a part of his habiliments, which we will suppose to have been his waistcoat. It was *not* that ; but for decorum we will so call it. The stray portion of his own supposed tunic was admonished of its errors by a forcible thrust-back into its proper home ; but still another *limbus* persisted to emerge, or seemed to persist, and still another, until the learned gentleman absolutely perspired with the labour of re-establishing order. And, after all, he saw with anguish that some arrears of the snowy indecorum still remained to reduce into obedience. To this remnant of rebellion he was proceeding to apply himself— strangely confounded, however, at the obstinacy of the insurrection—when the mistress of the house, rising to lead away the ladies from the table, and all parties naturally rising with her, it became suddenly apparent to every

eye that the worthy Orientalist had been most laboriously
stowing away, into the capacious receptacles of his own
habiliments—under the delusion that it was his own shirt
—the snowy folds of a lady's gown, belonging to his next
neighbour ; and so voluminously, that a very small portion
of it, indeed, remained for the lady's own use ; the natural
consequence of which was, of course, that the lady appeared
inextricably yoked to the learned theologian, and could not
in any way effect her release, until after certain operations
upon the vicar's dress, and a continued refunding and roll-
ing out of snowy mazes upon snowy mazes, in quantities
which at length proved too much for the gravity of the
company. Inextinguishable laughter arose from all parties,
except the erring and unhappy doctor, who, in dire perplexity, continued still refunding with all his might—perspiring
and refunding—until he had paid up the last arrears of
his long debt, and thus put an end to a case of distress
more memorable to himself and his parishioners than any
" quale-quare-quidditive" case that probably had ever perplexed his learning.

In his childish days, and when he had become an orphan,
Coleridge was removed to the heart of London, and placed
on the great foundation of Christ's Hospital. He there
found himself associated, as a school-fellow, with several
boys destined to distinction in after life ; particularly the
brilliant Leigh Hunt, and more closely with one, who,
if not endowed with powers equally large and comprehensive as his own, had, however, genius not less original or
exquisite—viz., the inimitable Charles Lamb. But, in
learning, Coleridge outstripped all competitors, and rose to
be the captain of the school. It is, indeed, a memorable
fact to be recorded of a boy, that, before completing his
fifteenth year, he had translated the Greek Hymns of

Synesius into English Anacreontic verse. This was not a
school task, but a labour of love and choice. Before leaving
school, Coleridge had an opportunity of reading the sonnets
of Bowles, which so powerfully impressed his poetic sensibility, that he made forty transcripts of them with his
own pen, by way of presents to youthful friends. From
Christ's Hospital, by the privilege of his station at school,
he was transferred to Jesus College, Cambridge. It was
here, no doubt, that his acquaintance began with the
philosophic system of Hartley, for that eminent person had
been a Jesus man. Frend also, the mathematician, of here-
tical memory (he was judicially tried, and expelled from
his fellowship, on some issue connected with the doctrine
of the Trinity), belonged to that college, and was probably
contemporary with Coleridge. What accident, or impru-
dence, carried him away from Cambridge before he had
completed the usual period of study, I never heard. He
had certainly won some distinction as a scholar, having
obtained the prize for a Greek ode in Sapphic metre, of
which the sentiments (as he observes himself) were better
than the Greek. Porson was accustomed, meanly enough,
to ridicule the Greek *lexis* of this ode, which was to break
a fly upon the wheel. The ode was clever enough for a
boy ; but to such skill in Greek as could have enabled him
to compose with critical accuracy, Coleridge never made
pretensions.

The incidents of Coleridge's life about this period, and
some account of a heavy disappointment in love, which
probably it was that carried him away from Cambridge,
are to be found embodied (with what modifications I know
not) in the novel of " Edmund Oliver," written by Charles
Lloyd. It is well known that, in a frenzy of unhappy
feeling at the rejection he met with from the lady of his

choice, Coleridge enlisted as a private into a dragoon regiment. He fell off his horse on several occasions, but perhaps not more than raw recruits are apt to do when first put under the riding-master. But Coleridge was naturally ill framed for a good horseman. He is also represented in "Edmund Oliver" as having found peculiar difficulty or annoyance in grooming his horse. But the most romantic incident in that scene of his life was in the circumstances of his discharge. It is said (but I vouch for no part of the story) that Coleridge as a private, mounted guard at the door of a room in which his officers were giving a ball. Two of them had a dispute upon some Greek word or passage when close to Coleridge's station. He interposed his authentic decision of the case. The officers stared as though one of their own horses had sung "Rule Britannia;" questioned him; heard his story; pitied his misfortune; and finally subscribed to purchase his discharge. So the story has been told; and also otherwise. Not very long after this, Coleridge became acquainted with the two celebrated Wedgwoods of Etruria, both of whom, admiring his fine powers, subscribed to send him into North Germany, where, at the University of Gottingen, he completed his education according to his own scheme. The most celebrated professor whose lectures he attended was the far-famed Blumenbach, of whom he continued to speak through life with almost filial reverence. Returning to England, he attended Mr. Thomas Wedgwood, as a friend, throughout the afflicting and anomalous illness which brought him to the grave. It was supposed by medical men that the cause of Mr. Wedgwood's continued misery was a stricture of the colon. The external symptoms were torpor and morbid irritability, together with everlasting restlessness. By way of some relief to this latter symptom, Mr. Wedgwood purchased a travelling carriage, and wandered up and down England, taking Coleridge as his companion. And, as a desperate attempt to rouse and irritate the decaying sensibility of his system, I have been assured, by a surviving friend, that Mr. Wedgwood at one time opened a butcher's shop, conceiving that the affronts and disputes to which such a situation would expose him, might act beneficially upon his increasing torpor. This strange expedient* served only to express the anguish which had now mastered his nature; it was soon abandoned; and this accomplished but miserable man at length sank under his sufferings. What made the case more memorable, was the combination of worldly prosperity which forced into strong relief and fiery contrast this curse written in the flesh. He was rich, he was young, he was popular, distinguished for his scientific attainments, publicly honoured for patriotic services, and had before him, when he first fell ill, every prospect of a career even nationally splendid.

By the death of Mr. Wedgwood, Coleridge succeeded to a regular annuity of £75, which that gentleman had bequeathed to him. The other Mr. Wedgwood granted him an equal allowance. Now came his marriage, his connexion with politics and political journals, his residence in various parts of Somersetshire, and his consequent intro-

---

* Which, however, his brother denied as a pure fable. On reading this account, he wrote to me, and in very courteous terms assured me that I had been misinformed. I now retain the story, simply as a version, partially erroneous, no doubt, of perhaps some true anecdote that may have escaped the surviving Mr. Wedgwood's knowledge; my reason for thinking thus being, that the same anecdote essentially, but varied in the circumstances, has reached me at different periods from parties having no connexion whatsoever.

duction to Mr. Wordsworth. In his politics, Mr. Coleridge was most sincere and most enthusiastic. No man hailed with profounder sympathy the French Revolution ; and, though he saw cause to withdraw his regard from many of the democratic zealots in this country, and even from the revolutionary interest as it was subsequently conducted, he continued to worship the original revolutionary cause in a pure Miltonic spirit ; and he continued also to abominate the policy of Mr. Pitt in a degree which I myself find it difficult to understand. The very spirited little poem of "Fire, Famine, and Slaughter," who are supposed to meet in conference, to describe their horrid triumphs, and then to ask in a whisper *who* it was that unchained them ; to which each in turn replies,

"Letters four do form his name !"

expresses his horror of Mr. Pitt personally in a most extravagant shape, but merely for the purpose of poetic effect ; for he had no real unkindness in his heart towards any human being ; and I have often heard him disclaim the hatred which is here expressed for Mr. Pitt, as he did also very elaborately and earnestly in print. Somewhere about this time, Coleridge attempted, under Sheridan's countenance, to bring a tragedy upon the stage of Drury Lane ; but his prospect of success, as I once heard or read, was suddenly marred by Mr. Sheridan's inability to sacrifice what he thought a good jest. One scene presented a cave with streams of water weeping down the sides ; and the first words were, in a sort of mimicry of the sound, "Drip, drip, drip !" Upon which Sheridan repeated aloud to the assembled green-room, expressly convoked for the purpose of hearing the play read, "Drip, drip, drip !— why, God bless me, there's nothing here but *dripping !*"

and so arose a chorus of laughter amongst the actors fatal for the moment to the probationary play.

About the latter end of the century, Coleridge visited North Germany again, in company with Mr. and Miss Wordsworth. Their tour was chiefly confined to the Hartz Forest and its neighbourhood. But the incident most worthy of remembrance in their excursion, was a visit made to Klopstock; either at Hamburgh, or, perhaps, at the Danish town of Altona, on the same river Elbe; for Klopstock was a pensioner of the Danish king. An anonymous writer, who attacked Coleridge most truculently in an early number of "Blackwood," and with an *acharnement* that must astonish the neutral reader, has made the mistake of supposing Coleridge to have been the chief speaker, who did not speak at all. The case was this : Klopstock could not speak English, though everybody remembers the pretty broken English * of his second wife. Neither Coleridge nor Wordsworth, on the other hand, was able to *speak* German with any fluency. French, therefore, was the only medium of free communication ; that being pretty equally familiar to Wordsworth and to Klopstock. But Coleridge found so much difficulty even in *reading* French, that, wherever (as in the case of Leibnitz's "Theodicée") there was a choice between an original written in French, and a translation, though it might be a very faulty one, in German, he always preferred the latter. Hence it happened that Wordsworth, on behalf of the English party, was the sole supporter of the dialogue. The anonymous critic says another thing, which certainly has an air of truth— viz., that Klopstock plays a very secondary *rôle* in the interview (or words to that effect). But how was this to

---

* Published in Richardson's Correspondence.

be avoided in reporting the case, supposing the fact to
have been such ?   Now, the plain truth is, that Wordsworth, upon his own ground, was an incomparable talker ;
whereas " Klubstick " (as Coleridge used to call him) was
always a feeble and slovenly one, because a loose and incoherent thinker.   Besides, he was now old and decaying.
Nor at any time, nor in any accomplishment, could Klopstock have shone, unless in the respectable art of skating.   *There* he had a real advantage.   The author of " The
Messiah," I have authority for saying, skated with the
ease and grace of a regular artist ; whereas the poet of the
" Excursion " sprawled upon the ice like a cow dancing a
cotillon.   Wordsworth did the very opposite of that with
which he was taxed ; for, happening to look down at Klopstock's swollen legs, and recollecting his age, he felt touched
by a sort of filial pity for his helplessness.   And he came
to the conclusion, that it would not seem becoming in a
young, and as yet obscure author, to report too consciously
the real superiority which he found it easy to maintain in
such a colloquy.

But neither had Klopstock the pretensions as a poet,
which the Blackwood writer seems to take for granted.
Germany, the truth is, wanted a great epic poet.   Not
having produced one in that early and plastic stage of her
literary soil when such a growth is natural and spontaneous, the next thing was to bespeak a substitute.   The force
of Coleridge's well-known repartee, when, in reply to a
foreigner asserting for Klopstock the rank of German
Milton, he said, " True, sir ; a very *German* Milton," cannot be fully appreciated but by one who is familiar with
the German poetry, and the small proportion in which it is
a natural, racy, and domestic growth.   It has been often
noticed as the misfortune of the Roman literature, that

it grew up too much under the oppression of Grecian models, and of Grecian models depraved by Alexandrian art—a fact, so far as it *was* a fact, which tended to cripple the *genial* and characteristic spirit of the national mind. But this evil, after all, did not take effect except in a partial sense. Rome had cast much of her literature in her own moulds before these exotic models had begun to domineer. In fact, the reproach is in a very narrow sense true. Not so with Germany. Her literature, since its revival in the last century (and the revival upon the impulse of what cattle!—Bodmer on the one hand, and Gottsched—the never-enough-to-be-despised Gottsched—on the other!), has hardly moved a step in the freedom of natural grace. England for nineteen, and France for the twentieth of all her capital works, has given the too servile law : and with regard to Klopstock, if ever there was a good exemplification of the spurious and the counterfeit in literature, seek it in " The Messiah." He is verily and indeed the *Birmingham* Milton. This Klopstockian dialogue, by the way, was first printed (hardly *published*) in the original, or Lake edition of " The Friend." In the recast of that work it was omitted ; nor has it been printed anywhere else, that I am aware of.

About the close of the first revolutionary war, it must have been, or in the brief interval of peace, that Coleridge resorted to the English Lakes as a place of residence. Wordsworth had a natural connexion with that region, by birth, breeding, and family alliances. Wordsworth must have attracted Coleridge to the Lakes ; and Coleridge, through his affinity to Southey, eventually attracted *him*. Southey, as is known to all who take an interest in the Lake colony, married a sister of Mrs. Coleridge's ; and, as a singular eccentricity in the circumstances of that marriage, I may mention, that, on his wedding-day, and from the very portico of the church, Southey left his bride to embark for Lisbon. His uncle, Dr. Herbert, was chaplain to the English factory in that city ; and it was to benefit by the facilities in that way opened to him for seeing Portugal, that Southey now went abroad. He extended his tour to Spain ; and the result of his notices was communicated to the world in a volume of travels. By such accidents of personal or family connexion as I have mentioned, was the Lake colony gathered ; and the critics of the day, unaware of the real facts, supposed them to have assembled under common views in literature— particularly with regard to the true functions of poetry, and the true theory of poetic diction. Under this original blunder, laughable it is to mention, that they went on to *find* in their writings all the agreements and common characteristics which their blunder had presumed ; and they incorporated the whole community under the name of the *Lake School.* Yet Wordsworth and Southey never had one principle in common ; their hostility was even flagrant. Indeed, Southey troubled himself little about abstract principles in anything ; and, so far from agreeing with Wordsworth to the extent of setting up a separate school in poetry, he told me himself (August 1812), that he highly disapproved both of Mr. Wordsworth's theories and of his practice. It is very true, that one man may sympathize with another, or even follow his leading, unconscious that he does so ; or he may go so far as, in the very act of virtual imitation, to deem himself in opposition ; but this sort of blind agreement could hardly be supposed of two men so discerning and so self-examining as Wordsworth and Southey. And, in fact, a philosophic investigation of the difficult questions connected with this

whole slang about schools, Lake schools, &c., would show
that Southey has not, nor ever had, any *peculiarities* in
common with Wordsworth, beyond that of exchanging the
old prescriptive diction of poetry, introduced between the
periods of Milton and Cowper, for the simpler and profounder forms of daily life in some instances, and of the
Bible in others.   The bold and uniform practice of Wordsworth was here adopted, on perfectly independent views,
by Southey.   In this respect, however, Cowper had already
begun the reform ; and his influence, concurring with the
now larger influence of Wordsworth, has operated so extensively, as to make their own original differences at this day
less perceptible.

By the way, the word *colony* reminds me that I have
omitted to mention in its proper place some scheme for
migrating to America, which had been entertained by
Coleridge and Southey about the year 1794-95, under the
learned name of *Pantisocracy.*   So far as I ever heard,
it differed little, except in its Grecian name, from any
other scheme for mitigating the privations of a wilderness,
by settling in a cluster of families bound together by
congenial tastes and uniform principles, rather than in
self-depending, insulated households.   Steadily pursued,
it might, after all, have been a fortunate plan for Coleridge.   " Soliciting my food from daily toil," a line in
which Coleridge alludes to the scheme, implies a condition
of life that would have upheld Coleridge's health and happiness somewhat better than the habits of luxurious city
life as now constituted in Europe.   But, returning to the
Lakes, and to the Lake colony of poets : So little were
Southey and Wordsworth connected by any personal intercourse in those days, and so little disposed to be connected, that, whilst the latter had a cottage in Grasmere,

Southey pitched his tent at Greta Hall, on a little eminence rising immediately from the river Greta and the town of Keswick. Grasmere is in Westmoreland; Keswick in Cumberland; and they are thirteen good miles apart. Coleridge and his family were domiciliated in Greta Hall; sharing that house, a tolerably large one, on some principle of amicable division, with Mr. Southey. But Coleridge personally was more often to be found at Grasmere—which presented the threefold attractions of loveliness so complete as to eclipse even the scenery of Derwentwater; a pastoral state of society, free from the deformities of a little town like Keswick; and finally, for Samuel Taylor Coleridge, the society of Wordsworth. Not before 1815 or 1816, could it be said that Southey and Wordsworth were even upon friendly terms; so entirely is it untrue that they combined to frame a school of poetry. Up to that time, they viewed each other with mutual respect, but also with mutual dislike; almost, I might say, with mutual disgust. Wordsworth disliked in Southey the want of depth, or the apparent want, as regards the power of philosophic abstraction. Southey disliked in Wordsworth the air of dogmatism, and the unaffable haughtiness of his manner. Other more trivial reasons combined with these.

At this time, when Coleridge first settled at the Lakes, or not long after, a romantic and somewhat tragical affair drew the eyes of all England, and, for many years, continued to draw the steps of tourists, to one of the most secluded Cumberland valleys, so little visited previously, that it might be described almost as an undiscovered chamber-of that romantic district. Coleridge was brought into a closer connexion with this affair than merely by the general relation of neighbourhood; for an article of his

in a morning paper, I believe, unintentionally furnished
the original clue for unmasking the base impostor who
figured as the central actor in this tale.   The tale was
at that time dramatized, and scenically represented by
some of the minor theatres in London, as noticed by
Wordsworth in the " Prelude." But other generations
have arisen since that time, who must naturally be unacquainted with the circumstances ; and on their account I
will here recall them.   One day in the Lake season, there
drove up to the Royal Oak, the principal inn at Keswick, a handsome and well-appointed travelling carriage,
containing one gentleman of somewhat dashing exterior.
The stranger was a picturesque-hunter, but not of that
order who fly round the ordinary tour with the velocity
of lovers posting to Gretna, or of criminals running from
the police ; his purpose was to domiciliate himself in this
beautiful scenery, and to see it at his leisure.   From
Keswick, as his head-quarters, he made excursions in every
direction amongst the neighbouring valleys ; meeting generally a good deal of respect and attention, partly on
account of his handsome equipage, and still more from
his visiting cards, which designated him as " The Hon.
Augustus Hope."   Under this name, he gave himself out
for a brother of Lord Hopetoun's.   Some persons had discernment enough to doubt of this ; for the man's breeding
and deportment, though showy, had an under tone of vul-
garity about it ; and Coleridge assured me, that he was
grossly ungrammatical in his ordinary conversation.   However, one fact, soon dispersed by the people of a little
rustic post-office, laid asleep all demurs ; he not only received letters addressed to him under this assumed name
—*that* might be through collusion with accomplices—-
but he himself continually *franked* letters by that name.

Now, this being a capital offence, being not only a forgery, but (as a forgery on the Post-Office), sure to be prosecuted, nobody presumed to question his pretensions any longer ; and, henceforward, he went to all places with the consideration attached to an earl's brother. All doors flew open at his approach : boats, boatmen, nets, and the most unlimited sporting privileges, were placed at the disposal of the "Honourable" gentleman : and the hospitality of the district was put on its mettle, in offering a suitable reception to the patrician Scotsman. It could be no blame to a shepherd girl, bred in the sternest solitude which England has to show, that she should fall into a snare which many of her betters had not escaped. Nine miles from Keswick, by the nearest bridle-road through Newlands, but fourteen or fifteen by any route which the honourable gentleman's travelling-carriage could traverse, lies the Lake of Buttermere. Its margin, which is overhung by some of the loftiest and steepest of the Cumbrian mountains, exhibits on either side few traces of human neighbourhood ; the level area, where the hills recede enough to allow of any, is of a wild pastoral character, or almost savage ; the waters of the lake are deep and sullen ; and the barrier mountains, by excluding the sun for much of his daily course, strengthen the gloomy impressions. At the foot of this lake (that is, at the end where its waters issue), lie a few unornamented fields, through which rolls a little brook-like river, connecting it with the larger lake of Crummock ; and at the edge of this miniature domain, upon the roadside, stands a cluster of cottages, so small and few, that, in the richer tracts of England, they would scarcely be complimented with the name of hamlet. One of these, and I believe the principal, belonged to an independent

proprietor, called, in the local dialect, a " *Statesman;* " * and
more, perhaps, for the sake of attracting a little society,
than with much view to pecuniary profit at that era, this
cottage offered the accommodations of an inn to the
traveller and his horse.   Rare, however, must have been
the mounted traveller in those days, unless visiting Buttermere for itself, and as a *terminus ad quem ;* since the road
led to no further habitations of man, with the exception
of some four or five pastoral cabins, equally humble, in
Gatesgarthdale.

Hither, however, in an evil hour for the peace of this
little brotherhood of shepherds, came the cruel spoiler from
Keswick.   His errand was, to witness or to share in the
char-fishing ; for in Derwentwater (the Lake of Keswick)
no char is found, which breeds only in the deep waters,
such as Windermere, Crummock, Buttermere, and Coniston—never in the shallow ones.   But, whatever had been
his first object, *that* was speedily forgotten in one more
deeply interesting.   The daughter of the house, a fine
young woman of eighteen, acted as waiter.†   In a situation
so solitary, the stranger had unlimited facilities for enjoy-
ing her company, and recommending himself to her favour.
Doubts about his pretensions never arose in so simple a
place as this ; they were overruled before they could well

---

* *i. e.*—A 'Statesman elliptically for an Estatesman—a native
dalesman possessing and personally cultivating a patrimonial landed
estate.

† *Waiter :*—Since this was first written, social changes in London,
by introducing females very extensively into the office (once mono-
polized by men) of attending the visitors at the tables of eating-
houses) have introduced a corresponding new word—viz., *waitress;*
which word, twenty-five years back, would have been simply ludicrous ; but now is become as indispensable to precision of language
as the words, traitress, heiress, inheritrix, &c.

have arisen, by the opinion now general in Keswick, that he really was what he pretended to be : and thus, with little demur, except in the shape of a few natural words of parting anger from a defeated or rejected rustic admirer, the young woman gave her hand in marriage to the showy and unprincipled stranger. I know not whether the marriage was, or could have been, celebrated in the little mountain chapel of Buttermere. If it were, I persuade myself that the most hardened villain must have felt a momentary pang on violating the altar of such a chapel ; so touchingly does it express, by its miniature dimensions, the almost helpless humility of that little pastoral community to whose spiritual wants it has from generation to generation administered. It is not only the very smallest chapel by many degrees in all England, but is so mere a toy in outward appearance, that, were it not for its antiquity, its wild mountain exposure, and its consecrated connexion with the final hopes and fears of the adjacent pastoral hamlet—but for these considerations, the first movement of a stranger's feelings would be towards loud laughter ; for the little chapel looks not so much a mimic chapel in a drop-scene from the Opera House, as a miniature copy from such a scene ; and evidently could not receive within its walls more than half-a-dozen of households. From this sanctuary it was—from beneath the maternal shadow, if not from the very altar,* of this lonely chapel—that the heartless villain carried off the flower of the mountains. Between this place and Keswick

---

* My doubt is founded upon the varying tenure of these secluded chapels as to privileges of marrying or burying. The mere name of chapel, though of course, in regular connexion with some mother church, does not of itself imply whether it has or has not the power to solemnize a marriage.

they continued to move backwards and forwards, until at length, with the startling of a thunder-clap to the affrighted mountaineers, the bubble burst : officers of justice appeared : the stranger was easily intercepted from flight : and, upon a capital charge, was borne away to Carlisle. At the ensuing assizes he was tried for forgery on the prosecution of the Post-Office ; found guilty, left for execution, and executed accordingly. On the day of his condemnation, Wordsworth and Coleridge passed through Carlisle, and endeavoured to obtain an interview with him. Wordsworth succeeded ; but, for some unknown reason, the prisoner steadily refused to see Coleridge ; a caprice which could not be penetrated. It is true that he had, during his whole residence at Keswick, avoided Coleridge with a solicitude which had revived the original suspicions against him in some quarters, after they had generally gone to sleep. But for this his motive had then been sufficient : he was of a Devonshire family, and naturally feared the eye, or the inquisitive examination of one who bore a name immemorially associated with the southern part of that county.

Coleridge, however, had been transplanted so immaturely from his native region, that few people in England knew less of its family connexions. That, perhaps, was unknown to this malefactor ; but, at any rate, he knew that all motive was now at an end for disguise of any sort ; so that his reserve, in this particular, had now become unintelligible. However, if not him, Coleridge saw and examined his very interesting papers. These were chiefly letters from women whom he had injured, pretty much in the same way, and by the same impostures, as he had so recently practised in Cumberland ; and, as Coleridge assured me, were in part the most agonizing appeals that he had ever read to human justice and pity. The man's real name was, I think, Hatfield. And amongst the papers were two separate correspondences, of some length, with two young women, apparently of superior condition in life (one the daughter of an English clergyman), whom this villain had deluded by marriage, and, after some cohabitation, abandoned,—one of them with a family of young children. Great was the emotion of Coleridge when he recurred to his remembrance of these letters, and bitter, almost vindictive—was the indignation with which he spoke of Hatfield. One set of letters appeared to have been written under too certain a knowledge of *his* villany to whom they were addressed ; though still relying on some possible remains of humanity, or perhaps (the poor writer might think) on some lingering prefer-ence for herself. The other set was even more distressing ; they were written under the first conflicts of suspicions, alternately repelling with warmth the gloomy doubts which were fast arising, and then yielding to their afflicting evi-dence ; raving in one page under the misery of alarm, in another courting the delusions of hope, and luring back the perfidious deserter,—here resigning herself to despair, and there again labouring to show that all might yet be well. Coleridge said often, in looking back upon that frightful exposure of human guilt and misery, that the man who, when pursued by these heartrending apos-trophes, and with this litany of anguish sounding in his ears, from despairing women and from famishing children, could yet find it possible to enjoy the calm pleasures of a Lake tourist, and deliberately to hunt for the picturesque, must have been a fiend of that order which fortunately does not often emerge amongst men. It is painful to remember that, in those days, amongst the

multitudes who ended their career in the same ignomini-
ous way, and the majority for offences connected with the
forgery of bank notes, there must have been a considerable
number who perished from the very opposite cause—viz.,
because they felt, too passionately and profoundly for prudence, the claims of those who looked up to them for
support.   One common scaffold confounds the most flinty
hearts and the tenderest.   However, in this instance, it
was in some measure the heartless part of Hatfield's conduct which drew upon him his ruin : for the Cumberland
jury honestly declared their unwillingness to hang him for
having forged a frank ; and both they, and those who
refused to aid his escape when first apprehended, were
reconciled to this harshness entirely by what they heard
of his conduct to their injured young fellow-country-
woman.

   She, meantime, under the name of *The Beauty of Buttermere*, became an object of interest to all England ; melo-
dramas were produced in the London suburban* theatres

---

   * In connexion with this mention of " suburban" and minor theatres,
it is but fair to cite a passage expressly relating to Mary of Buttermere from the Seventh Book (entitled " Residence in London ") of
Wordsworth's " Prelude :"—

   " Here, too, were *forms and pressures of the time,*
      Rough, bold, as Grecian comedy display'd
      When Art was young ; dramas of living men,
      And recent things yet warm with life ; a sea-fight,
      Shipwreck, or some domestic incident
      Divulged by Truth, and magnified by Fame ;
      Such as the daring brotherhood of late
      Set forth, too serious theme for that light place—
      I mean, O distant friend ! a story drawn
      From our own ground—the Maid of Buttermere
      And how, unfaithful to a virtuous wife,
      Deserted and deceived, the spoiler came

BUTTERMERE.

upon her story ; and for many a year afterwards, shoals of
tourists crowded to the secluded lake, and the little homely
cabaret, which had been the scene of her brief romance.
It was fortunate for a person in her distressing situation,
that her home was not in a town : the few and simple
neighbours, who had witnessed her imaginary elevation,
having little knowledge of worldly feelings, never for an
instant connected with her disappointment any sense of
the ludicrous, or spoke of it as a calamity to which
her vanity might have co-operated.   They treated it as
unmixed injury, reflecting shame upon nobody but the
wicked perpetrator.   Hence, without much trial to her
womanly sensibilities, she found herself able to resume her

> And woo'd the artless daughter of the hills,
> And wedded her, in cruel mockery
> Of love and marriage bonds.   These words to thee
> Must needs bring back the moment when we first,
> Ere the broad world rang with the maiden's name,
> Beheld her serving at the cottage inn,
> Both stricken, as she enter'd or withdrew,
> With admiration of her modest mien
> And carriage, mark'd by unexampled grace.
> We since that time not unfamiliarly
> Have seen her—her discretion have observed,
> Her just opinions, delicate reserve,
> Her patience and humility of mind,
> Unspoil'd by commendation and th' excess
> Of public notice—an offensive light
> To a meek spirit suffering inwardly."

The " distant friend" here apostrophized is Coleridge, then at Malta.
But it is fair to record this memorial of the fair mountaineer—going
perhaps as much beyond the public estimate of her pretensions as my
own was below it.   It should be added, that William Wordsworth
and Samuel Taylor Coleridge (to whom the writer appeals, as in
general sympathy with himself) had seen Mary more frequently, and
had conversed with her much more freely than myself.

situation in the little inn; and this she continued to hold for many years. In that place, and that capacity, I saw her repeatedly, and shall here say a word upon her personal appearance, because the Lake poets all admired her greatly. Her figure was, in my eyes, good; but I doubt whether most of my readers would have thought it such. She was none of your evanescent, wasp-waisted beauties; on the contrary, she was rather large every way; tallish, and proportionably broad. Her face was fair, and her features feminine; and, unquestionably, she was what all the world would have agreed to call " good-looking." But, except in her arms, which had something of a statuesque beauty, and in her carriage, which expressed a womanly grace, together with some degree of dignity and self-possession, I confess that I looked in vain for any *positive* qualities of any sort or degree. *Beautiful*, in any emphatic sense, she was not. Everything about her face and bust was negative; simply without offence. Even this, however, was more than could be said at all times; for the expression of her countenance *could* be disagreeable. This arose out of her situation; connected as it was with defective sensibility and a misdirected pride. Nothing operates so differently upon different minds and different styles of beauty, as the inquisitive gaze of strangers, whether in the spirit of respectful admiration or of insolence. Some I have seen, upon whose angelic beauty this sort of confusion settled advantageously, and like a softening veil; others, in whom it meets with proud resentment, are sometimes disfigured by it. In Mary of Buttermere it roused mere anger and disdain; which, meeting with the sense of her humble and dependent situation, gave birth to a most unhappy aspect of countenance. Men who had no touch of a gentleman's nature in their com-

position sometimes insulted her by looks and by words ;
supposing that they purchased the right to do this by an
extra half-crown ; and she too readily attributed the same
spirit of impertinent curiosity to every man whose eyes
happened to settle steadily upon her face.   Yet, once at
least, I must have seen her under the most favourable circumstances : for, on my first visit to Buttermere, I had the
pleasure of Mr. Southey's company, who was incapable of
wounding anybody's feelings, and to Mary, in particular,
was well known by kind attentions, and I believe by some
services.   Then, at least, I saw her to advantage, and perhaps, for a figure of her build, at the best age ; for it was
about nine or ten years after her misfortune, when she
might be twenty-seven or twenty-eight years old.   We
were alone, a solitary pair of tourists : nothing arose to
confuse or distress her.   She waited upon us at dinner,
and talked to us freely.   "This is a respectable young
woman," I said to myself ; but nothing of that enthusiasm
could I feel, which beauty, such as I *have* beheld at the
Lakes, would have been apt to raise under a similar misfortune.   One lady, not very scrupulous in her embellishments
of facts, used to tell an anecdote of her, which I hope was
exaggerated.   Some friend of hers (as she affirmed), in
company with a large party, visited Buttermere, within one
day after that upon which Hatfield suffered ; and she protested that Mary threw upon the table, with an emphatic
gesture, the Carlisle paper containing an elaborate account
of his execution.

It is an instance of Coleridge's carelessness, that he, who
had as little of fixed ill-nature in his temper as any person
whom I have ever known, managed, in reporting this story
at the time of its occurrence, to get himself hooked into a
personal quarrel, which hung over his head unsettled for

nine or ten years. A Liverpool merchant, who was then
meditating a house in the Vale of Grasmere, and perhaps
might have incurred Coleridge's anger, by thus disturbing,
with inappropriate intrusions, this loveliest of all English
landscapes, had connected himself a good deal with Hatfield
during his Keswick masquerade; and was said even to
have carried his regard to that villain so far as to have
christened one of his own children by the names of
" Augustus Hope." With these and other circumstances,
expressing the extent of the infatuation amongst the
swindler's dupes, Coleridge made the public merry. Naturally, the Liverpool merchant was not amongst those who
admired the facetiousness of Coleridge on this occasion, but
swore vengeance whenever they should meet. They never
did meet, until ten years had gone by, and then, oddly
enough, it was in the Liverpool man's own house—in that
very nuisance of a house which had, I suppose, first armed
Coleridge's wrath against him. This house, by time and
accident, in no very wonderful way, had passed into the
hands of Wordsworth as tenant. Coleridge, as was still
less wonderful, had become the visitor of Wordsworth
on returning from Malta; and the Liverpool merchant, as
was also natural, either seeking his rent, or on the general
errand of a friendly visit, calling upon Wordsworth, met
Coleridge in the hall. Now came the hour for settling
old accounts. I was present, and can report the case.
Both looked grave, and coloured a little. But ten years
work wonders: an armistice of that duration heals many a
wound; and Samuel Taylor Coleridge, requesting his
enemy's company in the garden, entered upon a long metaphysical dissertation, bordering upon what you might call
philosophical rigmarole, and rather puzzling to answer. It
seemed to be an expansion, by Thomas Aquinas, of that

parody upon a well-known passage in Shenstone, where the
writer says—

> " He kick'd me down-stairs with such a sweet grace,
> That I thought he was handing me up."

And in the upshot, this conclusion *eventuated* (to speak
Yankeeishly), that, purely on principles of good neighbourhood and universal philanthropy, could Coleridge have
meditated or executed the insult offered in the " Morning
Post." The Liverpool merchant rubbed his forehead, and
seemed a little perplexed ; but he was a most good-natured
man ; and he was eminently a gentleman. At length, considering, perhaps, how very like Duns Scotus, or Albertus
Magnus, Coleridge had shown himself in this luminous explanation, he might begin to reflect, that, had any one of
those distinguished men offered a similar affront, it would
have been impossible to resent it ; for who could think of
kicking the " Doctor Seraphicus ?" or would it tell to any
man's advantage in history that he had caned Thomas
Aquinas ? On these principles, therefore, without saying
one word, Liverpoliensis held out his hand, and a lasting
reconciliation followed.

Not very long, I believe, after this affair of Hatfield,
Coleridge went to Malta. His inducement to such a step
must have been merely a desire to see the most interest·
ing regions of the Mediterranean, under the shelter and
advantageous introduction of an official station. It was,
however, an unfortunate chapter of his life : for, being
necessarily thrown a good deal upon his own resources in
the narrow society of a garrison, he there confirmed and
cherished, if he did not there form, his habit of taking
opium in large quantities. I am the last person in the
world to press conclusions harshly or uncandidly against
Coleridge ; but I believe it to be notorious, that he first

began the use of opium, not as a relief from any bodily pains or nervous irritations (since his constitution was strong and excellent), but as a source of luxurious sensations. It is a great misfortune, at least it is a great peril, to have tasted the enchanted cup of youthful rapture incident to the poetic temperament. That fountain of high-wrought sensibility once unlocked experimentally, it is rare to see a submission afterwards to the insipidities of daily life. Coleridge, to speak in the words of Cervantes, wanted better bread than was made of wheat ; and when youthful blood no longer sustained the riot of his animal spirits, he endeavoured to excite them by artificial stimulants.

At Malta he became acquainted with Commodore Decatur and other Americans of distinction ; and this brought him afterwards into connexion with Allston, the American artist. Of Sir Alexander Ball, one of Lord Nelson's captains in the battle of the Nile, and Governor of Malta, he spoke and wrote uniformly in a lavish style of panegyric, for which plainer men found it difficult to see the slightest ground. It was, indeed, Coleridge's infirmity to project his own mind, and his own very peculiar ideas, nay, even his own expressions and illustrative metaphors, upon other men, and to contemplate these reflex images from himself, as so many characters having an absolute ground in some separate object. "Ball and Bell "—" Bell and Ball," * were two of these pet subjects ;

---

* " *Ball and Bell* "—" *Bell and Ball :*"—viz., Sir Alexander Ball, Governor of Malta, and Dr. Andrew Bell, the importer into England from Madras of that machinery for facilitating popular education, which was afterwards fraudulently appropriated by Joseph Lancaster. The Bishop of Durham (Shute Barrington) gave to Dr. Bell, in reward of his Madras services the princely Mastership of Sherborne

he had a " craze" about each of them ; and to each he ascribed thoughts and words, to which, had they been put upon the rack, they never would have confessed.

From Malta, on his return homewards, he went to Rome and Naples. One of the cardinals, he tells us, warned him, by the Pope's wish, of some plot, set on foot by Bonaparte, for seizing him as an anti-Gallican writer. This statement was ridiculed by the anonymous assailant in " Blackwood" as the very consummation of moonstruck vanity ; and it is there compared to John Dennis's frenzy in retreating from the sea-coast, under the belief that Louis XIV. had commissioned emissaries to land on the English shore, and make a dash at his person. But, after all, the thing is not so entirely improbable. For it is certain that some orator of the Opposition (Charles Fox, as Coleridge asserts) had pointed out all the principal writers in the " Morning Post" to Napoleon's vengeance, by describing

---

Hospital. The doctor saved in this post £125,000, and with this money founded Trinity College, Glenalmond, in Perthshire. Most men have their enemies and calumniators: Dr. Bell had *his*, who happened rather indecorously to be his wife—from whom he was legally separated, or (as in Scotch law it is called) *divorced;* not, of course, divorced à *vinculo matrimonii* (which only amounts to a divorce in the English sense—such a divorce as enables the parties to contract another marriage), but simply divorced à *mensâ et thoro.* This legal separation, however, did not prevent the lady from persecuting the unhappy doctor with everlasting letters, indorsed outside with records of her enmity and spite. Sometimes she addressed her epistles thus :—" To that supreme of rogues, who looks the hang-dog that he is, Doctor (such a doctor!) Andrew Bell." Or again :—" To the ape of apes, and the knave of knaves, who is recorded to have once paid a debt—but a small one, you may be sure, it was that he selected for this wonderful experiment—in fact, it was 4½d. Had it been on the other side of 6d., he must have died before he could have achieved so dreadful a sacrifice." Many others, most ingeniously varied in the style of abuse, I have heard rehearsed by Coleridge,

the war as a war " of that journal's creation." And, as to
the insinuation that Napoleon was above throwing his
regards upon a simple writer of political essays, *that* is not
only abundantly confuted by many scores of established
cases, but also is specially put down by a case circum
stantially recorded in the second tour to Paris, by the celebrated John Scott of Aberdeen. It there appears, that, on
no other ground whatever than that of his connexion with
the London newspaper press, some friend of Mr. Scott's
had been courted most assiduously by Napoleon during the
Hundred Days. Assuredly Coleridge deserved, beyond all
other men that ever were connected with the daily press,
to be regarded with distinction. Worlds of fine thinking
lie buried in that vast abyss, never to be disentombed or
restored to human admiration. Like the sea, it has swallowed treasures without end, that no diving-bell will bring
up again. But nowhere, throughout its shoreless maga-

Southey, Lloyd, &c.; and one, in particular, addressed to the doctor,
when spending a summer at the cottage of Robert Newton, an old
soldier, in Grasmere, presented on the back two separate adjurations,
one specially addressed to Robert himself, pathetically urging him to
look sharply after the rent of his lodgings; and the other more generally addressed to the unfortunate person as yet undisclose l to the
British public (and in this case turning out to be myself), who might
be incautious enough to pay the postage at Ambleside. "Don't grant
him an hour's credit," she urged upon the person unknown, "if I had
any regard to my family." " *Cash down!*" she wrote twice over.
Why the doctor submitted to these annoyances, nobody knew. Some
said it was mere indolence; but others held it to be a cunning com-
promise with her inexorable malice. The letters were certainly open
to the " public" eye; but meantime the " public" was a very narrow
one; the clerks in the post-office had little time for digesting such
amenities of conjugal affection; and the chance bearer of the letters
to the doctor would naturally solve the mystery by supposing an
extra portion of madness in the writer, rather than an *extra* portion
of knavery in the reverend receiver.

mines of wealth, does there lie such a bed of pearls confounded with the rubbish and " purgamenta" of ages, as
in the political papers of Coleridge. No more *appreciable*
monument could be raised to the memory of Coleridge,
than a republication of his essays in the " Morning Post,"
and afterwards in the " Courier." And here, by the way,
it may be mentioned, that the sagacity of Coleridge, as
applied to the signs of the times, is illustrated by this fact,
that distinctly and solemnly he foretold the restoration of
the Bourbons, at a period when most people viewed such
an event as the most romantic of visions, and not less
chimerical than that "march upon Paris" of Lord Hawkes-
bury's, which for so many years supplied a theme of laughter
to the Whigs.

Why Coleridge left Malta, is as difficult to explain upon
any principles of ordinary business, as why he had ever
gone thither. The post of secretary, if it imposed any
official attendance of a regular kind, or any official correspondence, must have been but poorly filled by *him ;* and
Sir Alexander Ball, if I have collected his character justly,
was not likely to accept the gorgeous philosophy of Coleridge as an indemnification for irregular performance of his
public duties. Perhaps, therefore, though on the best terms
of mutual regard, mutually they might be pleased to part.
Part they did, at any rate, and poor Coleridge was sea-sick
the whole of his homeward (as he had been through the
whole of his outward) voyage.

It was not long after this event that my own introduction to Coleridge occurred. At that time some negotia-
tion was pending between him and the Royal Institution,
which ended in their engaging him to deliver a course of
lectures on Poetry and the Fine Arts during the ensuing
winter. For this series (twelve or sixteen, I think) he

II.—G

received a sum of one hundred guineas. And, considering
the slightness of the pains which he bestowed upon them,
he was well remunerated. I fear that they did not increase
his reputation; for never did any man treat his audience
with less respect, or his task with less careful attention.
I was in London for part of the time, and can report the
circumstances, having made a point of attending duly at
the appointed hours. Coleridge was at that time living
uncomfortably enough at the "Courier" office, in the
Strand. In such a situation, annoyed by the sound of feet
passing his chamber-door continually to the printing-rooms
of this great establishment, and with no gentle ministrations of female hands to sustain his cheerfulness, naturally
enough his spirits flagged; and he took more than ordinary
doses of opium. I called upon him daily, and pitied his for-
lorn condition. There was no bell in the room, which for
many months answered the double purpose of bedroom and
sitting-room. Consequently, I often saw him, picturesquely
enveloped in nightcaps, surmounted by handkerchiefs indorsed upon handkerchiefs, shouting from the attics of the
" Courier" office, down three or four flights of stairs, to a
certain "Mrs. Brainbridge," his sole attendant, whose dwelling was in the subterranean regions of the house. There
did I often see the philosopher, with the most lugubrious
of faces, invoking with all his might this uncouth name
of "Brainbridge," each syllable of which he intonated with
long-drawn emphasis, in order to overpower the hostile
hubbub coming downwards from the creaking press, and
the roar from the Strand, which entered at all the front
windows. "Mistress Brainbridge! I say, Mistress Brainbridge!" was the perpetual cry, until I expected to hear
the Strand, and distant Fleet Street, take up the echo of
" Brainbridge!" Thus unhappily situated, he sank more

than ever under the dominion of opium ; so that, at two
o'clock, when he should have been in attendance at the
Royal Institution, he was too often unable to rise from
bed.   Then came dismissals of audience after audience,
with pleas of illness ; and on many of his lecture days I
have seen all Albemarle Street closed by a " lock " of carriages, filled with women of distinction, until the servants
of the Institution or their own footmen advanced to the
carriage-doors with the intelligence that Mr. Coleridge had
been suddenly taken ill.   This plea, which at first had
been received with expressions of concern, repeated too
often, began to rouse disgust. Many in anger, and some in
real uncertainty, whether it would not be trouble thrown
away, ceased to attend.   And we that were more constant,
too often found reason to be disappointed with the quality
of his lecture.   His appearance was generally that of a
person struggling with pain and overmastering illness.
His lips were baked with feverish heat, and often black in
colour ; and, in spite of the water which he continued
drinking through the whole course of his lecture, he often
seemed to labour under an almost paralytic inability to
raise the upper jaw from the lower.   In such a state, it is
clear that nothing could save the lecture itself from reflecting his own feebleness and exhaustion, except the advantage of having been pre-composed in some happier mood.
But that never happened : most unfortunately he relied
upon his extempore ability to carry him through.   Now,
had he been in spirits, or had he gathered animation, and
kindled by his own motion, no written lecture could have
been more effectual than one of his unpremeditated colloquial harangues.   But either he was depressed originally
below the point from which any re-ascent was possible, or
else thi re-action was intercepted by continual disgust.

from looking back upon his own ill success ; for, assuredly, he never once recovered that free and eloquent movement of thought which he could command at any time in a private company.   The passages he read, moreover, in illustrating his doctrines, were generally unhappily chosen, because chosen at haphazard, from the difficulty of finding at a moment's summons those passages which his purpose required.   Nor do I remember any that produced much effect, except two or three, which I myself put ready marked into his hands, among the Metrical Romances edited by Ritson.

Generally speaking, the selections were as injudicious and as inappropriate, as they were ill delivered ; for, amongst Coleridge's accomplishments, good reading was not one ; he had neither voice (so, at least, *I* thought) nor management of voice.   This defect is unfortunate in a public lecturer ; for it is inconceivable how much weight and effectual pathos can be communicated by sonorous depth and melodious cadences of the human voice to sentiments the most trivial ; nor, on the other hand, how the grandest are emasculated by a style of reading, which fails in distributing the lights and shadows of a musical intonation.   However, this defect chiefly concerned the immediate impression ; the most afflicting to a friend of Coleridge's was the entire absence of his own peculiar and majestic intellect ; no heart, no soul, was in anything he said ; no strength of feeling in recalling universal truths ; no power of originality or compass of moral relations in his novelties—all was a poor faint reflection from jewels once scattered in the highway by himself, in the prodigality of his early opulence—a mendicant dependence on the alms dropped from his own overflowing treasury of happier times.

The next opportunity I had of seeing Coleridge was at the Lakes, in the winter of 1809, and up to the autumn of the following year. During this period it was that he carried on the original publication of "The Friend;" and for much the greater part of the time I saw him daily. He lived as a visitor in the house occupied by Mr. Wordsworth. This house (Allan Bank by name) was in Grasmere; and in another part of the same vale, at a distance of barely one mile, I myself had a cottage, and a considerable library. Many of my books being German, Coleridge borrowed them in great numbers. Having a general license from me to use them as he would, he was in the habit of accumulating them so largely at Allan Bank (the name of Mr. Wordsworth's house), that sometimes as many as five hundred were absent at once : which I mention, in order to notice a practice of Coleridge's, indicating his very scrupulous honour in what regarded the rights of ownership. Literary people are not always so strict in respecting property of this description; and I know more than one celebrated man, who professes as a maxim, that he holds it no duty of honour to restore a borrowed book; not to speak of many less celebrated persons, who, without openly professing such á principle, do however, in fact, exhibit a lax morality in such cases. The more honourable it was to poor Coleridge, who had means so trifling of buying books for himself—that, to prevent my flocks from mixing, and being confounded with the flocks already folded at Allan Bank (his own and Wordsworth's), or rather that they *might* mix without danger, he duly inscribed my name in the blank leaves of every volume; a fact which became rather painfully made known to me; for, as he had chosen to dub me *Esquire*, many years after this, it cost myself and a female friend some weeks of labour to hunt out these multitudinous memorials, **and to erase** this heraldic addition ; which else had the appearance to a stranger of having been conferred by myself.

"The Friend," in its original publication, was, as a pecuniary speculation, the least judicious, both for its objects and its means, I have ever known. It was printed at Penrith, a town in Cumberland, on the outer verge of the Lake district, and precisely twenty-eight miles removed from Coleridge's abode. This distance, enough of itself, in all conscience, was at least trebled in effect by the interposition of Kirkstone, a mountain which is scaled by a carriage ascent of three miles long, and so steep in parts, that, without four horses, no solitary traveller can persuade the neighbouring innkeepers to carry him. Another road, by way of Keswick, is subject to its own separate difficulties. And thus, in any practical sense, for ease, for certainty, and for despatch, Liverpool, ninety-five miles distant, was virtually nearer. Dublin even, or Cork, was more eligible. Yet, in this town, so situated, as I have stated, by way of purchasing such intolerable difficulties at the highest price, Coleridge was advised, and actually persuaded, to set up a printer, to buy, to lay in a stock of paper, types, &c., instead of resorting to some printer already established in Kendal, a large and opulent town not more than eighteen miles distant, and connected by a daily post, whereas, between himself and Penrith there was no post at all. Building his mechanical arrangements upon this utter "upside-down" inversion of all common sense, it is not surprising (as "madness ruled the hour") that in all other circumstances of plan or execution the work moved by principles of downright crazy disregard to all that a judicious counsel would have suggested. The subjects were chosen obstinately in defiance of the popular taste; they were treated in a style studiously disfigured by German modes of thinking, and by a German terminology; no attempt was made to win or conciliate public taste; and the plans adopted for obtaining payment were of a nature to insure a speedy bankruptcy to the concern. Coleridge had a list—nobody could ever say upon whose authority gathered together—of subscribers. He tells us himself that many of these renounced the work from an early period; and some (as Lord Corke) rebuked him for his presumption in sending it unordered, but (as Coleridge asserts) neither returned the copies, nor remitted the price. And even those who were conscientious enough to do this, could not remit four or five shillings for as many numbers, without putting Coleridge to an expense of treble postage at the least. This he complains of bitterly in his "Biographia Literaria," forgetting evidently that the evil was due exclusively to his own defective arrangements. People necessarily sent their subscriptions through such channels as were open to them, or such as were pointed out by Coleridge himself. It is also utterly unworthy of Coleridge to have taxed, as he does, many of his subscribers (or really, for anything that appears, the whole body) with neglecting to pay at all. Probably not one neglected. And some ladies, to my knowledge, scrupulously anxious about transmitting their subscriptions, paid three times over. Managed as the reader will collect from these indications, the work was going down-hill from the first. It never gained any accessions of new subscribers; from what source, then, was the continual dropping off of names to be supplied? The printer became a bankrupt: Coleridge was as much in arrear with his articles as with his lectures at the Royal Institution. *That* he was from the very first; but now he was disgusted and desponding; and

with No. 28 or 29 the work came to a final stop. Some
years after, it was re-cast and re-published. But, in fact,
this re-cast was altogether and absolutely a new work.
The sole contributors to the original work had been, first
of all, Wordsworth, who gave a very valuable paper on the
principles concerned in the composition of Epitaphs ; and,
secondly, Professor Wilson, who, in conjunction with Mr.
(now Dr.) Blair, an early friend, then visiting Mr. W. on
Windermere, wrote the letter signed " Mathetes," the reply
to which came from Wordsworth.

At the Lakes, and summoned abroad by scenery so exquisite—living, too, in the bosom of a family endeared to
him by long friendship and by sympathy the closest with
all his propensities and tastes—Coleridge (it may be
thought) could not sequester himself so profoundly as at
the " Courier" Office within his own shell, or shut himself
out so completely from that large dominion of eye and ear
amongst the hills, the fields, and the woods, which once
he had exercised so delightfully to himself, and with a par-
ticipation so immortal, through his exquisite poems, to all
generations.   He was not now reduced to depend upon
" Mrs. Brainbridge" [Mistress Brain—Brain—Brainbridge,
I say—— Oh heavens ! *is* there, *can* there, *was* there, *will*
there ever at any future period be, an undeniable use in
saying and in pressing upon the attention of the Strand
and Fleet Street at their earliest convenience the painful
subject of Mistress Brain—Brain—Brainbridge, I say——
Do you hear, Mrs. Brain—Brain—Brainbridge—— ? Brain
or Bain, it matters little—Bran or Brain, it's all one, I con-
ceive] ; here, on the contrary, he looked out from his study
windows upon the sublime hills of *Seat Sandal* and *Arthur's
Chair*, and upon pastoral cottages at their feet ; and all
around him, he heard hourly the murmurings of happy

life, the sound of female voices, and the innocent laughter of children. But apparently he was not happy; opium, was it, or what was it, that poisoned all natural pleasure at its sources? He burrowed continually deeper into scholastic subtleties and metaphysical abstractions; and, like that class described by Seneca, in the luxurious Rome of *his* days, he lived chiefly by candlelight. At two or four o'clock in the afternoon he would make his first appearance. Through the silence of the night, when all other lights had disappeared in the quiet cottages of Grasmere, *his* lamp might be seen invariably by the belated traveller, as he descended the long steep from Dunmailraise; and at seven or eight o'clock in the morning, when man was going forth to his labour, this insulated son of reverie was retiring to bed.

Society he did not much court, because much was not to be had; but he did not shrink from any which wore the promise of novelty. At that time the leading person about the Lakes, as regarded rank and station, amongst those who had any connexion with literature, was Dr. Watson, the well-known Bishop of Llandaff. This dignitary I knew myself as much as I wished to know him; he *was* interesting; yet also *not* interesting; and I will speak of him circumstantially. Those who have read his Autobiography, or are otherwise acquainted with the outline of his career, will be aware that he was the son of a Westmoreland schoolmaster. Going to Cambridge, with no great store of classical knowledge, but with the more common accomplishment of Westmoreland men, and one better suited to Cambridge, viz., a sufficient basis of mathematics, and a robust though commonplace intellect, for improving his knowledge according to any direction which accident should prescribe—he obtained the Professorship

of Chemistry without one iota of chemical knowledge up
to the hour when he gained it; and then setting eagerly
to work, that he might not disgrace the choice which
had thus distinguished him, long before the time arrived
for commencing his prelections, he had made himself
capable of writing those beautiful essays on that science,
which, after a revolution, and a counter-revolution, so great
as succeeding times have witnessed, still remain a cardinal book of introductory discipline to such studies; an
opinion deliberately expressed to myself by the late Sir
Humphry Davy, and in answer to an earnest question
which I took the liberty of proposing to him on that
point.   Sir Humphry said—that he could scarcely imagine
a time, or a condition of the science, in which the Bishop's
" Essays" would be superannuated.   With this experi-
mental proof that a Chemical Chair might be won and
honoured without previous knowledge even of the chemical
alphabet, he resolved to play the same feat with the Royal
Chair of Divinity; one far more important for local honour
and for wealth.   Here, again, he succeeded; and this time
he extended his experiment; for, whereas both Chairs had
been won without *previous* knowledge, he resolved that in
this case it should be maintained without *after* knowledge.
He applied himself simply to the improvement of its income, which he raised from £300 to at least £1000 per
annum.   All this he had accomplished before reaching the
age of thirty-five.

Riches are with us the parent of riches; and success, in
the hands of an active man, is the pledge of further success.   On the basis of this Cambridge preferment, Dr.
Watson built upwards, until he had raised himself, in one
way or other, to a seat in the House of Lords, and to a
commensurate income.   For the latter half of his life, he

—originally a village schoolmaster's son—was able to associate with the *magnates* of the land, upon equal terms. And that fact, of itself, without another word, implies, in this country, a degree of rank and fortune which one would think a sufficient reward even for merit as unquestionable as was that of Dr. Watson, considering that in *quality* it was merit of so vulgar a class. Yet he was always a discontented man, a railer at the government and the age which could permit merit such as his to pine away ingloriously in one of the humblest amongst the bishoprics, with no other addition to its emoluments than the richest professorship in Europe, and such other accidents in life as gave him in all, perhaps, not above five thousand per annum! Poor man!—only five thousand per annum! What a trial to a man's patience!—and how much he stood in need of philosophy, or even of religion, to face so dismal a condition.

This bishop was himself, in a secondary way, no uninteresting study. What I mean is, that, though originally the furthest removed from an interesting person, being a man remarkable indeed for robust faculties, but otherwise commonplace in his character, worldly-minded, and coarse, even to obtuseness, in his sensibilities, he yet became interesting from the strength of *degree* with which these otherwise repulsive characteristics were manifested. He was one of that numerous order in whom even the love of knowledge is subordinate to schemes of advancement; and to whom even his own success, and his own honour consequent upon that success, had no higher value than according to their use as instruments for winning further promotion. Hence it was, that, when by such aids he had mounted to a certain eminence, beyond which he saw little promise of further ascent, through any assistance of *theirs*

—since at this stage it was clear that party connexion in
politics must become his main reliance—he ceased to regard his favourite sciences with interest.   The very organs
of his early advancement were regarded with no gratitude
or tenderness, when it became clear that they could yield
no more.   Even chemistry was now neglected.   This, above
all, was perplexing to one who did not understand his
character.   For hither one would have supposed he might
have retreated from his political disappointments, and
have found a perpetual consolation in honours which no
intrigues could defeat, and in the esteem, so pure and un-
tainted, which still attended the honourable exertions of
his youth.   But he had not feeling enough for that view ;
he looked at the matter in a very different light.   Other
generations had come since then, and " other palms were
won."   To keep pace with the advancing science, and to
maintain his station amongst his youthful competitors,
would demand a youthful vigour and motives such as theirs.
But, as to himself, chemistry had given all it *could* give.
Having first raised himself to distinction by that, he had
since married into an ancient family—one of the leaders
amongst the landed aristocracy of his own county : he
had thus entitled himself to call the head of that family—a
territorial potentate with ten thousand per annum—by the
contemptuous sobriquet of " Dull Daniel ;" he looked down
upon numbers whom, twenty years before, he scarcely durst
have looked up to, except, perhaps, as a cat is privileged to
look at a king ; he had obtained a bishopric.   Chemistry
had done all this for him ; and had, besides, co-operating
with luck, put him in the way of reaping a large estate
from the gratitude and early death of his pupil, Mr. Luther.
All this chemistry had effected.   Could chemistry do anything more ?   Clearly not.   It was a burnt-out volcano.

And here it was, that, having lost his motives for cultivating it farther, he regarded the present improvers of the
science, not with the feelings natural to a disinterested
lover of such studies on their own account, but with
jealousy, as men who had eclipsed or had bedimmed his
own once brilliant reputation.   Two revolutions had occurred since his own " palmy days ;" Sir Humphry Davy,
he said, might be right ; and all might be gold that
glistened ; but, for his part, he was too old to learn new
theories—he must be content to hobble to his grave with
such old-fashioned creeds as had answered in his time,
when, for aught he could see, men prospered as much as
in this newfangled world.   Such was the tone of his ordinary talk ; and, in one sense—as regards personal claims,
I mean—it was illiberal enough ; for the leaders of modern
chemistry never overlooked *his* claims.   Professor Thomson of Glasgow always spoke of his " Essays" as of a book
which hardly any revolution could antiquate ; and Sir
Humphry Davy, in reply to a question which I put to
him upon that point in 1813, declared that he knew of no
book better qualified, as one of introductory discipline, to
the youthful experimenter, or as an apprenticeship to the
taste in elegant selection of topics.

Yet querulous and discontented as the bishop was, when
he adverted either to chemistry or to his own position in
life, the reader must not imagine to himself the ordinary
" complement" and appurtenances of that character—such
as moroseness, illiberality, or stinted hospitalities.   On the
contrary, his lordship was a joyous, jovial, and cordial host.
He was pleasant, and even kind in his manners ; most
hospitable in his reception of strangers, no matter of what
party ; and I must say that he was as little overbearing
in argument, and as little stood upon his privilege in

his character of a church dignitary, as any " big wig" I
have happened to know.   He was somewhat pompous, undoubtedly ; but that, in an old academic hero, was rather
agreeable, and had a characteristic effect.   He listened
patiently to all your objections ; and, though steeped to
the lips in prejudice, he was really candid.   I mean to
say, that although, generally speaking, the unconscious
pre-occupation of his understanding shut up all avenues to
new convictions, he yet did his best to open his mind to
any views that might be presented at the moment.   And,
with regard to his querulous egotism, though it may appear
laughable enough to all who contrast his real pretensions
with their public appreciation, as expressed in his acquired
opulence and rank ; and who contrast, also, *his* case with
that of other men in his own profession—with that of
Paley, for example—yet it cannot be denied that fortune
had crossed his path, latterly, with foul winds, no less
strikingly than his early life had been seconded by her
favouring gales.   In particular, Lord Holland* mentioned
to a friend of my own the following anecdote :—" What
you say of the bishop may be very true" (they were riding
past his grounds at the time, which had turned the conversation upon his character and public claims) : " but to *us*"
(Lord Holland meant to the Whig party) " he was truly
honourable and faithful ; insomuch, that my uncle" (meaning, of course, Charles Fox) " had agreed with Lord Grenville to make him Archbishop of York, *sede vacante ;*—all
was settled ; and had we staid in power a little longer, he
would, beyond a doubt, have had that dignity.'
    Now, if the reader happens to recollect how soon the

---

* It was *Lady* Holland.   I know not how I came to make such a
mistake.   And the friend was Wordsworth.

death of Dr. Markham followed the sudden dissolution of that short-lived administration in 1807, he will see how narrowly Dr. Watson missed this elevation ; a..d one must allow for a little occasional spleen under such circumstances. How grand a thing, how princely, to be an English archbishop ! Yet, what an archbishop ! He talked openly, at his own table, as a Socinian ; ridiculed the miracles of the New Testament, which he professed to explain as so many chemical tricks, or cases of legerdemain ; and certainly had as little of devotional feeling as any man that ever lived. It is, by comparison, a matter of little consequence, that, so slightly regarding the church of which he called himself a member in her spiritual interest, he should, in her temporal interests, have been ready to lay her open to any assaults from almost any quarter. He could naturally have little reverence for the rights of the shepherds, having so very little for the pastoral office itself, or for the manifold duties it imposes. All his public, all his professional duties, he systematically neglected. He was a lord in Parliament, and for many a year he never attended in his place : he was a bishop, and he scarcely knew any part of his diocese by sight, living three hundred miles away from it : he was a professor of divinity, holding the richest professorship in Europe—the weightiest, for its functions, in England—drawing, by his own admission, one thousand per annum from its endowments (deducting some stipend to his *locum tenens* at Cambridge), and for thirty years he never read a lecture, or performed a public exercise. Spheres how vast of usefulness to a man as able as himself !—subjects of what bitter anguish on his deathbed to one who had been tenderly conscientious ! In his political purism, and the unconscious partisanship of his constitutional scruples, he was a true Whig, and thoroughly

diverting.   That Lord Lonsdale or that the Duke of
Northumberland should interfere with elections, this he
thought scandalous and awful; but that a lord of the
house of Cavendish or Howard, a Duke of Devonshire or
Norfolk, or an Earl of Carlisle, should traffic in boroughs,
or exert the most despotic influence as landlords, *mutato
nomine*, he viewed as the mere natural right of property :
and so far was he from loving the pure-hearted and un-
factious champions of liberty, that, in one of his printed
works, he dared to tax Milton with having knowingly,
wilfully, deliberately told a falsehood.*

Could Coleridge—was it possible that he could reverence
a man like this?   Ordinary men might, because they were
told that he had defended Christianity against the vile
blasphemers and impotent theomachists of the day.   But
Coleridge had too pure an ideal of a Christian philosopher,
derived from the age of the English Titans in theology, to
share in that estimate.   It is singular enough, and interesting to a man who has ever heard Coleridge talk, but
especially to one who has *assisted* (to speak in French
phrase) at a talking party between Coleridge and the
bishop, to look back upon an article in the " Quarterly
Review," where, in connexion with the Bishop's Autobiography, some sneers are dropped with regard to the
intellectual character of the neighbourhood in which he
had settled.   I have been told, on pretty good authority,
that this article was written by the late Dr. Whittaker of
Craven, the topographical antiquarian ; a pretty sort of
person, doubtless, to assume such a tone, in speaking of a

---

* This supposed falsehood respected the sect called Brownists, and
occurs in the " Defensio pro Pop. Anglicano."   The whole charge is
a blunder, and rests upon the bishop's own imperfect Latinity.

neighbourhood so dazzling in its intellectual pretensions as that region at that time. Listen, reader, and judge !

The bishop had fixed his abode on the banks of Windermere. In a small, but by the necessity of its situation a beautiful park, he had himself raised a plain, but handsome and substantial mansion ; Calgarth, or Calgarth Park, was its name. Now, at Keswick (I am looking back to the sneer of the "Quarterly Review") lived Southey ; twenty miles distant, it is true, but still, for a bishop with a bishop's equipage, not beyond a morning's drive. At Grasmere, about eight miles from Calgarth, were to be found Wordsworth and Coleridge. At Brathay, about four miles from Calgarth, lived Charles Lloyd ; and he, far as he might be below the others I have mentioned, could not in candour be considered a common man. Common ! he was a man never to be forgotten ! He was somewhat too *Rousseauish ;* but he had, in conversation, the most extraordinary powers for analysis of a certain kind, applied to the philosophy of manners, and the most delicate *nuances* of social life ; and his translation of "Alfieri," together with his own poems, show him to have been an accomplished scholar. Then, not much above a mile from Calgarth, at his beautiful creation of Elleray, lived Professor Wilson ; of whom I need not speak. He, in fact, and Mr. Lloyd were on the most intimate terms with the Bishop's family. The meanest of these persons was able to have "taken the conceit" out of Dr. Whittaker and all his tribe. But even in the town of Kendal, about nine miles from Calgarth, there were many men of information, at least as extensive as Dr. Watson's, and amply qualified to have met him upon equal terms in conversation. Mathematics, it is well known, are extensively cultivated in the north of England. Sedburgh, for many years, was a sort

of nursery or rural chapel-of-ease to Cambridge.   Dawson
of Sedburgh was a luminary better known than ever Dr.
Watson was, by mathematicians both foreign and domestic.
Gough, the blind mathematician and botanist of Kendal,
is known to this day ; but many others in that town had
accomplishments equal to his ; and, indeed, so widely
has mathematical knowledge extended itself throughout
Northern England, that, even amongst the poor Lancashire
weavers, mechanic labourers for their daily bread, the
cultivation of pure geometry, in the most refined shape,
has long prevailed ; of which some accounts have been
recently published.   Local pique, therefore, must have been
at the bottom of Dr. Whittaker's sneer.   At all events, it
was ludicrously contrasted with the true state of the case,
as brought out by the meeting between Coleridge and the
bishop.

Coleridge was armed, at all points, with the scholastic
erudition which bore upon all questions that could arise
in polemic divinity.   The philosophy of ancient Greece,
through all its schools, the philosophy of the schoolmen,
technically so called, church history, &c., Coleridge had
within his call.   Having been personally acquainted, or
connected as a pupil, with Eichhorn and Michaelis, he
knew the whole cycle of schisms and audacious speculations through which Biblical criticism or Christian philosophy has revolved in Modern Germany.   All this was
ground upon which the Bishop of Llandaff trod with the
infirm footing of a child.   He listened to what Coleridge
reported with the same sort of pleasurable surprise, al-
ternating with starts of doubt or incredulity, as would
naturally attend a detailed report from Laputa—which
aërial region of speculation does but too often recur to a
sober-minded person, in reading of the endless freaks in

philosophy of Modern Germany, where the sceptre of Muta·
bility, that potentate celebrated by Spenser, gathers more
trophies in a year, than elsewhere in a century; " the
anarchy of dreams" presides in her philosophy; and the
restless elements of opinion, throughout every region of de-
bate, mould themselves eternally, like the billowy sands
of the desert, as beheld by Bruce, into towering columns,
soar upwards to a giddy altitude, then stalk about for a
minute, all a-glow with fiery colour, and finally unmould
and " dislimn," with a collapse as sudden as the motions
of that eddying breeze under which their vapoury architecture had arisen.   Hartley and Locke, both of whom the
bishop made into idols, were discussed; especially the
former, against whom Coleridge alleged some of those arguments which he has used in his " Biographia Literaria."
The bishop made but a feeble defence; and, upon some
points, none at all.   He seemed, I remember, much struck
with one remark of Coleridge's, to this effect :—" That,
whereas Hartley fancied that our very reasoning was an
aggregation, collected together under the law of association, on the contrary, we reason by counteracting that law :
just," said he, " as, in leaping, the law of gravitation
concurs to that act in its latter part; but no leap could
take place, were it not by a counteraction of the law."
One remark of the bishop's let me into the secret of his
very limited reading.   Coleridge had used the word " apperception," apparently without intention; for, on hearing
some objection to the word, as being " surely not a word
that Addison would have used," he substituted *transcen-
dental consciousness.*   Some months afterwards, going with
Charles Lloyd to call at Calgarth, during the time when
" The Friend" was appearing, the bishop again noticed
this obnoxious word, and in the very same terms :—" Now,

this word *apperception*, which Mr. Coleridge uses in the last number of ' The Friend,' surely, surely it would **not** have been approved by Addison; no, Mr. Lloyd, nor by Swift; nor even, I think, by Arbuthnot." Somebody suggested that the word was a new word of German mintage, and most probably due to Kant—of whom the bishop seemed never to have heard. Meantime the fact was, and to me an amusing one, that the word had been commonly used by Leibnitz, a *classical* author on such subjects, 120 years before.

In the autumn of 1810, Coleridge left the Lakes; and, so far as I am aware, for ever. I once, indeed, heard a rumour of his having passed through with some party of tourists—some reason struck me at the time for believing it untrue—but, at all events, he never returned to them as a resident. What might be his reason for this eternal self-banishment from scenes which he so well understood in all their shifting forms of beauty, I can only guess. Perhaps it was the very opposite reason to that which is most obvious: not, possibly, because he had become indifferent to their attractions, but because his undecaying sensibility to their commanding power had become associated with too afflicting remembrances, and flashes of personal recollections, suddenly restored and illuminated—recollections which will

"Sometimes leap
From hiding-places ten years deep,"

and bring into collision the present with some long-forgotten past, in a form too trying and too painful for endurance. I have a brilliant Scotch friend, who cannot walk on the sea-shore—within sight of its ανηριθμον γελασμα, the multitudinous laughter of its waves, or within hearing of its resounding uproar, because they bring up.

by links of old association, too insupportably to his mind
the agitations of his glittering, but too fervid youth.
There is a feeling—morbid, it may be, but for which no
anodyne is found in all the schools from Plato to Kant—
to which the human mind is liable at times : it is best
described in a little piece by Henry More, the " Platonist."
He there represents himself as a martyr to his own
too passionate sense of beauty, and his consequent too
pathetic sense of its decay.   Everywhere — above, below, around him, in the earth, in the clouds, in the
fields, and in their " garniture of flowers"—he beholds
a beauty carried to excess ; and this beauty becomes a
source of endless affliction to him, because everywhere he
sees it liable to the touch of decay and mortal change.
During one paroxysm of this sad passion, an angel appears to comfort him ; and, by the sudden revelation of
her immortal beauty, does, in fact, suspend his grief.   But
it is only a suspension ; for the sudden recollection that
her privileged condition, and her exemption from the
general fate of beauty, is only by way of exception to a
universal rule, restores his grief : " And thou thyself," he
says to the angel—

> " And thou thyself, that com'st to comfort me,
>   Wouldst strong occasion of deep sorrow bring,
>   If thou wert subject to mortality ! "

Every man, who has ever dwelt with passionate love upon
the fair face of some female companion through life, must
have had the same feeling ; and must often, in the exquisite language of Shakspere's sonnets, have commanded and
adjured all-conquering Time, there, at least, and upon that
one tablet of his adoration,

> " To write no wrinkle with his antique hand "

Vain prayer ! Empty adjuration ! Profitless rebellion
against the laws which season all things for the inexorable grave ! Yet not the less we rebel again and
again ; and, though wisdom counsels resignation, yet our
human passions, still cleaving to their object, force us
into endless rebellion. Feelings the same in kind as
these attach themselves to our mental power, and our
vital energies. Phantoms of lost power, sudden intuitions,
and shadowy restorations of forgotten feelings, sometimes
dim and perplexing, sometimes by bright but furtive
glimpses, sometimes by a full and steady revelation,
overcharged with light—throw us back in a moment
upon scenes and remembrances that we have left full
thirty years behind us. In solitude, and chiefly in the
solitudes of nature ; and, above all, amongst the great
and *enduring* features of nature, such as mountains, and
quiet dells, and the lawny recesses of forests, and the
silent shores of lakes, features with which (as being
themselves less liable to change) our feelings have a more
abiding association—under these circumstances it is, that
such evanescent hauntings of our past and forgotten
selves are most apt to startle and to waylay us. These
are *positive* torments from which the agitated mind shrinks
in fear ; but there are others *negative* in their nature—
that is, blank mementoes of powers extinct, and of faculties
burnt out within us. And from both forms of anguish—
from this twofold scourge—poor Coleridge fled, perhaps,
in flying from the beauty of external nature. In alluding
to this latter, or negative form of suffering—that form,
I mean, which presents not the too fugitive glimpses of
past power, but its blank annihilation—Coleridge himself
most beautifully insists upon, and illustrates the truth,
that all which we find in Nature must be created by

ourselves ; and that alike, whether Nature is so gorgeous
in her beauty as to seem apparelled in her wedding-gar-
ment, or so powerless and extinct as to seem palled in
her shroud ; in either case,

> " O, Lady, we receive but what we give,
> And in *our* life alone does nature *live;*
> Ours is her wedding-garment, ours her shroud.
>
> " It were a vain endeavour,
> Though I should gaze for ever
> On that green light that lingers in the west:
> I may not hope from *outward* forms to win
> The passion and the life whose fountains are *within.*"

This was one, and the most common shape of extinguished
power from which Coleridge fled to the great city. But
sometimes the same decay came back upon his heart in the
more poignant shape of intimations and vanishing glimpses,
recovered for one moment from the paradise of youth,
and from fields of joy and power, over which, for him,
too certainly, he felt that the cloud of night was settling
for ever. Both modes of the same torment exiled him from
nature ; and for the same reason he fled from poetry and all
commerce with his own soul ; burying himself in the profoundest abstractions, from life and human sensibilities.

> " For not to think of what I needs must feel,
> But to be still and patient all I can ;
> And haply *by abstruse research to steal,*
> *From my own nature, all the natural man ;*
> This was my sole resource, my only plan ;
> Till *that,* which suits a part, infects the whole,
> And now is almost grown the habit of my soul."

Such were, doubtless, the true and radical causes which,
for the final twenty-four years of Coleridge's life, drew
him away from those scenes of natural beauty in which
only, at an earlier stage of life, he found strength and
restoration. These scenes still survived ; but their power

was gone, because *that* had been derived from himself ; and his ancient self had altered. Such were the *causes;* but the immediate *occasion* of his departure from the Lakes, in the autumn of 1810, was the favourable opportunity then presented to him of migrating in a pleasant way. Mr. Basil Montagu, the Chancery barrister, happened at that time to be returning to London with Mrs. Montagu, from a visit to the Lakes, or to Wordsworth. His travelling carriage was roomy enough to allow of his offering Coleridge a seat in it ; and his admiration of Coleridge was just then fervent enough to prompt a friendly wish for that sort of close connexion (viz., by domestication as a guest under Mr. Basil Montagu's roof) which is the most trying to friendship, and which in this instance led to a perpetual rupture of it. The domestic habits of eccentric men of genius, much more those of a man so irreclaimably irregular as Coleridge, can hardly be supposed to promise very auspiciously for any connexion so close as this. A very extensive house and household, together with the unlimited license of action which belongs to the *ménage* of some great Dons amongst the nobility, could alone have made Coleridge an inmate perfectly desirable. Probably many little jealousies and offences had been mutually suppressed ; but the particular spark which at length fell amongst the combustible materials already prepared, and thus produced the final explosion, took the following shape :—Mr. Montagu had published a book against the use of wine and intoxicating liquors of every sort. Not out of parsimony or under any suspicion of inhospitality, but in mere self-consistency and obedience to his own conscientious scruples, Mr. Montagu would not countenance the use of wine at his own table. So far all was right. But doubtless, on such a system, under the known habits of modern life, it should

have been made a rule to ask no man to dinner: for to force
men, without warning, to a *single* (and, therefore, thoroughly
useless) act of painful abstinence, is what neither I nor any
man can have a right to do.   In point of sense, it is, in
fact, precisely the freak of Sir Roger de Coverley, who
drenches his friend the "Spectator" with a hideous decoc-
tion : not, as his confiding visitor had supposed, for some
certain and immediate benefit to follow, but simply as having
a *tendency* (if well supported by many years' continuance of
similar drenches) to abate the remote contingency of the
stone.   Hear this, ye Gods of the Future !   I am required
to perform a most difficult sacrifice ; and forty years hence
I *may*, by persisting so long, have some dim chance of reward.   One day's abstinence could do no good on *any*
scheme : and no man was likely to offer himself for a second.
However, such being the law of the castle, and that law well
known to Coleridge, he nevertheless, thought fit to ask to
dinner Colonel (then Captain) Pasley, of the Engineers, well
known in those days for his book on the "Military Policy
of England ;" and since, for his "System of Professional
Instruction."   Now, where or in what land abides that

"Captain, or Colonel, or Knight-in-arms,"

to whom wine in the analysis of dinner is a neutral or
indifferent element ?   Wine, therefore, as it was not of a
nature to be omitted, Coleridge took care to furnish at his
own private cost.   And so far, again, all was right.   But
why must Coleridge give his dinner to the captain in Mr.
Montagu's house ?   There lay the affront ; and doubtless,
it was a very inconsiderate act on the part of Coleridge.   I report the case simply as it was then generally borne upon the
breath, not of scandal, but of jest and merriment.   The result, however, was no jest ; for bitter words ensued—words

that festered in the remembrance; and a rupture between the parties followed, which no reconciliation has ever healed.

Meantime, on reviewing this story, as generally adopted by the learned in literary scandal, one demur rises up.   Dr. Parr, a lisping Whig pedant, without personal dignity or conspicuous power of mind, was a frequent and privileged inmate at Mr. Montagu's.   Him now—this Parr—there was no conceivable motive for enduring; that point is satisfactorily settled by the pompous inanities of his works.   Yet, on the other hand, his habits were in their own nature far less endurable than Samuel Taylor Coleridge's; for the monster smoked;—and how? How did the " Birmingham Doctor " * smoke?   Not as you, or I, or other civilized people smoke, with a gentle cigar—but with the very coarsest tobacco.   And those who know how that abomination lodges and nestles in the draperies of window-curtains, will guess the horror and detestation in which the old Whig's memory is held by all enlightened women.   Surely, in a house where the Doctor had any toleration at all, Samuel Taylor Coleridge might have enjoyed an unlimited toleration.

---

* " *Birmingham Doctor*."—This was a *sobriquet* imposed on Dr Parr by " The Pursuits of Literature," that most popular of satires at the end of the eighteenth and opening of the nineteenth centuries. The name had a mixed reference to the Doctor's personal connexion with Warwickshire, but chiefly to the Doctor's spurious and windy imitation of Dr. Johnson. He was viewed as the Birmingham (or mock) Dr. Johnson. Why the word *Birmingham* has come for the last sixty or seventy years to indicate in every class of articles the spurious in opposition to the genuine, I suppose to have arisen from the Birmingham habit of reproducing all sorts of London or Paris trinkets, *bijouterie*, &c., in cheaper materials and with inferior workmanship.

WILLIAM WORDSWORTH.

In 1807 it was, at the beginning of winter, that I first saw William Wordsworth. I have already mentioned that I had introduced myself to his notice by letter as early as the spring of 1803. To this hour it has continued, I believe, a mystery to Wordsworth, why it was that I suffered an interval of four and a half years to slip away before availing myself of the standing invitation with which I had been honoured to the poet's house. Very probably he accounted for this delay by supposing that the new-born liberty of an Oxford life, with its multiplied enjoyments, acting upon a boy just emancipated from the restraints of a school, and, in one hour, elevated into what we Oxonians so proudly and so exclusively denominate

" a man," * might have tempted me into pursuits alien
from the pure intellectual passions which had so powerfully
mastered my youthful heart some years before.   Extinguished such a passion could not be ; nor could he think,
if remembering the fervour with which I had expressed it,
the sort of " nympholepsy" which had seized upon me,
and which, in some imperfect way, I had avowed with
reference to the very lakes and mountains amongst which
the scenery of this most original poetry had chiefly grown
up and moved.   The very names of the ancient hills—
Fairfield, Seat Sandal, Helvellyn, Blencathara, Glaramara ;
the names of the sequestered glens—such as Borrowdale,
Martindale, Mardale, Wasdale, and Ennerdale ; but, above
all, the shy pastoral recesses, not garishly in the world's
eye, like Windermere or Derwentwater, but lurking half
unknown to the traveller of that day—Grasmere, for
instance, the lovely abode of the poet himself, solitary, and
yet sowed, as it were, with a thin diffusion of humble
dwellings—here a scattering, and there a clustering, as
in the starry heavens—sufficient to afford, at every turn
and angle, human remembrances and memorials of time-
honoured affections, or of passions (as the " Churchyard
amongst the Mountains" will amply demonstrate) not
wanting even in scenic and tragical interest—these were
so many local spells upon me, equally poetic and elevating with the Miltonic names of Valdarno and Vallom-
brosa.

Deep are the voices which seem to call, deep is the

---

* At the Universities of Oxford and Cambridge, where the town is
viewed as a mere ministerial appendage to the numerous colleges—the
civic Oxford, for instance, existing for the sake of the academic Oxford,
and not *vice versâ*—it has naturally happened that the students honour
with the name of " *a man*" him only who wears a cap and gown.

lesson which would be taught even to the most thoughtless of men—

> " Could field, or grove, or any spot of earth,
> Show to his eye an image of the pangs
> Which it hath witness'd ; render back an echo
> Of the sad steps by which it hath been trod."*

Meantime, my delay was due to anything rather than to waning interest. On the contrary, the real cause of my delay was the too great profundity, and the increasing profundity, of my interest in this regeneration of our national poetry ; and the increasing awe, in due proportion to the decaying thoughtlessness of boyhood, which possessed me for the character of its author. So far from neglecting Wordsworth, it is a fact that twice I had undertaken a long journey expressly for the purpose of paying my respects to Wordsworth ; twice I came so far as the little rustic inn (then the sole inn of the neighbourhood) at Church Coniston ; and on neither occasion could I summon confidence enough to present myself before him. It was not that I had any want of proper boldness for facing the most numerous company of a mixed or ordinary character : reserved, indeed, I was, perhaps even shy.—from the character of my mind, so profoundly meditative, and the character of my life, so profoundly sequestered—but still, from counteracting causes, I was not deficient in a reasonable self-confidence towards the world generally. But the very image of Wordsworth, as I prefigured it to my own planet-struck eye, crushed my faculties as before Elijah or St. Paul. Twice, as I have said, did I advance as far as the Lake of Coniston ; which is about eight miles

---

* See the divine passage (in the Sixth Book of " The Excursion ") beginning—

> " Ah, what a lesson to a thoughtless man," &c.

from the church of Grasmere, and once I absolutely went
forwards from Coniston to the very gorge of Hammerscar,
from which the whole Vale of Grasmere suddenly breaks
upon the view in a style of almost theatrical surprise, with
its lovely valley stretching before the eye in the distance,
the lake lying immediately below, with its solemn ark-like
island of four and a half acres in size seemingly floating on
its surface, and its exquisite outline on the opposite shore,
revealing all its little bays* and wild sylvan margin,
feathered to the edge with wild flowers and ferns. In
one quarter, a little wood, stretching for about half a mile
towards the outlet of the lake ; more directly in opposition
to the spectator, a few green fields ; and beyond them,
just two bowshots from the water, a little white cottage
gleaming from the midst of trees, with a vast and seemingly
never-ending series of ascents, rising above it to the height
of more than three thousand feet. That little cottage was
Wordsworth's from the time of his marriage, and earlier ;
in fact, from the beginning of the century to the year 1808.
Afterwards, for many a year, it was mine. Catching one
hasty glimpse of this loveliest of landscapes, I retreated
like a guilty thing, for fear I might be surprised by Wordsworth, and then returned faintheartedly to Coniston, and
so to Oxford, *re infectâ.*

This was in 1806. And thus far, from mere excess of
nervous distrust in my own powers for sustaining a conversation with Wordsworth, I had for nearly five years
shrunk from a meeting for which, beyond all things under
heaven, I longed. In early youth I laboured under a

---

* All which inimitable graces of nature have, by the hands of
mechanic art, by solid masonry, by whitewashing, &c., been exter-
minated as a growth of weeds and nuisances for thirty years.—
August 17, 1853.

EDMUND EVANS SC

GRASMERE.

Page 126.

peculiar embarrassment and penury of words, when I
sought to convey my thoughts adequately upon interesting subjects : neither was it words only that I wanted ; but
I could not unravel, I could not even make perfectly conscious to myself, the subsidiary thoughts into which one
leading thought often radiates ; or, at least, I could not
do this with anything like the rapidity requisite for conversation.   I laboured like a sibyl instinct with the burden
of prophetic woe, as often as I found myself dealing with
any topic in which the understanding combined with deep
feelings to suggest mixed and tangled thoughts : and thus
partly—partly also from my invincible habit of reverie—
at that era of my life, I had a most distinguished talent
"*pour le silence*."   Wordsworth, from something of the
same causes, suffered (by his own report to myself) at the
same age from pretty much the same infirmity.   And yet,
in more advanced years—probably about twenty-eight or
thirty—both of us acquired a remarkable fluency in the
art of unfolding our thoughts colloquially.   However, at
that period my deficiencies were what I have described.
And after all, though I had no absolute cause for anticipating contempt, I was so far right in my fears, that since
that time I have had occasion to perceive a worldly tone of
sentiment in Wordsworth, not less than in Mrs. Hannah
More and other literary people, by which they were led to
set a higher value upon a limited respect from a person
high in the world's esteem, than upon the most lavish
spirit of devotion from an obscure quarter.   Now, in that
point, *my* feelings are far otherwise.

Meantime, the world went on ; events kept moving ;
and, amongst them, in the course of 1807, occurred the
event of Coleridge's return to England from his official
station in the Governor's family at Malta.   At Bridge-

water, as I have already recorded, in the summer of 1807, I was introduced to him. Several weeks after he came with his family to the Bristol Hot-Wells, at which, by accident, I was then visiting. On calling upon him, I found that he had been engaged by the Royal Institution to lecture at their theatre in Albemarle Street, during the coming winter of 1807-8 ; and, consequently, was embarrassed about the mode of conveying his family to Keswick. Upon this, I offered my services to escort them in a post-chaise. This offer was cheerfully accepted ; and at the latter end of October we set forwards—Mrs. Coleridge, viz., with her two sons—Hartley, aged nine, Derwent, about seven—her beautiful little daughter,* about five ; and, finally, myself. Going by the direct route through Gloucester, Bridgenorth, &c., on the third day we reached Liverpool, where I took up my quarters at a hotel, whilst Mrs. Coleridge paid a visit of a few days to a very interesting family, who had become friends of Southey during his visit to Portugal. These were the Misses Koster, daughters of an English gold merchant of celebrity, who had recently quitted Lisbon on the approach of the French army under Junot. Mr. Koster did me the honour to call at my quarters, and invite me to his house ; an invitation which I very readily accepted, and had thus an opportunity of becoming acquainted with a family the most

---

* That most accomplished, and to Coleridge most pious daughter, whose recent death afflicted so very many who knew her only by her writings. She had married her cousin, Mr. Serjeant Coleridge, and in that way retained her illustrious maiden name as a wife. At seventeen, when last I saw her, she was the most perfect of all pensive, nun-like, intellectual beauties that I have seen in real breathing life. The upper parts of her face were verily divine. See, for an artist's opinion, the Life of that admirable man Collins, by his son.

accomplished I had ever known. At dinner there appeared only the family party—several daughters, and one son, a fine young man of twenty, but who was *consciously* dying of asthma. Mr. Koster, the head of the family, was distinguished for his good sense and practical information ; but, in Liverpool, even more so by his eccentric and obstinate denial of certain notorious events ; in particular, some two years later, he denied that any such battle as Talavera had ever been fought, and had a large wager depending upon the decision. His house was the resort of distinguished foreigners ; and, on the first evening of my dining there, as well as afterwards, I there met that marvel of women, Madame Catalani. I had heard her repeatedly ; but never before been near enough to see her smile and converse— even to be honoured with a smile myself. She and Lady Hamilton were the most effectively brilliant women I ever saw. However, on this occasion, the Misses Koster outshone even La Catalani ; to her they talked in the most fluent Italian ; to some foreign men, in Portuguese ; to one in French ; and to most of the party in English ; and each, by turns, seemed to be their native tongue. Nor did they shrink, even in the presence of the mighty enchantress, from exhibiting their musical skill.

Leaving Liverpool, after about a week's delay, we pursued our journey northwards. We had slept on the first day at Lancaster. Consequently, at the rate of motion which then prevailed throughout England—which, however, was rarely equalled on that western road, where all things were in arrear by comparison with the eastern and southern roads of the kingdom—we found ourselves, about three o'clock in the afternoon, at Ambleside, fourteen miles to the north-west of Kendal, and thirty-six from Lancaster. There, for the last time, we stopped to change horses ; and

about four o'clock we found ourselves on the summit of
the White Moss, a hill which rises between the second and
third milestones on the stage from Ambleside to Keswick,
and which then retarded the traveller's advance by a full
fifteen minutes, but is now evaded by a lower line of road.
In ascending this hill, from weariness of moving so slowly,
I, with the two Coleridges, had alighted ; and, as we all
chose to refresh ourselves by running down the hill into
Grasmere, we had left the chaise behind us, and had even
lost the sound of the wheels at times, when all at once we
came, at an abrupt turn of the road, in sight of a white
cottage, with two yew-trees breaking the glare of its white
walls.   A sudden shock seized me on recognising this
cottage, of which, in the previous year, I had gained a
momentary glimpse from Hammerscar, on the opposite
side of the lake.   I paused, and felt my old panic returning upon me ; but just then, as if to take away all doubt
upon the subject, I saw Hartley Coleridge, who had gained
upon me considerably, suddenly turn in at a garden gate ;
this motion to the right at once confirmed me in my
belief that here at last we had reached our port ; that this
little cottage was tenanted by that man whom, of all the
men from the beginning of time, I most fervently desired
to see ; that in less than a minute, I should meet Wordsworth face to face.   Coleridge was of opinion that, if a
man were really and *consciously* to see an apparition, in
such circumstances death would be the inevitable result ;
and, if so, the wish which we hear so commonly expressed
for such experience is as thoughtless as that of Semele in
the Grecian Mythology, so natural in a female, that her
lover should visit her *en grande costume*—presumptuous
ambition, that unexpectedly wrought its own ruinous chas-
tisement !   Judged by Coleridge's test, my situation could

not have been so terrific as *his* who anticipates a ghost ; for, certainly, I survived this meeting ; but at that instant it seemed pretty much the same to my own feelings.

Never before or since can I reproach myself with having trembled at the approaching presence of any creature that is born of woman, excepting only, for once or twice in my life, woman herself. Now, however, I *did* tremble ; and I forgot, what in no other circumstances I could have for gotten, to stop for the coming up of the chaise, that I might be ready to hand Mrs. Coleridge out. Had Charlemagne and all his peerage been behind me, or Cæsar and his equipage, or Death on his pale horse, I should have foi gotten them at that moment of intense expectation, and of eyes fascinated to what lay before me, or what might in a moment appear. Through the little gate I pressed forward ; ten steps beyond it lay the principal door of the house. To this, no longer clearly conscious of my own feelings, I passed on rapidly ; I heard a step, a voice, and like a flash of lightning, I saw the figure emerge of a tallish man, who held out his hand, and saluted me with most cordial expressions of welcome. The chaise, however, drawing up to the gate at that moment, he (and there needed no Roman nomenclator to tell me that this *he* was Wordsworth) felt himself summoned to advance and receive Mrs. Coleridge. I, therefore, stunned almost with the actual accomplishment of a catastrophe so long anti-cipated and so long postponed, mechanically went forward into the house. A little semi-vestibule between two doors prefaced the entrance into what might be considered the principal room of the cottage. It was an oblong square, not above eight and a half feet high, sixteen feet long, and twelve broad ; very prettily wainscoted from the floor to the ceiling with dark polished oak, slightly embellished

with carving.   One window there was—a perfect and **un**-
pretending cottage window, with little diamond panes, em-
bowered at almost every season of the year with roses ;
and, in the summer and autumn, with a profusion of jas-
mine· and other fragrant shrubs.   From the exuberant luxu-
riance of the vegetation around it, and from the dark hue
of the wainscoting, this window, though tolerably large,
did not furnish a very powerful light to one who entered
from the open air.   However, I saw sufficiently to be
aware of two ladies just entering the room, through a door-
way opening upon a little staircase.   The foremost, a tallish
young woman, with the most winning expression of benignity upon her features, advanced to me, presenting her
hand with so frank an air, that all embarrassment must
have fled in a moment before the native goodness of her
manner.   This was Mrs. Wordsworth, cousin of the poet ;
and, for the last five years or more, his wife.   She was
now mother of two children, a son and a daughter ; and
she furnished a remarkable proof how possible it is for a
woman neither handsome nor even comely, according to the
rigour of criticism—nay, generally pronounced very plain—
to exercise all the practical fascination of beauty, through
the mere compensatory charms of sweetness all but angelic,
of simplicity the most entire, womanly self-respect and
purity of heart speaking through all her looks, acts, and
movements.   *Words*, I was going to have added ; but her
words were few.   In reality, she talked so little, that Mr.
Slave-Trade Clarkson used to allege against her, that she
could only say, " *God bless you !* "   Certainly, her intellect
was not of an active order ; but, in a quiescent, reposing,
meditative way, she appeared always to have a genial enjoyment from her own thoughts ; and it would have been
strange, indeed, if she, who enjoyed such eminent advan-

tages of training, from the daily society of her husband and his sister, failed to acquire some power of judging for herself, and putting forth some functions of activity. But undoubtedly that was not her element : to feel and to enjoy in a luxurious repose of mind—there was her *forte* and her peculiar privilege ; and how much better this was adapted to her husband's taste, how much more adapted to uphold the comfort of his daily life, than a blue-stocking loquacity, or even a legitimate talent for discussion, may be inferred from his verses, beginning—

> " She was a phantom of delight,
> When first she gleam'd upon my sight."

Once for all,* these exquisite lines were dedicated to Mrs. Wordsworth ; were understood to describe her—to have been prompted by the feminine graces of her character ; hers they are, and will remain for ever. To these, therefore, I may refer the reader for an idea of what was most important in the partner and second self of the poet. And I will add to this abstract of her *moral* portrait, these few concluding traits of her appearance in a physical sense. Her figure was tolerably good. In complexion she was fair, and there was something peculiarly pleasing even in this accident of the skin, for it was accompanied by an animated expression of health, a blessing which, in fact, she possessed uninterruptedly. Her eyes, the reader may already know, were

> " Like stars of twilight fair ;
> Like twilight, too, her dark brown hair ;
> But all things else about her drawn
> From May-time and the cheerful dawn."

---

* *Once for all*, I say—on recollecting that Coleridge's verses to *Sara* were made transferable to any Sara who reigned at the time. At least three Saras appropriated them ; all three long since in the grave.

Yet strange it is to tell that, in these eyes of vesper gentleness, there was a considerable obliquity of vision; and
much beyond that slight obliquity which is often supposed to be an attractive foible in the countenance : this
ought to have been displeasing or repulsive ; yet, in fact, it
was not.   Indeed all faults, had they been ten times more
and greater, would have been neutralized by that supreme
expression of her features, to the unity of which every
lineament in the fixed parts, and every undulation in the
moving parts of her countenance, concurred, viz., a sunny
benignity—a radiant graciousness—such as in this world
I never saw surpassed.

Immediately behind her moved a lady, shorter, slighter,
and perhaps, in all other respects, as different from her
in personal characteristics, as could have been wished for
the most effective contrast.   " Her face was of Egyptian
brown ;" rarely, in a woman of English birth, had I seen
a more determinate gipsy tan.   Her eyes were not soft, as
Mrs. Wordsworth's, nor were they fierce or bold ; but
they were wild and startling, and hurried in their motion.
Her manner was warm and even ardent ; her sensibility
seemed constitutionally deep ; and some subtle fire of impassioned intellect apparently burned within her, which,
being alternately pushed forward into a conspicuous expression by the irrepressible instincts of her temperament,
and then immediately checked, in obedience to the decorum of her sex and age, and her maidenly condition,
gave to her whole demeanour, and to her conversation, an
air of embarrassment, and even of self-conflict, that was
almost distressing to witness.   Even her very utterance
and enunciation often suffered in point of clearness and
steadiness, from the agitation of her excessive organic
sensibility.   At times, the self-counteraction and self-

baffling of her feelings caused her even to stammer, and so determinately to stammer, that a stranger who should have seen her and quitted her in that state of feeling, would have certainly set her down for one plagued with that infirmity of speech, as distressingly as Charles Lamb himself. This was Miss Wordsworth, the only sister of the poet—his " Dorothy ;" who naturally owed so much to the lifelong intercourse with her great brother, in his most solitary and sequestered years ; but, on the other hand, to whom he has acknowledged obligations of the profoundest nature ; and, in particular, this mighty one, through which we also, the admirers and the worshippers of this great poet, are become equally her debtors—that, whereas the intellect of Wordsworth was, by its original tendency, too stern, too austere, too much enamoured of an ascetic harsh sublimity, she it was—the lady who paced by his side continually through sylvan and mountain tracks, in Highland glens, and in the dim recesses of German charcoal-burners—that first *couched* his eye to the sense of beauty, humanized him by the gentler charities, and engrafted, with her delicate female touch, those graces upon the ruder growths of his nature, which have since clothed the forest of his genius with a foliage corresponding in loveliness and beauty to the strength of its boughs and the massiness of its trunks. The greatest deductions from Miss Wordsworth's attractions, and from the exceeding interest which surrounded her in right of her character, of her history, and of the relation which she fulfilled towards her brother, was the glancing quickness of her motions, and other circumstances in her deportment (such as her stooping attitude when walking), which gave an ungraceful, and even an unsexual character to her appearance when out-of-doors. She did not cul-

tivate the graces which preside over the person and its
carriage. But, on the other hand, she was a person of
very remarkable endowments intellectually ; and, in addition to the other great services which she rendered to
her brother, this I may mention, as greater than all the
rest, and it was one which equally operated to the benefit
of every casual companion in a walk—viz., the exceeding
sympathy, always ready and always profound, by which
she made all that one could tell her, all that one could
describe, all that one could quote from a foreign author,
reverberate, as it were, *à plusieurs reprises,* to one's own
feelings, by the manifest impression it made upon *hers.*
The pulses of light are not more quick or more inevitable
in their flow and undulation, than were the answering and
echoing movements of her sympathizing attention. Her
knowledge of literature was irregular, and thoroughly un-
systematic. She was content to be ignorant of many
things ; but what she knew and had really mastered lay
where it could not be disturbed—in the temple of her own
most fervid heart.

Such were the two ladies, who, with himself and two
children, and at that time one servant, composed the poet's
household. They were both, I believe, about twenty-eight
years old ; and, if the reader inquires about the single
point which I have left untouched in their portraiture—
viz., the style of their manners—I may say that it was, in
some points, naturally of a plain household simplicity, but
every way pleasing, unaffected, and (as respects Mrs. Wordsworth) even dignified. Few persons had seen so little as
this lady of the world. She had seen nothing of high life,
for she had seen little of any. Consequently, she was unacquainted with the conventional modes of behaviour, prescribed in particular situations by high breeding. But, as

these modes are little more than the product of dispassion-
ate good sense, applied to the circumstances of the case,
it is surprising how few deficiencies are perceptible, even to
the most vigilant eye—or, at least, essential deficiencies—
in the general demeanour of any unaffected young woman,
acting habitually under a sense of sexual dignity and
natural courtesy.   Miss Wordsworth had seen more of life,
and even of good company ; for she had lived, when quite
a girl, under the protection of Dr. Cookson, a near relative,
canon of Windsor, and a personal favourite of the Royal
Family, especially of George III.   Consequently, she ought
to have been the more polished of the two ; and yet, from
greater natural aptitudes for refinement of manner in her
sister-in-law, and partly, perhaps, from her more quiet and
subdued manner, Mrs. Wordsworth would have been pronounced very much the more lady-like person.

From the interest which attaches to anybody so nearly
connected as these two ladies with a great poet, I have
allowed myself a larger latitude than else might have
been justifiable in describing them.   I now go on with my
narrative :—

I was ushered up a little flight of stairs, fourteen in all,
to a little drawing-room, or whatever the reader chooses to
call it.   Wordsworth himself has described the fireplace
of this room as his

" Half-kitchen and half-parlour fire."

It was not fully seven feet six inches high, and, in other
respects, pretty nearly of the same dimensions as the rustic
hall below.   There was, however, in a small recess, a
library of perhaps three hundred volumes, which seemed
to consecrate the room as the poet's study and composing
room ; and such occasionally it was.   But far oftener he

both studied, as I found, and composed on the high road. I had not been two minutes at the fireside, when in came Wordsworth, returning from his friendly attentions to the travellers below, who, it seemed, had been over-persuaded by hospitable solicitations to stay for this night in Grasmere, and to make out the remaining thirteen miles of their road to Keswick on the following day. Wordsworth entered. And "*what-like*"—to use a Westmoreland as well as a Scottish expression—"*what-like*" was Wordsworth? A reviewer in "Tait's Magazine,"* noticing some recent collection of literary portraits, gives it as his opinion that Charles Lamb's head was the finest among them. This remark may have been justified by the engraved portraits; but, certainly, the critic would have cancelled it, had he seen the original heads—at least, had he seen them in youth or in maturity; for Charles Lamb bore age with less disadvantage to the intellectual expression of his appearance than Wordsworth, in whom a sanguine complexion had, of late years, usurped upon the original bronze-tint; and this change of hue, and change in the quality of skin, had been made fourfold more conspicuous, and more unfavourable in its general effect, by the harsh contrast of grizzled hair which had displaced the original brown. No change in personal appearance ever can have been so unfortunate; for, generally speaking, whatever other disadvantages old age may bring along with it, one effect, at least, in male subjects, has a compensating tendency—that it removes any tone of vigour too harsh, and mitigates the expression of power too unsubdued. But, in Wordsworth, the effect of the change has been to substitute an air of animal vigour, or, at least, hardiness, as if derived from constant exposure

---

* Vol. iv. page 793 (Dec. 1837).

to the wind and weather, for the fine sombre complexion which he once wore, resembling that of a Venetian senator or a Spanish monk.

Here, however, in describing the personal appearance of Wordsworth, I go back, of course, to the point of time at which I am speaking. He was, upon the whole, not a well-made man. His legs were pointedly condemned by all female connoisseurs in legs; not that they were bad in any way which *would* force itself upon your notice—there was no absolute deformity about them; and undoubtedly they had been serviceable legs beyond the average standard of human requisition; for I calculate, upon good data, that with these identical legs Wordsworth must have traversed a distance of 175,000 to 180,000 English miles—a mode of exertion which, to him, stood in the stead of alcohol and all other stimulants whatsoever to the animal spirits; to which, indeed, he was indebted for a life of unclouded happiness, and we for much of what is most excellent in his writings. But, useful as they have proved themselves, the Wordsworthian legs were certainly not ornamental; and it was really a pity, as I agreed with a lady in thinking, that he had not another pair for evening dress parties —when no boots lend their friendly aid to mask our imperfections from the eyes of female rigorists—those *elegantes formarum spectatrices.* A sculptor would certainly have disapproved of their contour. But the worst part of Wordsworth's person was the bust; there was a narrowness and a droop about the shoulders which became striking, and had an effect of meanness, when brought into close juxtaposition with a figure of a more statuesque build. Once on a summer evening, walking in the Vale of Langdale with Wordsworth, his sister, and Mr. J——, a native Westmoreland clergyman, I remember that Miss Words-

worth was positively mortified by the peculiar illustration
which settled upon this defective conformation. Mr. J———,
a fine towering figure, six feet high, massy and columnar
in his proportions, happened to be walking, a little in
advance, with Wordsworth ; Miss Wordsworth and myself
being in the rear ; and from the nature of the conversation
which then prevailed in our front rank, something or other
about money, devises, buying and selling, we of the rear-
guard thought it requisite to preserve this arrangement
for a space of three miles or more ; during which time,
at intervals, Miss Wordsworth would exclaim, in a tone of
vexation, " Is it possible,—can that be William ? How
very mean he looks !" And she did not conceal a morti-
fication that seemed really painful, until I, for my part,
could not forbear laughing outright at the serious interest
which she carried into this trifle. She was, however, right,
as regarded the mere visual judgment. Wordsworth's figure,
with all its defects, was brought into powerful relief by one
which had been cast in a more square and massy mould ;
and in such a case it impressed a spectator with a sense of
absolute meanness, more especially when viewed from
behind, and not counteracted by his countenance ; and yet
Wordsworth was of a good height (five feet ten), and not
a slender man ; on the contrary, by the side of Southey,
his limbs looked thick, almost in a disproportionate degree.
But the total effect of Wordsworth's person was always
worst in a state of motion. Meantime, his face—that was
one which would have made amends for greater defects of
figure. Many such, and finer, I have seen amongst the
portraits of Titian, and, in a later period, amongst those of
Vandyke, from the great era of Charles i., as also from the
court of Elizabeth and of Charles ii., but none which has
more impressed me in my own time.

Haydon, in his great picture of " Christ's Entry into Jerusalem," has introduced Wordsworth in the character of a disciple attending his Divine Master, and Voltaire in the character of a sneering Jewish elder. This fact is well known ; and, as the picture itself is tolerably well known to the public eye, there are multitudes now living who will have seen a very impressive likeness of Wordsworth—some consciously ; some not suspecting it. There will, however, always be many who have *not* seen any portrait at all of Wordsworth ; and therefore I will describe its general outline and effect. It was a face of the long order, often falsely classed as oval ; but a greater mistake is made by many people in supposing the long face which prevailed so remarkably in the Elizabethan and Carolinian periods, to have become extinct in our own. Miss Ferrier, in one of her novels (" Marriage," I think), makes a Highland girl protest that " no Englishman *with his round face*" shall ever wean her heart from her own country ; but England is not the land of round faces ; and those have observed little, indeed, who think so : France it is that grows the round face, and in so large a majority of her provinces, that it has become one of the national characteristics. And the remarkable impression which an Englishman receives from the eternal recurrence of the orbicular countenance, proves of itself, without any *conscious* testimony, how the fact stands ; in the blind sense of a monotony, not felt elsewhere, lies involved an argument that cannot be gainsaid. Besides, even upon an *à priori* argument, how is it possible that the long face so prevalent in England, by all confession, in certain splendid eras of our history, should have had time, in some five or six generations, to grow extinct ? Again, the character of face varies essentially in different provinces. Wales has no connexion in this respect with

Devonshire, nor Kent with Yorkshire, nor either with Westmoreland.   England, it is true, tends, beyond all known examples, to a general amalgamation of differences, by means of its unrivalled freedom of intercourse.   Yet, even in England, law and necessity have opposed as yet such and so many obstacles to the free diffusion of labour, that every generation occupies, by at least five-sixths of its numbers, the ground of its ancestors.

The moveable part of a population is chiefly the higher part ; and it is the lower classes that, in every nation, compose the *fundus*, in which lies latent the national face, as well as the national character.   Each exists here in racy purity and integrity, not disturbed in the one by alien intermarriages, nor in the other by novelties of opinion, or other casual effects, derived from education and reading. Now, look into this *fundus*, and you will find, in many districts, no such prevalence of the round orbicular face, as some people erroneously suppose ; and in Westmoreland, especially, the ancient long face of the Elizabethan period, powerfully resembling in all its lineaments the ancient Roman face, and often (though not so uniformly) the face of northern Italy in modern times.   The face of Sir Walter Scott, as Irving, the pulpit orator, once remarked to me, was the indigenous face of the Border : the mouth, which was bad, and the entire lower part of the face, are seen repeated in thousands of working-men ; or, as Irving chose to illustrate his position, " in thousands of Border horse-jockeys."   In like manner, Wordsworth's face was, if not absolutely the indigenous face of the Lake district, at any rate a variety of that face, a modification of that original type.   The head was well filled out ; and there, to begin with, was a great advantage over the head of Charles Lamb, which was absolutely truncated in the posterior region—sawn off, as it were, by no timid sawyer. The forehead was not remarkably lofty—and, by the way, some artists, in their ardour for realizing their phreno-logical preconceptions, not suffering nature to surrender quietly and by slow degrees her real alphabet of signs and hieroglyphic characters, but forcing her language prematurely into conformity with their own crude speculations, have given to Sir Walter Scott a pile of forehead which is unpleasing and cataphysical, in fact, a caricature of anything that is ever seen in nature, and would (if real) be esteemed a deformity; in one instance—that which was introduced in some annual or other—the forehead makes about two-thirds of the entire face. Wordsworth's forehead is also liable to caricature misrepresentations in these days of phrenology : but, whatever it may appear to be in any man's fanciful portrait, the real living forehead, as I have been in the habit of seeing it for more than five-and-twenty years, is not remarkable for its height ; but it *is*, perhaps, remarkable for its breadth and expansive development. Neither are the eyes of Wordsworth "large," as is erroneously stated somewhere in "Peter's Letters ;" on the contrary, they are (I think) rather small ; but *that* does not interfere with their effect, which at times is fine, and suitable to his intellectual character. At times, I say, for the depth and subtlety of eyes, even their colouring (as to condensation or dilution), varies exceedingly with the state of the stomach ; and if young ladies were aware of the magical transformations which can be wrought in the depth and sweetness of the eye by a few weeks' walking exercise, I fancy we should see their habits in this point altered greatly for the better. I have seen Wordsworth's eyes oftentimes affected powerfully in this respect ; his eyes are not, under any circumstances, bright, lustrous, or piercing ;

but, after a long day's toil in walking, I have seen them
assume an appearance the most solemn and spiritual that
it is possible for the human eye to wear. The light which
resides in them is at no time a superficial light ; but, under
favourable accidents, it is a light which seems to come
from unfathomed depths : in fact, it is more truly entitled
to be held " the light that never was on land or sea," a
light radiating from some far spiritual world, than any the
most idealizing that ever yet a painter's hand created. The
nose, a little arched, and large ; which, by the way (according to a natural phrenology, existing centuries ago amongst
some of the lowest amongst the human species), has always
been accounted an unequivocal expression of animal appe-
tites organically strong. And that expressed the simple
truth : Wordsworth's intellectual passions were fervent and
strong : but they rested upon a basis of preternatural animal
sensibility diffused through *all* the animal passions (or ap-
petites) ; and something of that will be found to hold of all
poets who have been great by original force and power,
not (as Virgil) by means of fine management and exquisite artifice of composition applied to their conceptions.
The mouth, and the whole circumjacencies of the mouth,
composed the strongest feature in Wordsworth's face; there
was nothing specially to be noticed that I know of, in the
mere outline of the lips ; but the swell and protrusion of
the parts above and around the mouth, are both noticeable
in themselves, and also because they remind me of a very
interesting fact which I discovered about three years after
this my first visit to Wordsworth.

Being a great collector of everything relating to Milton,
I had naturally possessed myself, whilst yet very young,
of Richardson the painter's thick octavo volume of notes
on the " Paradise Lost." It happened, however, that my

copy, in consequence of that mania for portrait collecting which has stripped so many English classics of their engraved portraits, wanted the portrait of Milton. Subsequently I ascertained that it ought to have had a very good likeness of the great poet; and I never rested until I procured a copy of the book which had not suffered in this respect by the fatal admiration of the amateur. The particular copy offered to me was one which had been priced unusually high, on account of the unusually fine specimen which it contained of the engraved portrait. This, for a particular reason, I was exceedingly anxious to see; and the reason was—that, according to an anecdote reported by Richardson himself, this portrait, of all that were shown to her, was the only one acknowledged by Milton's last surviving daughter to be a strong likeness of her father. And her involuntary gestures concurred with her deliberate words :—for, on seeing all the rest, she was silent and inanimate; but the very instant she beheld that crayon drawing, from which is derived the engraved head in Richardson's book, she burst out into a rapture of passionate recognition; exclaiming—" That is my father! that is my dear father! " Naturally, therefore, after such a testimony, so much stronger than any other person in the world could offer to the authentic value of this portrait, I was eager to see it.

Judge of my astonishment, when, in this portrait of Milton, I saw a likeness nearly perfect of Wordsworth, better by much than any which I have since seen of those expressly painted for himself. The likeness is tolerably preserved in that by Carruthers, in which one of the little Rydal waterfalls, &c., composes a background; yet this is much inferior, as a mere portrait of Wordsworth, to the Richardson head of Milton; and this, I believe, is the

last which represents Wordsworth in the vigour of his
power. The rest, which I have not seen, may be better
as works of art (for anything I know to the contrary),
but they must labour under the great disadvantage of presenting the features when " defeatured " in the degree and
the way I have described, by the peculiar ravages of old
age, as it affects this family; for it is noticed of the Wordsworths, by those who are familiar with their peculiarities,
that, in their very blood and constitutional differences,.
lie hidden causes that are able, in some mysterious way,

> " Those shocks of passion to prepare
> That kill the bloom before its time,
> And blanch, without the owner's crime,
> The most resplendent hair."

Some people, it is notorious, live faster by much than
others ; the oil is burned out sooner in one constitution
than another : and the cause of this may be various ; but.
in the Wordsworths, one part of the cause is, no doubt,
the secret fire of a temperament too fervid ; the self-consuming energies of the brain, that gnaw at the heart and
life-strings for ever. In that account which " The Excursion " presents to us of an imaginary Scotsman, who, to
still the tumult of his heart, when visiting the cataracts of
a mountainous region, obliges himself to study the laws
of light and colour, as they affect the rainbow of the stormy
waters ; vainly attempting to mitigate the fever which
consumed him, by entangling his mind in profound speculations ; raising a cross-fire of artillery from the subtilizing
intellect, under the vain conceit that in this way he could
silence the mighty battery of his impassioned heart—there
we read a picture of Wordsworth and his own youth. In
Miss Wordsworth, every thoughtful observer might read
the same self-consuming style of thought. And the effect

upon each was so powerful for the promotion of a premature old age, and of a premature expression of old age, that strangers invariably supposed them fifteen to twenty years older then they were. And I remember Wordsworth once laughingly reporting to me, on returning from a short journey in 1809, a little personal anecdote, which sufficiently showed what was the spontaneous impression upon that subject of casual strangers, whose feelings were not confused by previous knowledge of the truth. He was travelling by a stage-coach, and seated outside, amongst a good half-dozen of fellow-passengers. One of these, an elderly man, who confessed to having passed the grand climacterical year (9 multiplied into 7) of 63, though he did not say precisely by how many years, said to Wordsworth, upon some anticipations which they had been mutually discussing of changes likely to result from enclosures, &c., then going on or projecting—" Ay, ay, another dozen of years will show us strange sights ; but you and I can hardly expect to see them."—" How so ?" said Wordsworth. " How so, my friend ? How old do you take me to be ?"—" Oh, I beg pardon," said the other ; " I meant no offence—but what ?" looking at Wordsworth more attentively—" you'll never see threescore, I'm of opinion ;" meaning to say that Wordsworth *had* seen it already. And, to show that he was not singular in so thinking, he appealed to all the other passengers ; and the motion passed (*nem. con.*), that Wordsworth was rather over than under sixty. Upon this he told them the literal truth—that he had not yet accomplished his thirty-ninth year. " God bless me !" said the climacterical man ; " so then, after all, you'll have a chance to see your childer get up like, and get settled ! Only to think of that !" And so closed the conversation. leaving to Wordsworth an un-

deniable record of his own prematurely expressed old age
in this unaffected astonishment, amongst a whole party of
plain men, that he could really belong to a generation of
the forward-looking, who live by hope ; and might reason-
ably expect to see a child of seven years old matured into
a man.   And yet as Wordsworth lived into his 82d year,
it is plain that the premature expression of decay does not
argue any real decay.

Returning to the question of portraits, I would observe
that this Richardson engraving of Milton has the advantage
of presenting, not only by far the best likeness of Wordsworth, but of Wordsworth in the prime of his powers—a
point essential in the case of one so liable to premature
decay.   It may be supposed that I took an early opportunity of carrying the book down to Grasmere, and calling
for the opinions of Wordsworth's family upon this most
remarkable coincidence.   Not one member of that family
but was as much impressed as myself with the accuracy of
the likeness.   All the peculiarities even were retained—a
drooping appearance of the eyelids, that remarkable swell
which I have noticed about the mouth, the way in which
the hair lay upon the forehead.   In two points only there
was a deviation from the rigorous truth of Wordsworth's
features—the face was a little too short and too broad, and
the eyes were too large.   There was also a wreath of laurel
about the head, which (as Wordsworth remarked) disturbed
the natural expression of the whole picture ; else, and with
these few allowances, he also admitted that the resemblance
was, *for that period of his life*, perfect, or as nearly so as
art could accomplish.

I have gone into so large and circumstantial a review
of my recollections on this point, as would have been
trifling and tedious in excess, had these recollections re-

lated to a less important man ; but I have a certain knowledge that the least of them will possess a lasting and a
growing interest in connexion with William Wordsworth.
How peculiar, how different from the interest which we
grant to the ideas of a great philosopher, a great mathematician, or a great reformer, is that burning interest
which settles on the great poets who have made themselves necessary to the human heart ; who have first
brought into consciousness, and have clothed in words,
those grand catholic feelings that belong to the grand
catholic situations of life through all its stages ; who have
clothed them in such words that human wit despairs of
bettering them ! Mighty were the powers, solemn and serene
is the memory, of Archimedes ; and Apollonius shines like
" the starry Galileo" in the firmament of human genius ;
yet how frosty is the feeling associated with these names
by comparison with that which, upon every sunny lawn,
by the side of every ancient forest, even in the farthest
depths of Canada, many a young innocent girl, perhaps at
this very moment—looking now with fear to the dark
recesses of the infinite forest, and now with love to the
pages of the infinite poet, until the fear is absorbed and
forgotten in the love—cherishes in her heart for the name
and person of Shakspere !

The English language is travelling fast towards the
fulfilment of its destiny. Through the influence of the
dreadful Republic,* that within the thirty last years has

---

* Not many months ago, the blind hostility of the Irish newspaper
editors in America forged a ludicrous estimate of the Irish numerical
preponderance in the United States, from which it was inferred, as
at least a possibility, that the Irish Celtic language might come to
dispute the pre-eminence with the English. Others anticipated the
same destiny for the German. But, in the meantime, the unresting

run through all the stages of infancy into the first stage
of maturity, and through the English colonies—African,
Canadian, Indian, Australian—the English language (and,
therefore, the English literature) is running forward towards its ultimate mission of eating up, like Aaron's rod,
all other languages. Even the German and the Spanish
will inevitably sink before it ; perhaps within 100 or 150
years. In the recesses of California, in the vast solitudes
of Australia, *The Churchyard amongst the Mountains,* from
Wordsworth's " Excursion," and many a scene of his shorter
poems, will be read, even as now Shakspere is read amongst
the forests of Canada. All which relates to the writer of
these poems will then bear a value of the same kind as
that which attaches to our personal memorials (unhappily
so slender) of Shakspere.

Let me now attempt to trace, in a brief outline, the chief
incidents in the life of William Wordsworth, which are
interesting, not only in virtue of their illustrious subject,
but also as exhibiting a most remarkable (almost a providential) arrangement of circumstances, all tending to
one result—that of insulating from worldly cares, and
carrying onward from childhood to the grave, in a state of
serene happiness, one who was unfitted for daily toil, and,
at all events, who could not, under such demands upon his

---

career of the law-courts, of commerce, and of the national senate,
that cannot suspend themselves for an hour, reduce the case to this
dilemma : If the Irish and the Germans in the United States adapt
their general schemes of education to the service of their public ambition, they must begin by training themselves to the use of the language now prevailing on all the available stages of ambition. On the
other hand, by refusing to do this, they lose in the very outset every
point of advantage. In other words, adopting the English, they
renounce the contest—*not* adopting it, they disqualify themselves for
the contest.

time and anxieties, have prosecuted those genial labours in which all mankind have an interest.

William Wordsworth was born at Cockermouth, a small town of Cumberland, lying about a dozen miles to the north-west of Keswick, on the high road from that town to Whitehaven. His father was a solicitor, and acted as an agent for that Lord Lonsdale, the immediate predecessor of the present,* who is not unfrequently described by those who still remember him, as "the bad Lord Lonsdale." In what was he bad ? Chiefly, I believe, in this—that, being a man of great local power, founded on his rank, on his official station of Lord-Lieutenant over two counties, and on a very large estate, he used his power at times in a most oppressive way. I have heard it said that he was mad ; and, at any rate, he was inordinately capricious—capricious even to eccentricity. But, perhaps, his madness was nothing more than the intemperance of a haughty and a headstrong will, encouraged by the consciousness of power, and tempted to abuses of it by the abject servility which poverty and dependence presented in one direction, embittering the contrast of that defiance which inevitably faced him in another, throughout a land of freedom and amongst spirits as haughty as his own. He was a true feudal chieftain ; and, in the very approaches to his mansion, in the style of his equipage, or whatever else was likely to meet the public eye, he delighted to express his disdain of modern refinements, and the haughty carelessness of his magnificence. The coach in which he used to visit Penrith, the nearest town to his principal house of Lowther, was old and neglected ; his horses fine, but untrimmed ; and such

---

* " *The present :*"—This was written about 1835, when the present Earl of Lonsdale meant the late Earl.

was the impression diffused about him by his gloomy temper and his habits of oppression, that the streets were silent as he traversed them, and an awe sat upon many faces (so, at least, I have heard a Penrith contemporary of the old despot declare), pretty much like that which may be supposed to attend the entry into a guilty town of some royal commission for trying state criminals. In his park, you saw some of the most magnificent timber in the kingdom—trees that were coeval with the feuds of York and Lancaster, yews that possibly had furnished bows to Cœur de Lion, and oaks that might have built a navy. All was savage grandeur about these native forests : their sweeping lawns and glades had been unapproached, for centuries it might be, by the hand of art ; and amongst them roamed—not the timid fallow deer—but thundering droves of wild horses.

Lord Londsdale went to London less frequently than else he might have done, because at home he was allowed to forget that in this world there was any greater man than himself. Even in London, however, his haughty injustice found occasions for making itself known. On a court day (I revive an anecdote once familiarly known), St. James's Street was lined by cavalry, and the orders were peremptory that no carriages should be allowed to pass, except those which were carrying parties to court. Whether it were by accident or by way of wilfully provoking such a collision, Lord Lonsdale's carriage advanced ; and the coachman, in obedience to orders shouted out from the window, was turning down the forbidden route, when a trooper rode up to the horses' heads, and stopped them ; the thundering menaces of Lord Lonsdale perplexed the soldier, who did not know but he might be bringing himself into a scrape by persisting in his opposition ; but the officer on duty, observing the scene, rode up, and, in a determined tone, enforced the order, causing two of his men to turn the horses' heads round into Piccadilly. Lord Lonsdale threw his card to the officer, and a duel followed ; in which, however, the outrageous injustice of his lordship met with a pointed rebuke ; for the first person whom he summoned to his aid, in the quality of second, though a friend, and, I believe, a relative of his own, declined to sanction by any interference so scandalous a quarrel with an officer for simply executing an official duty. In this dilemma (for probably he was aware that few military men would fail to take the same disapproving view of the affair) he applied to the present * Earl of Lonsdale, then Sir William Lowther. Either there must have been some needless discourtesy in the officer's mode of fulfilling his duty, or else Sir William thought the necessity of the case, however wantonly provoked, a sufficient justification for a relative giving his assistance, even under circumstances of such egregious injustice. At any rate, it is due to Sir William, in mere candour, to suppose that he did nothing in this instance but what his conscience approved ; seeing, that in all others his conduct has been such as to win him the universal respect of the two counties in which he is best known. He it was that acted as second ; and by a will which is said to have been dated the same day, he became eventually possessed of a large property, which did not necessarily accompany the title.

Another anecdote is told of the same Lord Lonsdale. which expresses, in a more eccentric way, and a way that to many people will be affecting—to some shocking—the

---

* Who must now (1854) be classed as the *late* Earl.

moody energy of his passions. He loved, with passionate fervour, a fine young woman, of humble parentage, in a Cumberland farmhouse. Her he had persuaded to leave her father, and put herself under his protection. Whilst yet young and beautiful, she died : Lord Lonsdale's sorrow was profound ; he could not bear the thought of a final parting from that face which had become so familiar to his heart : he caused her to be embalmed ; a glass was placed over her features ; and at intervals, when his thoughts reverted to her memory, he found a consolation (or perhaps a luxurious irritation) of his sorrow, in visiting this sad memorial of his former happiness. This story, which I have often heard repeated by the country-people of Cumberland, strengthened the general feeling of this eccentric nobleman's self-willed character, though in this instance complicated with a trait of character that argued nobler capacities. By what rules he guided himself in dealing with the various lawyers, agents, or stewards whom his extensive estates brought into a dependency upon his justice or his moderation—whether, in fact, he had no rule, but left all to accident or caprice— I have never learned. Generally, I have heard it said, that in some years of his life he resisted the payment of all bills indiscriminately, which he had any colourable plea for supposing to contain overcharges ; some fared ill, because they were neighbours, and his lordship could say, that "he knew them to be knaves ;" others fared worse, because they were so remote, that "how could his lordship know what they were ?" Of this number, and possibly for this reason left unpaid, was Wordsworth's father. He died whilst his four sons and one daughter were yet helpless children, leaving to them respectable fortunes ; but which, as yet, were unrealized and tolerably

hypothetic, as they happened to depend upon so shadowy
a basis as the justice of Lord Lonsdale. The executors
of the will, and trustees of the children's interests, in one
point acted wisely : foreseeing the result of a legal contest with so potent a defendant as this leviathan of two
counties, and that, under any nominal award, the whole
estate of the orphans might be swallowed up in the costs
of any suit that should be carried into Chancery, they
prudently withdrew from all active measures of opposition,
confiding the event to Lord Lonsdale's returning sense of
justice. Unfortunately for that nobleman's reputation, and
also, as was thought, for the children's prosperity, before
this somewhat rusty quality of justice could have time to
operate, his lordship died.

However, for once the world was wrong in its malicious anticipations : the successor to Lord Lonsdale's titles
and Cumberland estates was made aware of the entire
case, in all its circumstances ; and he very honourably gave
directions for full restitution being made. This was done ;
and in one respect the result was more fortunate for the
children than if they had been trained from youth to rely
upon their expectations : for, by the time this repayment
was made, three out of the five children were already settled
in life, with the very amplest prospects opening before them
—so ample as to make their private patrimonial fortunes
of inconsiderable importance in their eyes ; and very probably the withholding of their inheritance it was, however
unjust, and however little contemplated as an occasion of
any such effect, that urged these three persons to the exertions requisite for their present success. Two only of
the children remained to whom the restoration of their
patrimony was a matter of grave importance ; but it was
precisely those two whom no circumstances could have

made independent of their hereditary means by personal
exertions—viz., William Wordsworth, the poet, and Dorothy, the sole daughter of the house.   The three others
were : Richard, the eldest ; he had become a thriving
solicitor, at one of the inns of court in London ; and, if
he died only moderately rich, and much below the expectations of his acquaintance, in the final result of his labo-
rious life, it was because he was moderate in his desires ;
and, in his later years, reverting to the pastoral region of
his infancy and boyhood, chose rather to sit down by a
hearth of his own amongst the Cumberland mountains,
and wisely to woo the deities of domestic pleasures and
health, than to follow the chase after wealth in the feverish
crowds of the capital.   The third son (I believe) was
Christopher (Dr. Wordsworth), who, at an early age, became a man of importance in the English Church, being
made one of the chaplains and librarians of the Archbishop
of Canterbury (Dr. Manners Sutton, father of the late
Speaker, Lord Canterbury).   He has since risen to the
important and dignified station—once held by Barrow,
and afterwards by Bentley—of Master of Trinity in Cambridge.   Trinity in Oxford is not a first-rate college ; but
Trinity, Cambridge, answers in rank and authority to
Christ Church in Oxford ; and to be the head of that college is rightly considered a very splendid distinction.

    Dr. Wordsworth has distinguished himself as an author
by a very useful republication, entitled, " Ecclesiastical
Biography," which he has enriched with valuable notes.
And in his own person, besides other works more professional, he is the author of one very interesting work of
historical research upon the difficult question of " Who
wrote the ' Eicon Basilike ?' " a question still unsettled, but
much nearer to a settlement, in consequence of the strong

presumptions which Dr. Wordsworth has adduced on behalf of the King's claim.* The fourth and youngest son, John, was in the service of the East India Company, and perished most unhappily at the very outset of the voyage which he had meant to be his last, off the coast of Dorsetshire, in the Company's ship Abergavenny. A calumny was current in some quarters, that Captain Wordsworth was in a state of intoxication at the time of the calamity. But the printed report of the affair, revised by survivors, entirely disproves this calumny; which, besides, was in itself incredible to all who were acquainted with Captain Words-

---

* *"Eicon Basilike:"*—By the way, in the lamented Eliot Warburton's "Prince Rupert," this book, by a very excusable mistake, is always cited as the "Eicon Basilicon:" he was thinking of the "Doron Basilicon," written by Charles's father: each of the nouns *Eicon* and *Doron*, having the same terminal syllable—*on*—it was most excusable to forget that the first belonged to an imparisyllabic declension, so as to be feminine, the second not so; which made it neuter. With respect to the great standing question as to the authorship of the work, I have myself always held, that the natural freedom of judgment in this case has been intercepted by one strong prepossession (entirely false) from the very beginning. The minds of all people have been pre-occupied with the notion, that Dr. Gauden, the reputed author, obtained his bishopric confessedly on the credit of that service. Lord Clarendon, it is said, who hated the Doctor, nevertheless gave him a bishopric, on the sole ground of his having written the "Eicon." The inference therefore is—that the Prime Minister, who gave so reluctantly, must have given under an irresistible weight of proof that the Doctor really had done the work for which so unwillingly he paid him. Any shade of doubt, such as could have justified Lord Clarendon in suspending this gift, would have been eagerly snatched at. Such a shade, therefore, there was not. Meantime the whole of this reasoning rests upon a false assumption: Dr. Gauden did *not* owe his bishopric to a belief (true or false) that he had written the "Eicon." The bishopric was given on another account: consequently it cannot, in any way of using the fact, at all affect the presumptions, small or great, which may exist separately for or against the Doctor's claim on that head.

worth's most temperate and even philosophic habits of life.
So peculiarly, indeed, was Captain Wordsworth's temperament, and the whole system of his life, coloured by a grave
and meditative turn of thought, that amongst his brother
officers in the Company's service, he bore the surname of
" The Philosopher." And William Wordsworth, the poet, not
only always spoke of him with a sort of respect, that argued
him to have been no ordinary man, but he has frequently
assured me of one fact, which, as implying some want of
sincerity in himself, gave me pain to hear—viz., that in
the fine lines entitled " The Happy Warrior," reciting the
main elements which enter into the composition of a hero,
he had in view chiefly his brother John's character.   That
was true, I daresay, but it was inconsistent in some measure with the note attached to the lines, by which the
reader learns, that it was out of reverence for Lord Nelson,
as one who transcended the estimate here made, that the
poem had not been openly connected with his name, as
the real suggester of the thoughts.   Now, privately, though
still professing a lively admiration for the mighty Admiral,
as one of the few men who carried into his professional
labours a real and vivid genius (and thus far Wordsworth
often testified a deep admiration for Lord Nelson), yet, in
reference to these particular lines, he uniformily declared
that Lord Nelson was much below the ideal there contemplated, and that, in fact, it had been suggested by the recollection of his brother.   But, if so, why should it have
been dissembled ?   And surely, in some of the first passages, this cannot be so ; for example, when he makes it
one trait of the heaven-born hero, that he, if called upon
to face some mighty day of trial—

> " To which Heaven has join'd
> Great issues, good or bad, for human kind—

Is happy as a lover, and attired
With a supernal brightness, like a man inspired "—

then, at least, he must have had Lord Nelson's idea pre-
dominating in his thoughts ; for Captain Wordsworth was
scarcely tried in such a situation.   There can be no doubt,
however, that he merited the praises of his brother ; and
it was indeed an idle tale, that he should first of all deviate
from this philosophic temperance upon an occasion where
his utmost energies and the fullest self-possession were all
likely to prove little enough.   In reality it was the pilot,
the incompetent pilot, who caused the fatal catastrophe :—
" O pilot, you have ruined me !" were amongst the last
words that Captain Wordsworth was heard to utter—
pathetic words, and fit for him, " a meek man, and a brave,"
to use in addressing a last reproach to one who, not through
misfortune or overruling will of Providence, but through
miserable conceit and unprincipled levity, had brought
total ruin upon so many gallant countrymen.   Captain
Wordsworth might have saved his own life ; but the perfect loyalty of his nature to the claims upon him, that
sublime fidelity to duty which is so often found amongst men
of his profession, kept him to the last upon the wreck ; and
after *that*, it is probable that the almost total wreck of his
own fortunes (which, but for this overthrow, would have
amounted to twenty thousand pounds, upon the successful
termination of this one voyage), but still more, the total
ruin of the new and splendid Indiaman confided to his
care, had so much dejected his spirits, that he was not in a
condition for making such efforts as, under a more hopeful
prospect, he might have been able to make.   Six weeks his
body lay unrecovered ; at the end of that time, it was
found, and carried to the Isle of Wight, and buried in close
neighbourhood to the quiet fields which he had so recently

described in letters to his sister at Grasmere, as a Paradise of English peace, to which his mind would be likely oftentimes to revert, amidst the agitations of the sea.

Such were the modes of life pursued by three of the orphan children : such the termination of life to the youngest. Meantime, the one daughter of the house was reared liberally, in the family of a relative at Windsor ; and she might have pursued a quiet and decorous career, of a character, perhaps, somewhat tame, under the same dignified auspices ; but, at an early age, her good angel threw open to her a vista of nobler prospects, in the opportunity which then arose, and which she did not hesitate to seize, of becoming the companion, through a life of delightful wanderings—of what, to her more elevated friends, seemed little short of vagrancy—the companion and the confidential friend, and, with a view to the enlargement of her own intellect, the pupil of a brother, the most original and most meditative man of his own age. William had passed his infancy on the very margin of the Lake district, just six miles, in fact, beyond the rocky screen of Whinlatter, and within one hour's ride of Bassenthwaite Water. To those who live in the tame scenery of Cockermouth, the blue mountains in the distance, the sublime peaks of Borrowdale and of Buttermere, raise aloft a signal, as it were, of a new country, a country of romance and mystery, to which the thoughts are habitually turning. Children are fascinated and haunted with vague temptations, when standing on the frontiers of such a foreign land ; and so was Wordsworth fascinated, so haunted. Fortunate for Wordsworth that, at an early age, he was transferred to a quiet nook of this lovely district. At the little town of Hawkshead, seated on the north-west angle of Esthwaite Water, a grammar-school (which, in English usage, means a school for classical literature) was founded, in Queen Elizabeth's reign, by Archbishop Sandys, who belonged to the very ancient family of that name, still seated in the neighbourhood. Hither were sent all the four brothers; and here it was that Wordsworth passed his life, from the age of nine until the time arrived for his removal to college. Taking into consideration the peculiar tastes of the person, and the peculiar advantages of the place, I conceive that no pupil of a public school can ever have passed a more luxurious boyhood than Wordsworth. The school discipline was not by many evidences very strict; the mode of living out of school very much resembled that of Eton for Oppidans; less elegant, no doubt, and less costly in its provisions for accommodation, but not less comfortable; and in that part of the arrangements which was chiefly Etonian, even more so; for in both places the boys, instead of being gathered into one fold, and at night into one or two huge dormitories, were distributed amongst motherly old " dames," technically so called at Eton, but not at Hawkshead. In the latter place, agreeably to the inferior scale of the whole establishment, the houses were smaller, and more cottage-like, consequently more like private households : and the old lady of the *ménage* was more constantly amongst them, providing, with maternal tenderness and with a professional pride, for the comfort of her young flock, and protecting the weak from oppression. The humble cares to which these poor matrons dedicated themselves, may be collected from several allusions scattered through the poems of Wordsworth; that entitled "Nutting," for instance, in which his own early Spinosistic feeling is introduced, of a mysterious presence diffused through the solitudes of woods, a presence that was disturbed by the intrusion of careless and noisy outrage, and which is brought into a strong

II.—L

relief by the previous homely picture of the old housewife
equipping her young charge with beggar's weeds, in crder
to prepare him for a struggle with thorns and brambles.
Indeed, not only the moderate rank of the boys, and the
peculiar kind of relation assumed by these matrons, equally
suggested this humble class of motherly attentions, but
the whole spirit of the place and neighbourhood was favourable to an old English homeliness of domestic and personal
economy.   Hawkshead, most fortunately for its own manners and the primitive style of its habits, even to this day,
stands about six miles out of the fashionable line for the
" Lakers."

Esthwaite, though a lovely scene in its summer garniture of woods, has no features of permanent grandeur to
rely upon.   A wet or gloomy day, even in summer, re-
duces it to little more than a wildish pond, surrounded by
miniature hills : and the sole circumstances which restore
the sense of a romantic region and an Alpine character,
are the towering groups of Langdale and Grasmere fells,
which look over the little pastoral barriers of Esthwaite,
from distances of eight, ten, and fourteen miles.   Esthwaite, therefore, being no object for itself, and the sublime
head of Coniston being accessible by a road which evades
Hawkshead, few tourists ever trouble the repose of this
little village town.   And in the days of which I am speaking (1778-1787), tourists were as yet few and infrequent
to *any* parts of the country.   Mrs. Radcliffe had not begun
to cultivate the sense of the picturesque in her popular
romances ; guide-books, with the sole exception of " Gray's
Posthumous Letters," had not arisen to direct public attention to this domestic Calabria ; roads were rude, and, in
many instances, not wide enough to admit post-chaises ;
but, above all, the whole system of travelling accommo-

dations was barbarous and antediluvian for the requisitions
of the pampered south. As yet the land had rest; the
annual fever did not shake the very hills; and (which was
the happiest immunity of the whole) false taste, the pseudo-
romantic rage, had not violated the most awful solitudes
amongst the ancient hills by opera-house decorations.
Wordsworth, therefore, enjoyed this labyrinth of valleys
in a perfection that no one can have experienced since
the opening of the present century. The whole was one
paradise of virgin beauty; the rare works of man, all over
the land, were hoar with the grey tints of an antique
picturesque; nothing was new, nothing was raw and
uncicatrized. Hawkshead, in particular, though tamely
seated in itself and its immediate purlieus, has a most fortunate and central locality, as regards the best (at least
the most interesting) scenes for a pedestrian rambler. The
gorgeous scenery of Borrowdale, the austere sublimities
of Wastdalehead, of Langdalehead, or Mardale—these are
too oppressive, in their colossal proportions and their
utter solitudes, for encouraging a perfectly human interest.
Now, taking Hawkshead as a centre, with a radius of
about eight miles, one might describe a little circular
tract which embosoms a perfect network of little valleys
—separate wards or cells, as it were, of one larger valley,
walled in by the great leading mountains of the region,
Grasmere, Easedale, Great and Little Langdale, Tilberth-
waite, Yewdale, Elter Water, Loughrigg Tarn, Skelwith, and
many other little quite nooks, lie within a single division of
this labyrinthine district. All these are within one summer
afternoon's ramble. And amongst these, for the years of
his boyhood, lay the daily excursions of Wordsworth.

I do not conceive that Wordsworth *could* have been an
amiable boy: he was austere and unsocial, I have reason

to think, in his habits ; not generous ; and not self-deny-
ing. I am pretty certain that no consideration would
ever have induced Wordsworth to burden himself with a
lady's reticule, parasol, shawl, or anything exacting trouble
and attention. Mighty must be the danger which would
induce him to lead her horse by the bridle. Nor would
he, without some demur, stop to offer her his hand over a
stile. Freedom——unlimited, careless, insolent freedom——
unoccupied possession of his own arms——absolute control
over his own legs and motions——these have always been
so essential to his comfort, that, in any case where they
were likely to become questionable, he would have declined to make one of the party. Meantime, we are not
to suppose that Wordsworth the boy expressly sought
for solitary scenes of nature amongst woods and mountains, with a direct conscious anticipation of imaginative
pleasure, and loving them with a pure, disinterested love,
on their own separate account. These are feelings beyond
boyish nature, or, at all events, beyond boyish nature
trained amidst the selfishness of social intercourse. Wordsworth, like his companions, haunted the hills and the vales
for the sake of angling, snaring birds, swimming, and sometimes of hunting, according to the Westmoreland fashion (or
the Irish fashion in Galway), on foot ; for riding to the
chase is quite impossible, from the precipitous nature of
the ground. It was in the course of these pursuits, by an
indirect effect growing gradually upon him, that Wordsworth became a passionate lover of nature, at the time
when the growth of his intellectual faculties made it possible that he should combine those thoughtful passions with
the experience of the eye and the ear.

One of the most interesting among the winter amuse-
ments of the Hawkshead boys was that of skating on the

adjacent lake. Esthwaite Water is not one of the deep
lakes, as its neighbours of Windermere, Coniston, and
Grasmere are; consequently, a very slight duration of frost
is sufficient to freeze it into a bearing strength. In
this respect Wordsworth found the same advantages in
his boyhood as afterwards at the university; for the
county of Cambridge is generally liable to shallow waters;
and that university breeds more good skaters than all the
rest of England. About the year 1810, by way of expressing an interest in " The Friend," which was just at that
time appearing in weekly numbers, Wordsworth allowed
Coleridge to print an extract from the poem on his own
life, descriptive of the games celebrated upon the ice of
Esthwaite by all who were able to skate : the mimic
chases of hare and hounds, pursued long after the last
orange gleam of light had died away from the western
horizon—oftentimes far into the night ; a circumstance
which does not speak much for the discipline of the
schools, or rather, perhaps, *does* speak much for the advantages of a situation so pure, and free from the usual
perils of a town, as could allow of a discipline so lax.
Wordsworth, in this fine descriptive passage—which I wish
that I had at this moment the means of citing, in order
to amplify my account of his earliest tyrocinium—speaks
of himself as frequently wheeling aside from his joyous
companions to cut across the image of a star ; and thus,
already in the midst of sportiveness, and by a movement
of sportiveness, half unconsciously to himself expressing the
growing necessity of retirement to his habits of thought.
At another period of the year, when the golden summer
allowed the students a long season of early play before
the studies of the day began, he describes himself as
roaming, hand-in-hand, with one companion, along the

banks of Esthwaite Water, chanting, with one voice, the verses of Goldsmith and of Gray—verses which, at the time of recording the fact, he had come to look upon as either in parts false in the principles of their composition, or, at any rate, as far below the tone of high poetic passion ; but which, at that time of life, when the profounder feelings were as yet only germinating, filled them with an enthusiasm

"More bright than madness and the dreams of wine."

Meanwhile, how prospered the classical studies which formed the main business of Wordsworth at Hawkshead ? Not, in all probability, very well ; for, though Wordsworth finally became a very sufficient master of the Latin language, and read certain favourite authors, especially Horace, with a critical nicety, and with a feeling for the felicities of his composition, I have reason to think that little of this skill had been obtained at Hawkshead. As to Greek, that is a language which Wordsworth never had energy enough to cultivate with effect.

From Hawkshead, and, I believe, after he had entered his eighteenth year (a time which is tolerably early on the English plan), probably at the latter end of the year 1787, Wordsworth entered at St. John's College, Cambridge. St. John's ranks as the second college in Cambridge—the second as to numbers, and influence, and general consideration ; in the estimation of the Johnians as the first, or at least as co-equal in all things with Trinity ; from which, at any rate, the general reader will collect, that no such absolute supremacy is accorded to any society in Cambridge, as in Oxford is accorded necessarily to Christ Church. The advantages of a large college are considerable, both to the idle man, who wishes to lurk unnoticed in the crowd,

and to the brilliant man, whose vanity could not be gratified by pre-eminence amongst a few.   Wordsworth, though
not idle as regarded his own pursuits, was so as regarded
the pursuits of the place.   With respect to them he felt—
to use his own words—that his hour was not come ; and
that his doom for the present was a happy obscurity, which
left him, unvexed by the torments of competition, to the
genial enjoyment of life in its most genial hours.

It will excite some astonishment when I mention that,
on coming to Cambridge, Wordsworth actually assumed the
beau, or, in modern slang, the "dandy."   He dressed in
silk stockings, had his hair powdered, and in all things
plumed himself on his gentlemanly habits.   To those who
remember the slovenly dress of his middle and philosophic
life, this will furnish matter for a smile.

Stranger still it is to tell, that, for the first time in his
life, Wordsworth became inebriated at Cambridge.   It is
but fair to add, that the first time was also the last time.
But perhaps the strangest part of the story is the occasion
of this drunkenness ; which was in celebration of his first
visit to the very rooms at Christ College once occupied by
Milton—intoxication by way of homage to the most temperate of men ; and this homage offered by one who has
turned out himself to the full as temperate !   Every man,
meantime, who is not a churl, must grant a privilege and
charter of large enthusiasm to such an occasion.   And an
older man than Wordsworth (at that era not fully nineteen),
and a man even without a poet's blood in his veins, might
have leave to forget his sobriety in such circumstances.
Besides which, after all, I have heard from Wordsworth's
own lips, that he was not too far gone to attend chapel
decorously during the very acmé of his elevation.

The rooms which Wordsworth occupied at St. John's were

singularly circumstanced ; mementoes of what is highest and
what is lowest in human things solicited the eye and the
ear all day long.   If the occupant approached the out-
doors prospect, in one direction, there was visible, through
the great windows in the adjacent chapel of Trinity, the
statue of Newton " with his silent face and prism," memorials of the abstracting intellect, serene and absolute,
emancipated from fleshly bonds.   On the other hand, immediately below, stood the college kitchen ; and, in that
region, " from noon to dewy eve," resounded the shrill
voice of scolding from the female ministers of the head
cook, never suffering the mind to forget one of the meanest
amongst human necessities.   Wordsworth, however, as one
who passed much of his time in social gaiety, was less in
the way of this annoyance than a profounder student would
have been.   Probably he studied little beyond French and
Italian during his Cambridge life ; not, however, at any
time forgetting (as I had so much reason to complain,
when speaking of my Oxonian contemporaries) the literature of his own country.   It is true, that he took the regular degree of A.B., and in the regular course ; but this
was won in those days by a mere nominal examination,
unless where the mathematical attainments of the student
prompted his ambition to contest the splendid distinction
of Senior Wrangler.   This, in common with all other
honours of the university, is won in our days with far
severer effort than in that age of relaxed discipline ; but
at no period could it have been won, let the malicious say
what they will, without an amount of mathematical skill
very much beyond what has ever been exacted of its
alumni by any other European university.   Wordsworth
was a profound admirer of the sublimer mathematics ; at
least of the higher geometry.   The secret of this admira-

tion for geometry lay in the antagonism between this world of bodiless abstraction and the world of passion. And here I may mention appropriately, and I hope without any breach of confidence, that, in a great philosophic poem of Wordsworth's, which is still in MS., and will remain in MS. until after his death, there is, at the opening of one of the books, a dream, which reaches the very *ne plus ultra* of sublimity, in my opinion, expressly framed to illustrate the eternity and the independence of all social modes or fashions of existence, conceded to these two hemispheres, as it were, that compose the total world of human power—mathematics on the one hand, poetry on the other.

I scarcely know whether I am entitled to quote—as my memory (though not refreshed by a sight of the poem for more than twenty years) would well enable me to do—any long extract ; but thus much I may allowably say, as it cannot in any way affect Mr. Wordsworth's interests, that the form of the dream is as follows ; and, by the way, even this form is not arbitrary ; but, with exquisite skill in the art of composition, is made to arise out of the situation in which the poet had previously found himself, and is faintly prefigured in the elements of that situation.   He had been reading " Don Quixote " by the sea-side ; and, oppressed by the heat of the sun, he had fallen asleep, whilst gazing on the barren sands before him.   Even in these circumstances of the case—as, first, the adventurous and half-lunatic knight riding about the world, on missions of universal philanthropy ; and, secondly, the barren sands of the seashore—one may read the germinal principles of the dream. He dreams that, walking in some sandy wilderness of Africa, some endless Zahara, he sees at a distance

> " An Arab of the desert, lance in rest,
> Mounted upon a dromedary."

The Arab rides forward to meet him; and the dreamer
perceives, in the countenance of the rider, the agitation of
fear, and that he often looks behind him in a troubled way,
whilst in his hand he holds two books—one of which is
Euclid's " Elements ;" the other (which is a book and yet
not a book) seeming, in fact, a shell as well as a book—
seeming neither, and yet both at once.   The Arab directs
him to apply the shell to his ear ; upon which,

> " In an unknown tongue, which yet I understood,"

the dreamer says that he heard

> " A wild prophetic blast of harmony,
>   An ode, as if in passion utter'd, that foretold
>   Destruction to the people of this earth
>   By deluge near at hand."

The Arab, with grave countenance, assures him that it is
even so ; that all was true which had been said ; and that
he himself was riding upon a divine mission, having it in
charge

> " To bury those two books ;
>   The one that held acquaintance with the stars,
>   —— undisturb'd by Space or Time ;
>   The other, that was a god, yea, many gods,
>   Had voices more than all the winds, and was
>   A joy, a consolation, and a hope ! "

That is, in effect, his mission is to secure the two great
interests of poetry and mathematics from sharing in the
watery ruin.   As he talks, suddenly the dreamer perceives
that the Arab's

> " Countenance grew more disturb'd,"

and that his eye was often reverted ; upon which the
dreaming poet also looks along the desert in the same
direction ; and in the far horizon he descries

> " A glittering light."

What is it? he asks of the Arab rider. "It is," said the Arab, "the waters of the earth," that even then were travelling on their awful errand. Upon which, the poet sees this apostle of the desert riding

> " Hurrying o'er the illimitable waste,
> With the fleet waters of a drowning world
> In chase of him: whereat I [meaning the poet] waked in terror,
> And saw the sea before me, and the book
> In which I had been reading at my side."

The sketch I have here given of this sublime dream sufficiently attests the interest which Wordsworth took in the mathematic studies of the place, and the exalted privilege which he ascribed to them of co-eternity with " the vision and the faculty divine " of the poet—the destiny common to both, of an endless triumph over the ruins of nature and of time.   Meantime, he himself travelled no farther in these studies than through the six elementary books, usually selected from the fifteen of Euclid. Whatever might be the interests of his speculative understanding, whatever his admiration, practically he devoted himself to the more agitating interests of man, social and political, just then commencing that vast career of revolution which has never since been still or stationary ; interests which in his mind alternated, nevertheless, with another and different interest, in the grander forms of external nature, as found amongst mountains and forests.   In obedience to this latter passion it was—for a passion it had become—that during one of his long Cambridge vacations, stretching from June to November, he went over to Switzerland and Savoy, for a pedestrian excursion amongst the Alps ; taking with him for his travelling companion a certain Mr. J——, of whom (excepting that he is once apostrophized in a sonnet, written at Calais in the year 1802) I never happened to

hear him speak : whence I presume to infer, that Mr. J.——
owed this flattering distinction, not so much to any intellectual graces of his society, as, perhaps, to his powers of
administering " punishment " (in the language of the
" fancy ") to restive and mutinous landlords ; for such were
abroad in those days ; people who presented huge reckon-
ings with one hand, and with the other a huge cudgel, by
way of opening the traveller's eyes to the propriety of
settling them without demur, and without discount.   I do
not positively know this to have been the case ; but I have
heard Wordsworth speak of the ruffian landlords who
played upon his youth in the Grisons ; and, however well
qualified to fight his own battles, he might find, amongst
such savage mountaineers, two combatants better than
one.

Wordsworth's route, on this occasion, lay at first through
Austrian Flanders, then (1788, I think) on the fret for an
insurrectionary war against the capricious innovations of
the imperial coxcomb, Joseph II.   He passed through the
camps then forming, and thence ascended the Rhine to
Switzerland ; crossed the Great St. Bernard, visited the
Lake of Como, and other interesting scenes in the north of
Italy, where, by the way, the tourists were benighted in a
forest—having, in some way or other, been misled by the
Italian clocks, and their peculiar fashion of striking round
to twenty-four o'clock.   On his return, Wordsworth published a quarto pamphlet of verses, describing, with very considerable effect and brilliancy, the grand scenery amongst
which he had been moving.   This poem, as well as another
in the same quarto form, describing the English lake
scenery of Westmoreland and Cumberland, addressed by
way of letter " to a young lady" (viz., Miss Wordsworth),
are remarkable, in the first place, as the earliest effort of

Wordsworth in verse, at least as his earliest publication ;
but, in the second place, and still more so, from their style
of composition. "Pure description," even where it cannot
be said, sneeringly, "to hold the place of sense," is so little
attractive as the direct exclusive object of a poem, and
in reality it exacts so powerful an effort on the part of the
reader to realize visually, or make into an apprehensible
unity, the scattered elements and circumstances of external
landscapes painted only by words, that, inevitably, and rea-
sonably, it can never hope to be a popular form of composition ; else it is highly probable that these "Descriptive
Sketches" of Wordsworth, though afterwards condemned
as vicious in their principles of composition by his own
maturer taste, would really have gained him a high momentary notoriety with the public, had they been fairly
brought under its notice ; whilst, on the other hand, his revolutionary principles of composition, and his purer taste,
ended in obtaining for him nothing but scorn and ruffian
insolence.   This seems marvellous ; but, in fact, it is not
so ; it seems, I mean, *primâ facie,* marvellous that the inferior models should be fitted to gain a far higher reputation ; but the secret lies here—that these were in a style
of composition which, if sometimes false, had been long
reconciled to the public feelings, and which, besides, have
a specific charm for certain minds, even apart from all
fashions of the day ; whereas, his later poems had to struggle
against sympathies long trained in an opposite direction,
to which the recovery of a healthier tone (even where
nature had made it possible) presupposed a difficult process
of weaning, and an effort of discipline for re-organizing the
whole internal economy of the sensibilities, that is both
painful and mortifying : for—and that is worthy of deep
attention—the misgivings of any vicious or unhealthy state ;

the impulses and suspicious gleams of the truth struggling
with cherished error ; the instincts of light conflicting with
darkness—these are the real causes of that hatred and in-
tolerant scorn which is ever awakened by the first dawnings
of new and important systems of truth.   Therefore it is,
that Christianity was so much more hated than any mere
variety of error.   Therefore are the first feeble struggles
of nature towards a sounder state of health always harsh
and painful ; for the false system which this change for the
better disturbs had, at least, this soothing advantage—that
it was self-consistent.   Therefore, also, was the Wordsworthian restoration of elementary power, and of a higher
or transcendent truth of nature (or, as some people vaguely
expressed the case, of *simplicity*), received at first with such
malignant disgust.   For there was a galvanic awakening
in the shock of power, as it jarred against the ancient system of prejudices, which inevitably revealed so much of
truth as made the mind jealous ; enlightened it enough to
descry its own wanderings, but not enough to recover the
right road.   The more energetic, the more spasmodically
potent are the throes of nature towards her own re-estab-
lishment in the cases of suspended animation—by drowning,
strangling, &c.—the more keen is the anguish of revival.
And, universally, a transition state is a state of suffering
and disquiet.   Meantime, the early poems of Wordsworth,
that *might* have suited the public taste so much better than
his more serious efforts, if the fashion of the hour, or the
sanction of a leading review, or the *prestige* of a name, had
happened to bring them under the public eye, did, in fact,
drop unnoticed into the market.   Nowhere have I seen
them quoted—no, not even since the author's victorious
establishment in the public admiration.   The reason may
be, however, that not many copies were printed at first ; no

subsequent edition was ever called for ; and yet, from growing interest in the author, every copy of the small impression had been studiously bought up. Indeed, I myself went to the publisher's (Johnson's) as early as 1805 or 1806, and bought up all the remaining copies (which were but six or seven of the Foreign Sketches, and two or three of the English), as presents, and as *future* curiosities in literature to literary friends, whose interest in Wordsworth might assure one of a due value being put upon the poem. Were it not for this extreme scarcity, I am disposed to think that many lines or passages would long ere this have been made familiar to the public ear. Some are delicately, some forcibly picturesque ; and the selection of circumstances is occasionally very original and felicitous. In particular, I remember this one, which presents an accident in rural life that must by thousands of repetitions have become intimately known to every dweller in the country, and yet had never before been consciously taken up for a poet's use. After having described the domestic cock as " sweetly ferocious"—a prettiness of phraseology which he borrows from an Italian author—he notices those competitions or defiances which are so often carried on interchangeably between barn-door cocks from great distances :—

> " Echoed by faintly answering farms remote."

This is the beautiful line in which he has caught and preserved so ordinary an occurrence—one, in fact, of the commonplaces which lend animation and a moral interest to rural life.

After his return from this Swiss excursion, Wordsworth took up his parting residence at Cambridge, and prepared for a final adieu to academic pursuits and academic society.

It was about this period that the French Revolution

broke out ; and the reader who would understand its appalling effects—its convulsing, revolutionary effects upon Wordsworth's heart and soul—should consult the history of the Solitary, as given by himself in " The Excursion ;" for that picture is undoubtedly a leaf from the personal experience of Wordsworth :—

" From that dejection I was roused —but how ?"

Mighty was the transformation which it wrought in the whole economy of his thoughts ; miraculous almost was the expansion which it gave to his human sympathies ; chiefly in this it showed its effects—in throwing the thoughts inwards into grand meditations upon man, his final destiny, his ultimate capacities of elevation ; and, secondly, in giving to the whole system of the thoughts and feelings a firmer tone, and a sense of the awful *realities* which surround the mind ; by comparison with which the previous literary tastes seemed (even where they were fine and elegant, as in Collins or Gray, unless where they had the self-sufficing reality of religion, as in Cowper) fanciful and trivial.   In all lands this result was accomplished, and at the same time : Germany, above all, found her new literature the mere creation and rebound of this great moral tempest ; and, in Germany or England alike, the poetry was so entirely regenerated, thrown into moulds of thought and of feeling so new, that the poets everywhere felt themselves to be putting away childish things, and now first, among those of their own century, entering upon the dignity and the sincere thinking of mature manhood.

Wordsworth, it is well known to all who know anything of his history, felt himself so fascinated by the gorgeous festival era of the Revolution—that era when the sleeping snakes which afterwards stung the national felicity were yet covered with flowers—that he went over to Paris, and spent about one entire year between that city, Orleans, and Blois. There, in fact, he continued to reside almost too long. He had been sufficiently connected with public men, to have drawn upon himself some notice from those who afterwards composed the Committee of Public Safety. And, as an Englishman, when that partiality began to droop, which at an earlier period had protected the English name, he became an object of gloomy suspicion with those even who would have grieved that he should fall a victim to undistinguishing popular violence. Already *for* England, and in her behalf, he was thought to be that spy which (as Coleridge tells us in his " Biographia Literaria") afterwards he was accounted by Mr. Pitt's emissaries, in the worst of services *against* her. I doubt, however (let me say it without impeachment of Coleridge's veracity— for he was easily duped), this whole story about Mr. Pitt's Somersetshire spies ; and it has often struck me with astonishment, that Coleridge should have suffered his personal pride to take so false a direction as to court the humble distinction of having been suspected as a conspirator, in those very years when poor empty tympanies of men, such as Thelwall, Holcroft, &c., were actually recognised as enemies of the state, and worthy of a state surveillance, by ministers so blind and grossly misinformed as, on this point, were Pitt and Dundas. Had I been Coleridge, instead of saving Mr. Pitt's reputation with posterity, by ascribing to him a jealousy which he or his agents had not the discernment to cherish, I would have boldly planted myself upon the fact, the killing fact, that he had utterly ignored both myself (Coleridge, to wit), and Wordsworth—even with Dogberry, *I* would have insisted upon that—" Set down, also, that I am an ass !" clamorous should have been my exultation in this fact.*

In France, however, Wordsworth had a chance, in good earnest, of passing for the traitor, that, in England, no rational person ever thought him. He had chosen his friends carelessly ; nor could any man, the most sagacious, have chosen them safely, in a time when the internal schisms of the very same general party brought with them worse hostilities and more personal perils than even, upon the broader divisions of party, could have attended the most *ultra* professions of anti-national politics, and when the rapid changes of position shifted the peril from

---

* The reader, who may happen not to have seen Coleridge's "Biographia Literaria," is informed that Coleridge tells a long story about a man who followed and dogged himself and Wordsworth in all their rural excursions, under a commission (originally emanating from Mr. Pitt) for detecting some overt acts of treason, or treasonable correspondence ; or, in default of either, some words of treasonable conversation. Unfortunately for his own interests as an active servant, even in a whole month that spy had collected nothing at all as the basis of a report, excepting only something which they (Coleridge and Wordsworth, to wit) were continually saying to each other, now in blame, now in praise, of one *Spy Nosy;* and this, praise and blame alike, the honest spy very naturally took to himself, seeing that the world accused him of having a *nose* of unreasonable dimensions, and his own conscience accused him of being a spy. " Now," says Coleridge, " the very fact was, that Wordsworth and I were constantly talking about Spinosa." This story makes a very good Joe Miller ; but, for other purposes, is somewhat damaged. However, there *is* one excellent story in the case. Some country gentleman from the neighbourhood of Nether Stowey, upon a party happening to discuss the probabilities that Wordsworth and Coleridge might be traitors, and in correspondence with the French Directory, answered thus :— " Oh, as to that Coleridge, he's a rattlebrain, that will say more in a week than he will stand to in a twelvemonth. But Wordsworth—that's the traitor: why, bless you, he's so close, that you'll never hear him open his lips on the subject from year's end to year's end !"

month to month. One individual is especially recorded by Wordsworth, in the poem on his own life, as a man of the highest merit, and personal qualities the most brilliant, who ranked first upon the list of Wordsworth's friends; and this man was so far a safe friend, at one moment, as he was a republican general—finally, indeed, a commander-in-chief. This was Beaupuis; and the description of his character and position is singularly interesting. There is, in fact, a special value and a use about the case; it opens one's eyes feelingly to the fact, that, even in this thought-less people, so full of vanity and levity, nevertheless, the awful temper of the times, and the dread burden of human interests with which it was charged, had called to a con-sciousness of new duties, had summoned to an audit, as if at some great final tribunal, even the gay, radiant crea-tures that, under less solemn auspices, under the reign of a Francis I. or a Louis XIV., would have been the merest painted butterflies of the court sunshine. This Beaupuis was a man of superb person—beautiful in a degree which made him a painter's model, both as to face and figure; and, accordingly, in a land where conquests of that nature were so easy, and the subjects of so trifling an effort, he had been distinguished, to his own as well as the public eyes, by a rapid succession of *bonnes fortunes* amongst women. Such, and so glorified by triumphs the most unquestionable and flattering, had the earthquake of the Revolution found him. From that moment he had no leisure, not a thought, to bestow upon his former selfish and frivolous pursuits. He was hurried, as one inspired by some high apostolic passion, into the service of the unhappy and desolate serfs amongst his own countrymen—such as are described, at an earlier date, by Madame de Sevigné, as the victims of feudal institutions; and one day,

as he was walking with Wordsworth in the neighbourhood of Orleans, and they had turned into a little quiet
lane, leading off from a heath, suddenly they came upon
the following spectacle :—A girl, seventeen or eighteen
years old, hunger-bitten, and wasted to a meagre shadow,
was knitting, in a dejected, drooping way; whilst to her
arm was attached, by a rope, the horse, equally famished,
that earned the miserable support of her family.   Beaupuis
comprehended the scene in a moment ; and seizing Wordsworth by the arm, he said,—" Dear English friend !—
brother from a nation of freemen !—*that* it is which is
the curse of our people, in their widest section ; and to
cure this it is, as well as to maintain our work against
the kings of the earth, that blood must be shed and tears
must flow for many years to come !"   At that time the
Revolution had not fulfilled its tendencies ; as yet, the
king was on the throne ; the fatal 10th of August 1792,
had not dawned ; and thus far there was safety for a
subject of kings.*   The irresistible stream was hurrying

---

* How little has any adequate power as yet approached this great
theme ! Not the Grecian stage, not " the dark sorrows of the line
of Thebes," in any of its scenes, unfold such tragical grouping of
circumstances and situations as may be gathered from the memoirs
of the time.   The galleries and vast staircases of Versailles, at early
dawn, on some of the greatest days—filled with dreadful faces—the
figure of the Duke of Orleans obscurely detected amongst them—
the growing fury—the growing panic—the blind tumult—and the
dimness of the event,—all make up a scene worthy to blend with our
images of Babylon or of Nineveh with the enemy in all her gates,
Memphis or Jerusalem in their agonies.   But, amongst all the ex-
ponents of the growing agitation that besieged the public mind, none
is so profoundly impressive as the scene (every Sunday renewed) at
the Chapel Royal.   Even in the most penitential of the litanies, in
the presence when most immediately confessed of God himself—when
the antiphonies are chanted, one party singing, with fury and gnash-

forwards. The king fell; and (to pause for a moment) how divinely is the fact recorded by Wordsworth, in the MS. poem on his own life, placing the awful scenes past and passing in Paris, under a pathetic relief from the description of the golden, autumnal day, sleeping in sunshine—

> " When I
> Towards the fierce metropolis bent my steps
> The homeward road to England. From his throne
> The king had fallen," &c.

What a picture does he give of the fury which there possessed the public mind; of the frenzy which shone in every eye, and through every gesture; of the stormy groups assembled at the Palais Royal, or the Tuileries, with " hissing factionists" for ever in their centre, " hissing" from the self-baffling of their own madness, and incapable from wrath of speaking clearly; of fear already creeping over the manners of multitudes; of stealthy movements through back streets; plotting and counter-plotting in every family; feuds to extermination, dividing children of the same house for ever; scenes such as those of the Chapel Royal (now silenced on that *public* stage), repeating themselves daily amongst private friends; and, to show the universality of this maniacal possession—that it was no narrow storm discharging its fury by local concentra-

---

ing of teeth, *Salvum fac regem*, and another, with equal hatred and fervour, answering *Et Reginam* [the poor queen at this time engrossing the popular hatred]—the organ roared into thunder—the semi-chorus swelled into shouting—the menaces into defiance—again the crashing semi-choir sang with shouts their *Salvum fac regem*— again the vengeful antiphony hurled back its *Et Reginam*—and one person, an eye-witness of these scenes, which mounted in violence on each successive Sunday, declares, that oftentimes the semi-choral bodies were at the point of fighting with each other in the presence of the king.

tion upon a single city, but that it overspread the whole
realm of France—a picture is given, wearing the same
features, of what passed daily at Orleans, Blois, and other
towns.   The citizens are described in the attitudes they
assumed at the daily coming in of the post from Paris ;
the fierce sympathy is portrayed with which they echoed
back the feelings of their compatriots in the capital : men
of all parties had been there up to this time—aristocrats
as well as democrats ; and one, in particular, of the former
class is put forward as a representative of his class.   This
man, duly as the hour arrived which brought the Parisian
newspapers, read restlessly of the tumults and insults
amongst which the Royal Family now passed their days ;
of the decrees by which his own order were threatened or
assailed ; of the self-expatriation, now continually swelling
in amount, as a measure of despair on the part of myriads,
as well priests as gentry—all this and worse he read in
public : and still, as he read,

> " His hand
> Haunted his sword, like an uneasy spot
> In his own body."

In short, as there never has been so strong a national con-
vulsion diffused so widely, with equal truth it may be
asserted, that no describer, so powerful, or idealizing so
magnificently what he deals with, has ever been a real
living spectator of parallel scenes.   The French, indeed, it
may be said, are far enough from being a people profound
in feeling.   True ; but, of all people, they most exhibit
their feeling on the surface ; are the most *demonstrative* (to
use a modern term), and most of all (except Italians) mark
their feelings by outward expression of gesticulation : not
to insist upon the obvious truth—that even a people of
shallow feeling may be deeply moved by tempests which

uproot the forest of a thousand years' growth ; by changes
in the very organization of society, such as throw all things,
for a time, into one vast anarchy ; and by murderous passions, alternately the effect and the cause of that same
chaotic anarchy.   Now, it was in this autumn of 1792, as
I have already said, that Wordsworth parted finally from
his illustrious friend—for, all things considered, he may be
justly so entitled—the gallant Beaupuis.   This great season
of public trial had searched men's natures ; revealed their
real hearts ; brought into light and action qualities oftentimes not suspected by their possessors ; and had thrown
men, as in elementary states of society, each upon his own
native resources, unaided by the old conventional forces of
rank and birth.   Beaupuis had shone to unusual advantage
under this general trial ; he had discovered, even to the
philosophic eye of Wordsworth, a depth of benignity very
unusual in a Frenchman ; and not of local, contracted
benignity, but of large, illimitable, apostolic devotion to the
service of the poor and the oppressed—a fact the more remarkable, as he had all the pretensions in his own person
of high birth and high rank ; and, so far as he had any personal interest embarked in the struggle, should have allied
himself with the aristocracy.   But of selfishness in any
shape he had no vestiges ; or, if he had, it showed itself in
a slight tinge of vanity ; yet, no—it was not vanity, but
a radiant quickness of sympathy with the eye which expressed admiring love—sole relic of the chivalrous devotion
once dedicated to the service of ladies.   Now, again, he put
on the garb of chivalry ; it was a chivalry the noblest in
the world, which opened his ear to the Pariah and the oppressed all over his misorganized country.   A more apostolic
fervour of holy zealotry in this great cause had not been
seen since the days of Bartholomew las Casas, who showed

the same excess of feeling in another direction. This sublime dedication of his being to a cause which, in his conception of it, extinguished all petty considerations for himself, and made him thenceforwards a creature of the national will—"a son of France," in a more eminent and loftier sense than according to the heraldry of Europe—had extinguished even his sensibility to the voice of worldly honour : "Injuries," says Wordsworth—

> "Injuries
> Made him more gracious."

And so utterly had he submitted his own will or separate interests to the transcendent voice of his country, which, in the main, he believed to be now speaking authentically for the first time since the foundations of Christendom, that, even against the motions of his own heart, he adopted the hatreds of the young republic, growing cruel in his purposes towards the ancient oppressor, out of very excess of love for the oppressed ; and, against the voice of his own order, as well as in stern oblivion of many early friendships, he became the champion of democracy in the struggle everywhere commencing with prejudice or feudal privilege.   Nay, he went so far upon the line of this new crusade against the evils of the world, that he even accepted, with a conscientious defiance of his own quiet homage to the erring spirit of loyalty embarked upon that cause, a commission in the Republican armies preparing to move against La Vendée ; and, finally, in that cause, as commander-in-chief, he laid down his life.   "He perished," says Wordsworth—

> "Perish'd fighting in supreme command,
> Upon the banks of the unhappy Loire."

Homewards fled all the English from a land which now was fast making ready the shambles for its noblest citizens.

Thither also came Wordsworth; and there he spent his time for a year and more chiefly in London, overwhelmed with shame and despondency for the disgrace and scandal brought upon Liberty by the atrocities committed in that holy name. Upon this subject he dwells with deep emotion in the poem on his own life; and he records the awful triumph for retribution accomplished, which possessed him when crossing the sands of the great Bay of Morecamb from Lancaster to Ulverstone; and hearing from a horseman who passed him, in reply to the question—*Was there any news?*—" Yes, that Robespierre had perished." Immediately a passion seized him, a transport of almost epileptic fervour, prompting him, as he stood alone upon this perilous * waste of sands, to shout aloud anthems of thanksgiving for this great vindication of eternal justice. Still, though justice was done upon one great traitor to the cause, the cause itself was overcast with clouds too heavily to find support and employment for the hopes of a poet who had believed in a golden era ready to open upon

---

* That tract of the lake-country which stretches southwards from Hawkshead and the lakes of Esthwaite, Windermere, and Coniston, to the little town of Ulverstone (which may be regarded as the metropolis of the little romantic English Calabria, called Furness), is divided from the main part of Lancashire by the estuary of Morecamb. The sea retires with the ebb tide to a vast distance, leaving the sands passable through a few hours for horses and carriages. But, partly from the daily variation in these hours, partly from the intricacy of the pathless track which must be pursued, and partly from the galloping pace at which the returning tide comes in, many fatal accidents are continually occurring—sometimes to the too venturous traveller who has slighted the aid of guides—sometimes to the guides themselves, when baffled and perplexed by mists. Gray the poet mentions one of the latter class as having then recently occurred, under affecting circumstances. Local tradition records a long list of such cases.

H 2

the prospects of human nature. It gratified and solaced his heart, that the indignation of mankind should have wreaked itself upon the chief monsters that had outraged their nature and their hopes ; but for the present he found it necessary to comfort his disappointment, by turning away from politics to studies less capable of deceiving his expectations.

From this period, therefore—that is, from the year 1794-95—we may date the commencement of Wordsworth's entire self-dedication to poetry as the study and main business of his life. Somewhere about this period also (though, according to my remembrance of what Miss Wordsworth once told me, I think one year or so later), his sister joined him ; and they began * to keep house together : once at Race Down, in Dorsetshire ; once at Clevedon, on the coast of Somersetshire ; then amongst the Quantock Hills, in the same county, or in that neighbourhood ; particularly at Alfoxton, a beautiful country-house, with a grove and shrubbery attached, belonging to Mr. St. Aubyn, a minor, and let (I believe) on the terms of keeping the house in repair. Whilst resident at this last place it was, as I have generally understood, and in the year 1797 or 1798, that Wordsworth first became acquainted with Coleridge ; though, possibly, in the year I am wrong ; for it occurs to me that, in a poem of Coleridge's dated in 1796, there is an allusion to a young writer, of the name of Wordsworth, as one who had something austere in his style, but otherwise was more original than any other poet of the age ; and it is probable that this

---

* I do not, on consideration, know when they might begin to keep house together: but, by a passage in "The Prelude," they must have made a tour together as early as 1787.

knowledge of the poetry would be subsequent to a personal knowledge of the author, considering the little circulation which any poetry of a Wordsworthian stamp would be likely to attain at that time.

It was at Alfoxton that Miss Mary Hutchinson visited her cousins the Wordsworths ; and there, or previously, in the north of England, at Stockton-upon-Tees and Darlington, that the attachment began between Miss Mary Hutchinson and Wordsworth, which terminated in their marriage about the beginning of the present century. The marriage took place in the north ; somewhere, I believe, in Yorkshire ; and, immediately after the ceremony, Wordsworth brought his bride to Grasmere ; in which most lovely of English valleys he had previously obtained, upon a lease of seven or eight years, the cottage in which I found him living at my first visit to him in November 1807. I have heard that there was a paragraph inserted on this occasion in the " Morning Post" or " Courier"—and I have an indistinct remembrance of having once seen it myself— which described this event of the poet's marriage in the most ludicrous terms of silly pastoral sentimentality ; the cottage being described as " the abode of content and all the virtues," the vale itself in the same puerile slang, and the whole event in the style of allegorical trifling about the Muses, &c. The masculine and severe taste of Words- worth made him peculiarly open to annoyance from such absurd trifling ; and, unless his sense of the ludicrous over- powered his graver feelings, he must have been much dis- pleased with the paragraph. But, after all, I have under- stood that the whole affair was an unseasonable jest of Coleridge's or Lamb's.

To us who, in after years, were Wordsworth's friends, or, at least, intimate acquaintances—viz., to Professor

Wilson and myself—the most interesting circumstance in this marriage, the one which perplexed us exceedingly, was the very possibility that it should ever have been brought to bear. For we could not conceive of Wordsworth as submitting his faculties to the humilities and devotion of courtship. That self-surrender—that prostration of mind by which a man is too happy and proud to express the profundity of his service to the woman of his heart—it seemed a mere impossibility that ever Wordsworth should be brought to feel for a single instant ; and what he did not sincerely feel, assuredly he was not the person to profess. Wordsworth, I take it upon myself to say, had not the feelings within him which make this total devotion to a woman possible. There never lived a woman whom he would not have lectured and admonished under circumstances that should have seemed to require it ; nor would he have conversed with her in any mood whatever, without wearing an air of mild condescension to her understanding. To lie at her feet, to make her his idol, to worship her very caprices, and to adore the most unreasonable of her frowns—these things were impossible to Wordsworth ; and being so, never could he, in any emphatic sense, have been a lover.

A lover, I repeat, in any passionate sense of the word, Wordsworth could not have been. And, moreover, it is remarkable, that a woman who could dispense with that sort of homage in her suitor, is not of a nature to inspire such a passion. That same meekness which reconciles her to the tone of superiority and freedom in the manner of her suitor, and which may afterwards in a wife become a sweet domestic grace, strips her of that too charming irritation, captivating at once and tormenting, which lurks in feminine pride. If there be an enchantress's spell yet surviving in this age of ours, it is the haughty grace of maidenly pride—the womanly sense of dignity, even when most in excess, and expressed in the language of scorn— which tortures a man and lacerates his heart, at the same time that it pierces him with admiration :—

> " Oh, what a world of scorn looks beautiful
>   In the contempt and anger of her lip ! "

And she, who spares a man the agitations of this thraldom, robs him no less of its divinest transports.   Wordsworth, however, who never could have laid aside his own nature sufficiently to have played *his* part in such an impassioned courtship, by suiting himself to this high sexual pride with the humility of a lover, quite as little could have enjoyed the spectacle of such a pride, or have viewed it in any degree as an attraction : it would to him have been a pure vexation.   Looking down even upon the lady of his heart, as upon the rest of the world, from the eminence of his own intellectual superiority—viewing her, in fact, as a child—he would be much more disposed to regard any airs of feminine disdain she might assume, as the imper- tinence of girlish levity, than as the caprice of womanly pride ; and much I fear that, in any case of dispute, he would have called even his mistress, " Child ! child ! " and, perhaps, even (but this I do not say with the same cer- tainty) might have bid her hold her tongue.

If, however, no lover, in a proper sense ; though, from many exquisite passages, one might conceive that at some time of his life he was, as especially from the inimitable stanzas beginning—

> " When she I loved was strong and gay,
>   And like a rose in June ; "

or perhaps (but less powerfully so, because here the pas- sion, though profound, is less the *peculiar* passion of love)

from the impassioned lamentation for "the pretty Barbarn,"
beginning—

> " 'Tis said that some have died for love:
> And here and there, amidst unhallow'd ground
> In the cold north," &c.;

yet, if no lover, or (which some of us have sometimes
thought) a lover disappointed at some earlier period, by
the death of her he loved, or by some other fatal event
(for he always preserved a mysterious silence on the subject
of that "Lucy," repeatedly alluded to or apostrophized in
his poems); at all events he made, what for him turned
out, a happy marriage. Few people have lived on such
terms of entire harmony and affection, as he lived with
the woman of his final choice. Indeed, the sweetness,
almost unexampled, of temper, which shed so sunny a
radiance over Mrs. Wordsworth's manners, sustained by
the happy life she led, the purity of her conscience, and
the uniformity of her good health, made it impossible for
anybody to have quarrelled with *her;* and whatever fits
of ill-temper Wordsworth might have—for, with all his
philosophy, he had such fits—met with no fuel to support
them, except in the more irritable temperament of his sister.
She was all fire, and an ardour which, like that of the first
Lord Shaftesbury,

> " O'er-informed its tenement of clay;"

and, as this ardour looked out in every gleam of her wild
eyes (those "wild eyes" so finely noticed in the "Tintern
Abbey"), as it spoke in every word of her self-baffled
utterance, as it gave a trembling movement to her very
person and demeanour—easily enough it might happen,
that any apprehension of an unkind word should with her
kindle a dispute. It might have happened; and yet, to

the great honour of both, having such impassioned temperaments, rarely it did happen ; and this was the more remarkable, as I have been assured that both were, in childhood, irritable or even ill-tempered ; and they were constantly together ; for Miss Wordsworth was always ready to walk out—wet or dry, storm or sunshine, night or day ; whilst Mrs. Wordsworth was completely dedicated to her maternal duties, and rarely left the house, unless when the weather was tolerable, or, at least, only for short rambles. I should not have noticed this trait in Wordsworth's occasional manners, had it been gathered from domestic or confidential opportunities. But, on the contrary, the first two occasions on which, after months' domestic intercourse with Wordsworth, I became aware of his possible ill-humour and peevishness, were so public, that others, and those strangers, must have been equally made parties to the scene : this scene occurred in Kendal.

Having brought down the history of Wordsworth to the time of his marriage, I am reminded by that event to mention the singular good fortune, in all points of worldly prosperity, which has accompanied him through life. His marriage—the capital event of life—was fortunate, and inaugurated a long succession of other prosperities. He has himself described, in his " Leech-Gatherer," the fears that at one time, or at least in some occasional moments of his life, haunted him, lest at some period or other he might be reserved for poverty. " Cold, pain, and hunger, and all fleshly ills," occurred to his boding apprehension—

> " And mighty poets in their misery dead."

> " He thought of Chatterton, the marvellous boy,
>   The sleepless soul that perish'd in its pride ;
> Of him who walk'd in glory and in joy,
>   Beside his plough upon the mountain-side."

And, at starting on his career of life, certainly no man had
plainer reasons for anticipating the worst evils that have
ever persecuted poets, excepting only two reasons which
might warrant him in hoping better ; and these two were
—his great prudence, and the temperance of his daily life.
He could not be betrayed into foolish engagements ; he
could not be betrayed into expensive habits.   Profusion
and extravagance had no hold over him, by any one passion or taste.   He was not luxurious in anything ; was not
vain or even careful of external appearances (not, at least,
since he had left Cambridge, and visited a mighty nation
in civil convulsions) ; was not even in the article of books
expensive.   Very few books sufficed him ; he was careless
habitually of all the current literature, or indeed of any
literature that could not be considered as enshrining the
very ideal, capital, and elementary grandeur of the human
intellect.   In this extreme limitation of his literary sensibilities, he was as much assisted by that accident of his own
intellectual condition—viz., extreme, intense, unparalleled
onesidedness (*einseitigkeit*)—as by any peculiar sanity of feeling.   Thousands of books, that have given rapturous delight to millions of ingenuous minds, for Wordsworth were
absolutely a dead letter—closed and sealed up from his
sensibilities and his powers of appreciation, not less than
colours from a blind man's eye.   Even the few books
which his peculiar mind had made indispensable to him,
were not in such a sense indispensable, as they would have
been to a man of more sedentary habits.   He lived in the
open air ; and the enormity of pleasure which both he and
his sister drew from the common appearances of nature and
their everlasting variety—variety so infinite, that if no one
leaf of a tree or shrub ever exactly resembled another in
all its filaments, and their arrangement, still less did any

one day ever repeat another in all its pleasurable elements.
This pleasure was to him in the stead of many libraries :—

> "One impulse, from a vernal wood,
>   Could teach him more of Man,
> Of moral evil and of good,
>   Than all the sages can."

And he, we may be sure, who could draw,

> "Even from the meanest flower that blows,
>   Thoughts that do often lie too deep for tears ;"

to whom the mere daisy, the pansy, the primrose, could
furnish pleasures—not the puerile ones which his most
puerile and worldly insulters imagined, but pleasures
drawn from depths of reverie and meditative tenderness
far beyond all power of *their* hearts to conceive ; that
man would hardly need any large variety of books. In
fact, there were only two provinces of literature in which
Wordsworth could be looked upon as decently well read—
Poetry and Ancient History. Nor do I believe that he
would much have lamented, on his own account, if all
books had perished, excepting the entire body of English
poetry, and, perhaps, " Plutarch's Lives." *

With these simple or rather austere tastes, Wordsworth
(it might seem) had little reason to fear poverty, supposing
him in possession of any moderate income ; but meantime
he had none. About the time when he left college, I have
good grounds for believing that his whole regular income
was precisely = 0. Some fragments must have survived
from the funds devoted to his education ; and with these,

---

* I do not mean to insinuate that Wordsworth was at all in the
dark about the inaccuracy and want of authentic weight attaching to
Plutarch as a historian ; but his business with Plutarch was not for
purposes of research : he was satisfied with his fine moral effects.

no doubt, he supported the expenses of his Continental
tours, and his year's residence in France.   But, at length,
"cold, pain, and hunger, and all fleshly ills," must have
stared him in the face pretty earnestly.   And hope of
longer evading an unpleasant destiny of daily toil, in some
form or other, there seemed absolutely none.   "For," as
he himself expostulates with himself—

> "For how can *he* expect that others should
>   Sow for him, build for *him*, and, at his call,
>   Love him, who for himself will take no thought at all?"

In this dilemma, he had all but resolved, as Miss Wordsworth once told me, to take pupils; and perhaps *that*,
though odious enough, was the sole resource he had; for
Wordsworth never acquired any popular talent of writing
for the current press; and, at that period of his life, he
was gloomily unfitted for bending to such a yoke.   In this
crisis of his fate it was that Wordsworth, for once, and once
only, became a martyr to some nervous affection.   *That*
raised pity; but I could not forbear smiling at the remedy,
or palliation, which his few friends adopted.   Every night
they played at cards with him, as the best mode of beguiling his sense of distress, whatever that might be; *cards*,
which, in any part of the thirty-and-one years since *I* have
known Wordsworth, could have had as little power to interest him, or to cheat him of sorrow, as marbles or a top.
However, so it was; for my information could not be
questioned: it came from Miss Wordsworth.

The crisis, as I have said, had arrived for determining
the future colour of his life.   Memorable it is, that exactly
in those critical moments when some decisive step had first
become necessary, there happened the first instance of
Wordsworth's good luck; and equally memorable that, at
measured intervals throughout the long sequel of his life

since then, a regular succession of similar but superior
windfalls have fallen in, to sustain his expenditure, in exact
concurrence with the growing claims upon his purse. A
more fortunate man, I believe, does not exist than Wordsworth. The aid which now dropped from heaven, as it
were, to enable him to range at will in paths of his own
choosing, and

> " Finally array
> His temples with the Muses' diadem,"

came in the shape of a bequest from Raisley Calvert, a
young man of good family in Cumberland, who died about
this time of pulmonary consumption. A very remarkable
young man he must have been, this Raisley Calvert, to
have discerned, at this early period, that future superiority
in Wordsworth which so few people suspected. He was
the brother of a Cumberland gentleman, whom slightly I
know; a generous man, doubtless; for he made no sort
of objections (though legally, I have heard, he might) to
his brother's farewell memorial of regard; a good man to
all his dependants, as I have generally understood, in the
neighbourhood of Windy Brow, his mansion, near Keswick;
and, as Southey always said (who must know better than I
could do), a man of strong natural endowments; else, as
his talk was of oxen, I might have made the mistake of
supposing him to be, in heart and soul, what he was in profession—a mere farming country gentleman, whose ambition
was chiefly directed to the turning up mighty turnips.
The sum left by Raisley Calvert was £900; and it was
laid out in an annuity. This was the basis of Wordsworth's
prosperity in life; and upon this he has built up, by a
series of accessions, in which each step, taken separately for
itself, seems perfectly natural, whilst the total result has undoubtedly something wonderful about it, the present goodly

edifice of his fortunes. Next in the series came the present Lord Lonsdale's repayment of his predecessor's debt. Upon that, probably, it was that Wordsworth felt himself entitled to marry. Then, I believe, came some fortune with Miss Hutchinson ; then—that is, fourthly—some worthy uncle of the same lady was pleased to betake himself to a better world, leaving to various nieces, and especially to Mrs. Wordsworth, something or other—I forget what, but it was expressed by thousands of pounds. At this moment, Wordsworth's family had begun to increase ; and the worthy old uncle, like everybody else in Wordsworth's case, finding his property very clearly " wanted," and, as people would tell him, " bespoke," felt how very indelicate it would look for him to stay any longer in this world ; and so off he moved. But Wordsworth's family, and the wants of that family, still continued to increase ; and the next person—viz., the fifth—who stood in the way, and must, therefore, have considered himself rapidly growing into a nuisance, was the stamp-distributor for the county of Westmoreland. About March 1814, I think it was, that his very comfortable situation was wanted. Probably it took a month for the news to reach him ; because in April, and not before, feeling that he had received a proper notice to quit, he, good man (this stamp-distributor), like all the rest, distributed himself and his office into two different places—the latter falling, of course, into the hands of Wordsworth.

This office, which it was Wordsworth's pleasure to speak of as " a little one," yielded, I believe, somewhere about £500 a year. Gradually, even *that*, with all former sources of income, became insufficient ; which ought not to surprise anybody ; for a son at Oxford, as a gentleman commoner, would spend, at the least, £300 per annum :

and there were other children. Still, it is wrong to say,
that it *had* become insufficient; as usual, it had not come
to that; but, on the first symptoms arising that it soon
would come to that, somebody, of course, had notice to
consider himself a sort of nuisance-elect;—in this case, it
was the distributor of stamps for the county of Cumberland. His district was absurdly large; and what so reasonable as that he should submit to a Polish partition of
his profits—no, not Polish; for, on reflection, such a partition neither was nor could be attempted with regard to an
actual incumbent. But then, since people had such consideration for him as not to remodel the office so long as
he lived, on the other hand, the least he could do for
" people," in return—so as to show his sense of this consideration—was not to trespass on so much goodness longer
than necessary. Accordingly, here, as in all cases before,
the *Deus ex machinâ* who invariably interfered when any
nodus arose in Wordsworth's affairs, such as could be considered *vindice dignus*, caused the distributor to begone
into a region where no stamps are wanted, about the very
month, or so, when an additional £400 per annum became
desirable. This, or perhaps more, was understood to have
been added, by the new arrangement, to the Westmoreland distributorship; the small towns of Keswick and
Cockermouth, together with the important one of Whitehaven, being severed, under this remodelling, from their
old dependency on Cumberland (to which geographically
they belonged), and transferred to the small territory of
rocky Westmoreland, the sum total of whose inhabitants
was at that time not much above 50,000; of which number, one-third, or nearly so, was collected into the only
important town of Kendal; but, of the other two-thirds, a
larger proportion was a simple agricultural or pastoral

population, than anywhere else in England. In Westmoreland, therefore, it may be supposed that the stamp
demand could not have been so great, not perhaps by
three-quarters, as in Cumberland ; which, besides having a
population at least three times as large, had more and
larger towns. The result of this new distribution was
something that approached to an equalization of the districts—giving to each, as was said, in round terms, a thousand a year.

Thus I have traced Wordsworth's ascent through its
several steps and stages, to what, for his moderate desires
and habits so philosophic, may be fairly considered opulence. And it must rejoice every man, who joins in the
public.homage *now* rendered to his powers (and what man
is to be found that, more or less, does not ?) to hear, with
respect to one so lavishly endowed by nature, that he has
not been neglected by fortune ; that he has never had the
finer edge of his sensibilities dulled by the sad anxieties,
the degrading fears, the miserable dependencies of debt ;
that he has been blessed with competency even when
poorest ; has had hope and cheerful prospects in reversion,
through every stage of his life ; that at all times he has
been liberated from *reasonable* anxieties about the final
interests of his children ; that at all times he has been
blessed with leisure, the very amplest that ever man enjoyed, for intellectual pursuits the most delightful ; yes,
that, even as regards those delicate and coy pursuits, he
has possessed, in combination, all the conditions for their
most perfect culture—the leisure, the ease, the solitude,
the society, the domestic peace, the local scenery—Paradise for his eye, in Miltonic beauty, lying outside his windows ; Paradise for his heart, in the perpetual happiness
of his own fireside ; and, finally, when increasing years

might be supposed to demand something more of modern luxuries, and expanding intercourse with society something more of refined elegancies, that his means, still keeping pace in almost arithmetical ratio with his wants, had shed the graces of art upon the failing powers of nature, had stripped infirmity of discomfort, and (so far as the necessities of things will allow) had placed the final stages of life, by means of many compensations, by universal praise, by plaudits reverberated from senates, benedictions where-ever his poems have penetrated, honour, troops of friends— in short, by all that miraculous prosperity can do to evade the primal decrees of nature—had placed the final stages upon a level with the first.

But now, reverting to the subject of Wordsworth's prosperity, I have numbered up six separate stages of good luck—six instances of pecuniary showers emptying themselves into his very bosom, at the very moments when they *began* to be needed, on the first symptoms that they might be wanted—accesses of fortune stationed upon his road like repeating frigates, connecting, to all appearance, some preconcerted line of operations ; and, amidst the tumults of chance, wearing as much the air of purpose and design, as if they supported a human plan. I have come down to the sixth case. Whether there were any seventh, I do not know : but confident I feel that, had a seventh been required by circumstances, a seventh would have happened. So true it is, that still, as Wordsworth needed a place or a fortune, the holder of that place or fortune was immediately served with a summons to surrender it : so certainly was this impressed upon my belief, as one of the blind necessities, making up the prosperity and fixed destiny of Wordsworth, that, for myself, had I happened to know of any peculiar adaptation in an estate or office of

mine to an existing need of Wordsworth's, forthwith, and
with the speed of a man running for his life, I would have
laid it down at his feet.   " Take it," I should have said ;
" take it, or in three weeks I shall be a dead man."

Well, let me pause : I think the reader is likely by this
time to have a slight notion of *my* notion of Wordsworth's
inevitable prosperity, and the sort of *lien* that he had upon
the incomes of other men who happened to stand in his way.
The same prosperity attended the other branches of the
family, with the single exception of John, the brother who
perished in the Abergavenny : and even he was prosper-
ous up to the moment of his fatal accident.   As to Miss
Wordsworth, who will, by some people, be classed amongst
the non-prosperous, I rank her amongst the most fortunate
of women ; or, at least, if regard be had to that period of
life which is most capable of happiness.   Her fortune, after
its repayment by Lord Lonsdale, was, much of it, confided,
with a sisterly affection, to the use of her brother John ;
and part of it, I have heard, perished in his ship.   How
much, I never felt myself entitled to ask ; but certainly a
part was on that occasion understood to have been lost
irretrievably.   Either it was that only a partial insurance
had been effected ; or else the nature of the accident, being
in home waters (off the coast of Dorsetshire), might, by the
nature of the contract, have taken the case out of the benefit
of the policy.   This loss, however, had it even been total,
for a single sister amongst a family of flourishing brothers,
could not be of any lasting importance.   A much larger
number of voices would proclaim her to have been unfortunate in life, because she made no marriage connexion ;
and certainly, the insipid as well as unfeeling ridicule
which descends so plentifully upon those women who, perhaps from strength of character, have refused to make

such a connexion where it promised little of elevated happiness, *does* make the estate of singleness somewhat of a trial to the patience of many ; and to many the vexation of this trial has proved a snare for beguiling them of their honourable resolutions. Meantime, as the opportunities are rare in which all the conditions concur for happy marriage connexions, how important it is that the dignity of high-minded women should be upheld by society in the honourable election they make of a self-dependent virgin seclusion, by preference to a heartless marriage ! Such women, as Mrs. Trollope justly remarks, fill a place in society which in their default would *not* be filled, and are available for duties requiring a tenderness and a punctuality that could not be looked for from women pre-occupied with household or maternal claims. If there were no regular fund (so to speak) of women free from conjugal and maternal duties, upon what body could we draw for our " sisters of mercy," &c. ? In another point, Mrs. Trollope is probably right : few women live unmarried from necessity. Miss Wordsworth had several offers ; amongst them, to my knowledge, one from Hazlitt ; all of them she rejected decisively. And she did right. A happier life, by far, was hers in youth, coming as near as difference of scenery and difference of relations would permit, to that which was promised to Ruth—the Ruth of her brother's creation*—by the youth who came from

---

* " *The Ruth of her brother's creation:*"—So I express it ; because so much in the development of the story and situations necessarily belongs to the poet. Else, for the mere outline of the story, it was founded upon fact : Wordsworth himself told me, in general terms, that the case which suggested the poem was that of an American lady, whose husband forsook her at the very place of embarkation from England, under circumstances and under expectations, upon

Georgia's shore ; for, though not upon American savannas,
or Canadian lakes,

> " With all their fairy crowds
> Of islands, that together lie
> As quietly as spots of sky
> Amongst the evening clouds,"

yet, amongst the loveliest scenes of sylvan England, and
(at intervals) of sylvan Germany—amongst lakes, too, far
better fitted to give the *sense* of their own character than
the vast inland *seas* of America, and amongst mountains
more romantic than many of the chief ranges in that
country—her time fleeted away like some golden age, or
like the life of primeval man ; and she, like Ruth, was for
years allowed

> " To run, though *not* a bride,
>   A sylvan huntress, by the side "

of him to whom she, like Ruth, had dedicated her days ;
and to whose children, afterwards, she dedicated a love like
that of mothers.   Dear Miss Wordsworth !   How noble a
creature did she seem when I first knew her !—and when,
on the very first night which I passed in her brother's company, he read to me, in illustration of something he was
saying, a passage from Fairfax's " Tasso," ending pretty
nearly with these words,

> " Amidst the broad fields and the endless wood,
>   The lofty lady kept her maidenhood,"

I thought that, possibly, he had his sister in his thoughts.
Yet " lofty" was hardly the right word.   Miss Wordsworth

---

her part, very much the same as those of Ruth.   I am afraid, however, that the husband was an attorney ; which is intolerable ; *nisi
prius* cannot be harmonized with the dream-like fairyland of Georgia.

was too ardent and fiery a creature to maintain the reserve
essential to dignity; and dignity was the last thing one
thought of in the presence of one so natural, so fervent
in her feelings, and so embarrassed in their utterance—
sometimes, also, in the attempt to check them. It must
not, however, be supposed that there was any silliness or
weakness of enthusiasm about her. She was under the
continual restraint of severe good sense, though liberated
from that false shame which, in so many persons, accompanies all expressions of natural emotion; and she had too
long enjoyed the ennobling conversation of her brother,
and his admirable comments on the poets, which they read
in common, to fail in any essential point of logic or propriety of thought. Accordingly, her letters, though the
most careless and unelaborate—nay, the most hurried that
can be imagined—are models of good sense and just feeling. In short, beyond any person I have known in this
world, Miss Wordsworth was the creature of impulse;
but, as a woman most thoroughly virtuous and well-
principled, as one who could not fail to be kept right by
her own excellent heart, and as an intellectual creature
from her cradle, with much of her illustrious brother's
peculiarity of mind—finally, as one who had been, in
effect, educated and trained by that very brother—she
won the sympathy and the respectful regard of every man
worthy to approach her. Properly, and in a spirit of
prophecy, was she named *Dorothy ;* in its Greek meaning,*

---

* Of course, therefore, it is essentially the same name as *Theodora,*
the same elements being only differently arranged. Yet how opposite
is the impression upon the mind! and chiefly, I suppose, from the
too prominent emblazonment of this name in the person of Justinian's
scandalous wife; though, for my own part, I am far from believing
all the infamous stories which we read about her.

gift of God, well did this name prefigure the relation in
which she stood to Wordsworth, the mission with which she
was charged—to wait upon him as the tenderest and most
faithful of domestics ; to love him as a sister ; to sympathize with him as a confidante ; to counsel him ; to cheer
him and sustain him by the natural expression of her
feelings—so quick, so ardent, so unaffected—upon the
probable effect of whatever thoughts or images he might
conceive ; finally, and above all other ministrations, to
ingraft, by her sexual sense of beauty, upon his masculine
austerity that delicacy and those graces, which else (according to the grateful acknowledgments of his own maturest
retrospect) it never could have had :—

> " The blessing of my later years
>   Was with me when I was a boy:
> She gave me hopes, she gave me fears,
> A heart the fountain of sweet tears.
>   *   *   *   *
> And love, and thought, and joy."

And elsewhere he describes her, in a philosophic poem,
still in M S., as one who planted flowers and blossoms with
her feminine hand upon what might else have been an
arid rock—massy, indeed, and grand, but repulsive from
the severity of its features. I may sum up in one brief
abstract the amount of Miss Wordsworth's character, as
a companion, by saying, that she was the very wildest (in
the sense of the most natural) person I have ever known ;
and also the truest, most inevitable, and at the same time
the quickest and readiest in her sympathy with either joy
or sorrow, with laughter or with tears, with the realities
of life or the larger realities of the poets !

Meantime, amidst all this fascinating furniture of her
mind, won from nature, from solitude, from enlightened

companionship, Miss Wordsworth was as thoroughly deficient (some would say painfully deficient—I say charm-
ingly deficient) in ordinary female accomplishments, as
" *Cousin* Mary," in dear Miss Mitford's delightful sketch.
Of French, she might have barely enough to read a plain
modern page of narrative; Italian, I question whether any;
German, just enough to insult the German literati, by
showing how little she had found them or their writings
necessary to her heart. The " Luise" of Voss, the " Her-
mann und Dorothea" of Goethe she had begun to trans-
late, as young ladies do " Télémaque;" but, like them,
had chiefly cultivated the first two pages ; * with the third,
she had a slender acquaintance, and with the fourth, she
meditated an intimacy at some future day. Music, in her
solitary and out-of-doors life, she could have little reason
for cultivating ; nor is it possible that any woman can
draw the enormous energy requisite for this attainment,
upon a *modern* scale of perfection, out of any other principle than that of vanity (at least of great value for social
applause) or else of deep musical sensibility ; neither of
which belonged to Miss Wordsworth's constitution of mind.
But, as everybody agrees in our days to think this accomplishment of no value whatever, and, in fact, *unproduceable*,
unless existing in an exquisite state of culture, no complaint could be made on that score, nor any surprise felt.

---

* Viz., "Calypso ne savoit se consoler du départ," &c. For how
long a period (viz., nearly two centuries) has Calypso been inconsolable
in the morning studies of young ladies ! As Fénélon's most dreary
romance always opened at one or other of these three earliest and
dreary pages, naturally to my sympathetic fancy the poor unhappy
goddess seemed to be eternally aground on this Goodwin Sand of in-
consolability. It is amongst the standing hypocrisies of the world,
that most people affect a reverence for this book, which nobody reads.

But the case in which the irregularity of Miss Wordsworth's education *did* astonish one, was in that part which respected her literary knowledge. In whatever she read, or neglected to read, she had obeyed the single impulse of her own heart; where that led her, *there* she followed : where that was mute or indifferent, not a thought had she to bestow upon a writer's high reputation, or the call for some acquaintance with his works, to meet the demands of society. And thus the strange anomaly arose, of a woman deeply acquainted with some great authors, whose works lie pretty much out of the fashionable beat; able, moreover, in her own person, to produce brilliant effects; able on some subjects to write delightfully, and with the impress of originality upon all she uttered; and yet ignorant of great classical works in her own mother tongue, and careless of literary history in a degree which at once exiled her from the rank and privileges of *bluestockingism.*

The reader may, perhaps, have objected silently to the illustration drawn from Miss Mitford, that " Cousin Mary " does not effect her fascinations out of pure negations. Such negations, from the mere startling effect of their oddity in this present age, might fall in with the general current of her attractions; but Cousin Mary's undoubtedly lay in the *positive* witcheries of a manner and a character transcending, by force of irresistible nature (as in a similar case recorded by Wordsworth in " The Excursion "), all the pomp of nature and art united, as seen in ordinary creatures. Now, in Miss Wordsworth, there were certainly no " Cousin Mary " fascinations of manner and deportment, that snatch a grace beyond the reach of art : *there* she was, indeed, painfully deficient; for hurry mars and defeats even the most ordinary expression of the feminine character—viz., its gentleness : abruptness and trepidation leave often a joint impression of what seems for an instant both rudeness and ungracefulness : and the least painful impression was that of unsexual awkwardness. But the point in which Miss Wordsworth made the most ample amends for all that she wanted of more customary accomplishments, was this very originality and native freshness of intellect, which settled with so bewitching an effect upon some of her writings, and upon many a sudden remark or ejaculation, extorted by something or other that struck her eye, in the clouds, or in colouring, or in accidents of light and shade, of form or combination of form. To talk of her " writings," is too pompous an expression, or at least far beyond any pretensions that she ever made for herself. Of poetry she has written little indeed ; and that little not, in my opinion, of much merit. The verses published by her brother, and beginning, " Which way does the wind come ?" meant only as nursery lines, are certainly wild and pretty ; but the other specimen is likely to strike most readers as feeble and trivial in the sentiment. Meantime, the book which is in very deed a monument to her power of catching and expressing all the hidden beauties of natural scenery, with a felicity of diction, a truth, and strength, that far transcend Gilpin, or professional writers on those subjects, is her record of a *first* tour in Scotland, made about the year 1802. This MS. book [unless my recollection of it, from a period now gone by for thirty years, has deceived me greatly] is absolutely unique in its class ; and, though it never could be very popular, from the minuteness of its details, intelligible only to the eye, and the luxuriation of its descriptions, yet I believe no person has ever been favoured with a sight of it, that has not yearned for its publication. Its own extraordinary merit, apart from the interest which *now* invests the name of Wordsworth, could not fail to procure purchasers for one edition on its first appearance.

Coleridge was of the party at first ; but afterwards, under some attack of rheumatism, found or thought it necessary to leave them. Melancholy it would be at this time, thirty-six years and more from the era of that tour, to read it under the afflicting remembrances of all which has been suffered in the interval by two at least out of the three who composed the travelling party ; for I fear that Miss Words-worth has suffered not much less than Coleridge ; and, in any general expression of it, from the same cause, viz., an excess of pleasurable excitement and luxurious sensibility, sustained in youth by a constitutional glow from animal causes, but drooping as soon as that was withdrawn. It is painful to point a moral from any story connected with those whom one loves or has loved ; painful to look for one moment towards any " improvement" of such a case, espe-cially where there is no reason to tax the parties with any criminal contribution to their own sufferings, except through that relaxation of the will and its potential energies, through which most of us, at some time or other—I myself too deeply and sorrowfully—stand accountable to our own con-sciences. Not, therefore, with any intention of speaking in a monitorial or censorial character, do I here notice a defect in Miss Wordsworth's self-education of something that might have mitigated the sort of suffering which, more or less, ever since the period of her too genial, too radiant youth, I suppose her to have struggled with. I have mentioned the narrow basis on which her literary interests had been made to rest—the exclusive character of her reading, and the utter want of pretension, and of all that looks like *blue-stockingism*, in the style of her habitual conversation and mode of dealing with literature. Now, to me it appears, upon reflection, that it would have been far better had Miss Wordsworth condescended a little to the ordinary mode of pursuing literature ; better for her own happiness if she *had* been a bluestocking ; or, at least, if she had been, in good earnest, a writer for the press, with the pleasant cares and solicitudes of one who has some little ventures, as it were, on that vast ocean.

We all know with how womanly and serene a temper literature has been pursued by Joanna Baillie, by Miss Mitford, and other women of admirable genius—with how absolutely no sacrifice or loss of feminine dignity they have cultivated the profession of authorship ; and, if we could hear their report, I have no doubt that the little cares of correcting proofs, and the forward-looking solicitudes connected with the mere business arrangements of new publications, would be numbered amongst the minor pleasures of life ; whilst the more elevated cares, connected with the intellectual business of such projects, must inevitably have done much to solace the troubles which, as human beings, they cannot but have experienced ; and even to scatter flowers upon their path. Mrs. Johnstone of Edinburgh has pursued the profession of literature—the noblest of professions, and the only one open to both sexes alike—with even more assiduity, and as a *daily* occupation ; and, I have every reason to believe, with as much benefit to her own happiness, as to the instruction and amusement of her readers ; for the petty cares of authorship are agreeable, and its serious cares are ennobling. More especially is such an occupation useful to a woman without children, and without any *prospective* resources—resources in objects that involve hopes growing and unfulfilled. It is too much to expect of any woman (or man either) that her mind should support itself in a pleasurable activity, under the drooping

IL—O

energies of life, by resting on the past or on the present; some interest in reversion, some subject of hope from day to day, must be called in to reinforce the animal fountains of good spirits. Had that been opened for Miss Words-worth, I am satisfied that she would have passed a more cheerful middle-age, and would not, at any period, have yielded to that nervous depression (or is it, perhaps, nervous irritation?) which, I grieve to hear, has clouded her latter days. Nephews and nieces, whilst young and innocent, are as good almost as sons and daughters to a fervid and loving heart that has carried them in her arms from the hour they were born. But, after a nephew has grown into a huge hulk of a man, six feet high, and as stout as a bullock; after he has come to have children of his own, lives at a distance, and finds occasion to talk much of oxen and turnips—no offence to him!—he ceases to be an object of any very profound sentiment. There is nothing in such a subject to rouse the flagging pulses of the heart, and to sustain a fervid spirit, to whom, at the very best, human life offers little of an adequate or sufficing interest, unless when idealized by the magic of the mighty poets. Fare-well, Miss Wordsworth! farewell, impassioned Dorothy! I have not seen you for many a day—shall, too probably, never see you again; but shall attend your steps with tender interest so long as I hear of you living: so will Pro-fessor Wilson; and, from two hearts at least, that knew and admired you in your fervid prime, it may sometimes cheer the gloom of your depression to be assured of never-failing remembrance, full of love and respectful pity.

ROBERT SOUTHEY.

THAT night—the first of personal intercourse with Wordsworth—the first in which I saw him face to face—was
(it is little, indeed, to say) memorable : it was marked
by a change even in the physical condition of my nervous
system.   Long disappointment—hope for ever baffled (and
why should it be less painful because *self*-baffled ?)—
vexation and self-blame, almost self-contempt at my own
want of courage to face the man whom of all men I
yearned to behold—these feelings had impressed upon my
nervous sensibilities a character of irritation, restlessness,
eternal self-dissatisfaction, which were gradually gathering
into a distinct, well-defined type, that would, but for youth
—almighty youth—have shaped itself into some nervous
complaint, wearing symptoms *sui generis*.   To this result
things tended ; but in one hour all passed away.   It was
gone, never to return.   The spiritual being whom I had
anticipated—for, like Eloisa.

"My fancy framed him of th' angelic kind—
Some emanation of th' all-beauteous mind"—

this ideal creature had at length been seen—seen with
fleshly eyes ; and now, if he did not cease for years to wear
something of a glory about his head, yet it was no longer
as a being to be feared—it was as Raphael, the "affable"
angel, who conversed on the terms of man with man.

About four o'clock, it might be, when we arrived. At
that hour, in November, the daylight soon declined ; and,
in an hour and a half, we were all collected about the
tea-table. This, with the Wordsworths, under the simple
rustic system of habits which they cherished then, and for
twenty years after, was the most delightful meal in the
day ; just as dinner is in great cities, and for the same
reason—because it was prolonged into a meal of leisure
and conversation. That night I found myself, about
eleven at night, in a pretty bedroom, about fourteen feet
by twelve. Much I feared that this might turn out the
best room in the house ; and it illustrates the hospitality
of my new friends, to mention that it was. Early in
the morning I was awakened by a little voice, issuing
from a little cottage bed in an opposite corner, solilo-
quizing in a low tone. I soon recognised the words,
"Suffered under Pontius Pilate ; was crucified, dead, and
buried ;" and the voice I easily conjectured to be that of
the eldest amongst Wordsworth's children, a son, and at
that time about three years old. He was a remarkably
fine boy in strength and size, promising (which has in fact
been realized) a more powerful person, physically, than
that of his father. Miss Wordsworth I found making
breakfast in the little sitting-room. No urn was there ;
no glittering breakfast service ; a kettle boiled upon the
fire, and everything was in harmony with these unpre-
tending arrangements. I rarely had seen so humble a

ménage : and contrasting the dignity of the man with this honourable poverty, and this courageous avowal of it, his utter absence of all effort to disguise the simple truth of the case, I felt my admiration increased. This, thought I to myself, is, indeed, in his own words,

" Plain living, and high thinking."

This, is, indeed, to reserve the humility and the parsimonies of life for its bodily enjoyments, and to apply its lavishness and its luxury to its enjoyments of the intellect. So might Milton have lived ; so Marvel. Throughout the day—which was rainy—the same style of modest hospitality prevailed. Wordsworth and his sister—myself being of the party—walked out in spite of the rain, and made the circuit of the two lakes, Grasmere and its dependency Rydal—a walk of about six miles. On the third day, Mrs. Coleridge having now pursued her journey northward to Keswick, and having, at her departure, invited me, in her own name as well as Southey's, to come and see them, Wordsworth proposed that we should go thither in company, but not by the direct route—a distance of only thirteen miles : that route we were to take in our road homeward ; our outward-bound journey was to be by way of Ulleswater—a circuit of forty-three miles.

On the third morning after my arrival in Grasmere, I found the whole family, except the two children, prepared for the expedition across the mountains. I had heard of no horses, and took it for granted that we were to walk ; however, at the moment of starting, a cart—the common farmer's cart of the country—made its appearance ; and the driver was a bonnie young woman of the vale. Accordingly, we were all carted along to the little town or large village, of Ambleside—three and a half miles distant. Our style of travelling occasioned no astonishment ; on the contrary, we met a smiling salutation wherever we appeared—Miss Wordsworth being, as I observed, the person most familiarly known of our party, and the one who took upon herself the whole expenses of the flying colloquies exchanged with stragglers on the road. What struck me with most astonishment, however, was the liberal manner of our fair driver, who made no scruple of taking a leap, with the reins in her hand, and seating herself dexterously upon the shafts of the cart. From Ambleside —and without one foot of intervening flat ground—begins to rise the famous ascent of Kirkstone; after which, for three long miles, all riding in a cart drawn by one horse becomes impossible. The ascent is computed at three miles, but is probably a little more. In some parts it is almost frightfully steep; for the road being only the original mountain track of shepherds, gradually widened and improved from age to age (especially since the era of tourists began), is carried over ground which no engineer, even in Alpine countries, would have viewed as practicable In ascending, this is felt chiefly as an obstruction, and not as a peril, unless where there is a risk of the horses backing; but, in the reverse order, some of these precipitous descents are terrific: and yet, once, in utter darkness, after midnight, and the darkness irradiated only by continual streams of lightning, I was driven down this whole descent, at a full gallop, by a young woman—the carriage being a light one, the horses frightened, and the descents, at some critical parts of the road, so literally like the sides of a house, that it was difficult to keep the fore-wheels from pressing upon the hind-legs of the horses. The innkeepers of Ambleside, or Lowwood, will not mount this formidable hill without four horses. The leaders you are not required to take beyond the first three miles; but, of course, they are glad if you will take them on through the whole stage to Patterdale; and in that case, there is a real luxury at hand for those who enjoy velocity of motion. The descent into Patterdale is above two miles ; but such is the propensity for flying down hills in Westmoreland, that I have found the descent accomplished in about six minutes, which is at the rate of eighteen miles an hour ; the various turnings of the road making the speed much more sensible to the traveller. The pass, at the summit of this ascent, is nothing to be compared in sublimity with the pass under Great Gavel from Wastdalehead ; but it is solemn, and profoundly impressive. At a height so awful as this, it may be easily supposed that all human dwellings have been long left behind : no sound of human life, no bells of churches or chapels, ever ascend so far. And, as is noticed in Wordsworth's fine verses upon this memorable pass, the only sound that, even at noonday, disturbs the sleep of the weary pedestrian, is that of the bee murmuring amongst the mountain flowers—a sound as ancient

"As man's imperial front, and woman's roseate bloom."

This way, and (which, to the sentiment of the case, is an important point) this way of *necessity*, and not simply in obedience to a motive of convenience, passed the Roman legions ; for it is a mathematic impossibility that any other route could be found for an army nearer to the eastward of this pass than by way of Kendal and Shap ; nearer to the westward, than by way of Legberthwaite and St. John's Vale (and so by Threlkeld to Penrith). Now, these two roads are twenty-five miles apart ; and, since a Roman cohort was stationed at Ambleside (*Amboglana*), it is pretty evident that this cohort would not correspond with the more northerly stations by either of these remote routes— having immediately before it this direct though difficult

pass of Kirkstone.   On the solitary area of table-land
which you find at the summit, there are only two objects
to remind you of man and his workmanship.   One is a
guide-post—always a picturesque and interesting object,
because it expresses a wild country and a labyrinth of
roads, and often made much more interesting (as in this
case) by the lichens which cover it, and which record the
generations of men to whom it has done its office ; as also
by the crucifix form, which inevitably recalls, in all mountainous regions, the crosses of Catholic lands, raised to the
memory of wayfaring men who have perished by the hand
of the assassin.

The other memorial of man is even more interesting :—
Amongst the fragments of rock which lie in the confusion
of a ruin on each side of the road, one there is which ex-
ceeds the rest in height, and which, in shape, presents a
very close resemblance to a miniature church.   This lies
to the left of the road as you are going from Ambleside ;
and from its name, Churchstone (Kirkstone), is derived the
name of the pass, and from the pass the name of the mountain.   This church, which is but a playful mimicry from
the hand of nature of man's handiwork, might, however,
really be mistaken for such, were it not that the rude and
almost inaccessible state of the adjacent ground proclaims
the truth.   As to size, *that* is remarkably difficult to estimate upon wild heaths or mountain solitudes, where there
are no leadings through gradations of distance, nor any
artificial standards, from which height or breadth can be
properly produced.   This mimic church, however, has a
peculiarly fine effect in this wild situation, which leaves so
far below the tumults of this world : the phantom church,
by suggesting the phantom and evanescent image of a congregation, where never congregation met ; of the pealing

"THE TRAVELLER'S REST"—KIRKSTONE PASS.

organ, where never sound was heard except of wild natural
notes, or else of the wind rushing through these mighty
gates of everlasting rock—in this way, the fanciful image
of populous life that accompanies the traveller on his road,
for half a mile or more, serves to bring out the antagonist
feeling of intense and awful solitude, which is the natural
and presiding sentiment—the *religio loci*—that broods for
ever over the romantic pass.

Having walked up Kirkstone, we ascended our cart
again ; then rapidly descended to Brothers' Water—a lake
which lies immediately below ; and, about three miles further, through endless woods and under the shade of mighty
fells, immediate dependencies and processes of the still
more mighty Helvellyn, we approached the Vale of Patterdale, where, by moonlight, we reached the inn.   Here we
found horses—by whom furnished, I never asked nor heard
perhaps I owe somebody for a horse to this day.   All I
remember is, that through those most romantic woods and
rocks of Stybarrow—through those silent glens of Glencoin
and Glenridding—through that most romantic of parks,
then belonging to the Duke of Norfolk—viz., Gobarrow
Park—we saw alternately, for four miles, the most gro-
tesque and the most awful spectacles—

> " Abbey windows,
> With Moorish temples of the Hindoos"—

all fantastic, all as unreal and shadowy as the moonlight
which created them ; whilst, at every angle of the road,
broad gleams came upwards of Ulleswater, stretching for
nine miles northward, but, fortunately for its effect, broken
into three watery chambers of almost equal length, and
never all visible at once.   At the foot of the lake, in a
house called Ewsmere, we passed the night, having accomplished about twenty-two miles only in our day's walking

and riding. The next day, Wordsworth and I, leaving at
Ewsmere the rest of our party, spent the morning in roaming through the woods of Lowther ; and, towards evening,
we dined together at Emont Bridge, one mile short of
Penrith. Afterwards we walked into Penrith. On this
day, which must have been the Sunday next after the 5th
of November in 1807, I may record it, as an incident most
memorable to myself, that Wordsworth read to me the
" White Doe of Rylstone." In Penrith, Wordsworth left
me. Whither he himself adjourned I know not, nor on
what business ; however, it occupied him throughout the
next day ; and that day, therefore, I employed in sauntering
along the road, about seventeen miles, to Keswick. There
I had been directed to ask for Greta Hall, which, with
some little difficulty, I found ; for it stands out of the
town a few hundred yards, upon a little eminence overhanging the river Greta. It was about seven o'clock when
I reached Southey's door ; for I had stopped to dine at a
little public-house in Threlkeld, and had walked slowly
for the last two hours in the dark. The arrival of a
stranger occasioned a little sensation in the house ; and by
the time the front door could be opened, I saw Mrs. Coleridge, and a gentleman of very striking appearance, whom
I could not doubt to be Southey, standing to greet my
entrance.

On the next day arrived Wordsworth. I could read at
once, in the manner of the two poets, that they were not
on particularly friendly, or rather, I should say, not on
confidential terms. It seemed to me as if both had
silently said—we are too much men of sense to quarrel,
because we do not happen particularly to like each other's
writings : we are neighbours, or what passes for such
in the country. Let us show each other the courtesies

which are becoming to men of letters ; and, for any closer
connexion, our distance of thirteen miles may be always
sufficient to keep us from *that*. In after life, it is true—
fifteen years, perhaps, from this time—many circumstances
combined to bring Southey and Wordsworth into more
intimate terms of friendship : agreement in politics, sorrows which had happened to both alike in their domestic
relations, and the sort of tolerance for different opinions
in literature, or, indeed, in anything else which advancing
years are sure to bring with them. At present, however,
Southey and Wordsworth entertained a mutual esteem,
but did not cordially like each other. Indeed, it would
have been odd if they had. Wordsworth lived in the
open air : Southey in his library, which Coleridge used to
call his wife. Southey had particularly elegant habits
(Wordsworth called them finical) in the use of books.
Wordsworth, on the other hand, was so negligent, and so
self-indulgent in the same case, that, as Southey laughingly
expressed it to me some years afterwards, " to introduce
Wordsworth into one's library, is like letting a bear into
a tulip-garden."

Returning to Southey and Greta Hall, both the house
and the master may deserve a few words more of description. For the master, his hair was black, and yet his
complexion was fair : his eyes I believe to be hazel and
large ; but I will not vouch for that fact : his nose aquiline ;
and he has a remarkable habit of looking up into the air,
as if looking at abstractions. The expression of his face
was that of a very aspiring man. So far, it was even
noble, as it conveyed a feeling of a serene and gentle pride,
habitually familiar with elevating subjects of contemplation.
And yet it was impossible that this pride could have been
offensive to anybody chastened as it was by the most

unaffected modesty, and this modesty made evident and
prominent by the constant expression of reverence for the
really great men of the age, and for all the great patriarchs
of our literature.   The point in which Southey's manner
failed the most in conciliating regard, was, perhaps, in what
related to the external expressions of friendliness.   No
man could be more sincerely hospitable—no man more
essentially disposed to give up even his time (the possession which he most valued) to the service of his friends.
But there was an air of reserve and distance about him
—the reserve of a lofty, self-respecting mind, but, perhaps,
a little too freezing—in his treatment of all persons who
were not amongst the *corps* of his ancient fireside friends.
Still, even towards the veriest strangers, it is but justice
to notice his extreme courtesy in sacrificing his literary
employments for the day, whatever they might be, to the
duty (for such he made it) of doing the honours of the lake
and the adjacent mountains.

   Southey was at that time (1807), and has continued ever
since, the most industrious of all literary men on record.
A certain task he prescribed to himself every morning
before breakfast.   This could not be a very long one, for
he breakfasted at nine, or soon after, and *never* rose before
eight, though he went to bed duly at half-past ten ; but,
as I have many times heard him say, less than nine hours'
sleep he found insufficient.   From breakfast to a latish
dinner, was his main period of literary toil.   After dinner,
according to the accident of having or not having visitors
in the house, he sat over his wine, or he retired to his
library again, from which, about eight, he was summoned
to tea.   But, generally speaking, he closed his *literary* toils
at dinner ; the whole of the hours after that meal being
dedicated to his correspondence.   This, it may be supposed,

was unusually large, to occupy so much of his time, since his letters rarely extended to any length. At that period, the post, by way of Penrith, reached Keswick about six or seven in the evening. And so pointedly regular was Southey in all his habits, that, short as the time was, all letters were answered on the same evening which brought them. At tea, he read the London papers. It was perfectly astonishing to find how much he got through of elaborate business by his unvarying system of arrangement in the distribution of his time. We often hear it said, in accounts of pattern ladies and gentlemen, that they found time for everything; that business never interrupted pleasure; that labours of duty or charity never stood in the way of courtesy or personal enjoyment. This is easy to say— easy to put down as one feature of an imaginary portrait: but I must say, that, in actual life, I have seen few such cases. Southey, however, *did* find time for everything. It moved the sneers of some people, that even his poetry was composed according to a predetermined rule; that so many lines should be produced, by contract, as it were, before breakfast; so many at such another definite interval. Meantime, the prose of Southey was that by which he lived. The " Quarterly Review" it was by which, as he expressed it laughingly to myself in 1810, he " *made the pot boil.*" One single paper, for instance—viz., a review of Lord Nelson's life, which subsequently was expanded into his own very popular little work on that subject— brought him the splendid *honorarium* of £150.

About the same time, possibly as early as 1808 (for I think that I remember in that journal an account of the Battle of Vimiera), Southey was engaged by an Edinburgh publisher to write the entire historical part of " The Edinburgh Annual Register," at a salary of £400 per annum.

Afterwards, the publisher, who was intensely national, and, doubtless, never from the first had cordially relished the notion of importing English aid into a city teeming with briefless barristers and variety of talent, threw out a hint that perhaps he might reduce the salary to £300. Just about this time I happened to visit Southey, who said, laughingly, "If the man of Edinburgh does this, I shall *strike* for an advance of wages." I presume that he *did* strike, and, like many other "operatives," without effect. Somebody was found in Edinburgh, some youthful advocate, who accepted £300 per annum, and thenceforward Southey lost this part of his income. I once possessed the whole work ; and in one part—viz., "The Domestic Chronicle"— I know that it is executed with a most culpable careless-ness : the beginnings of cases being given without the ends, the ends without the beginnings ; a defect but too common in public journals. The credit of the work, however, was staked upon its treatment of the current public history of Europe, and the tone of its politics in times so full of agitation, and teeming with new births in every year, some fated to prove abortive, but others bearing golden promises for the human race. Now, whatever might be the talent with which Southey's successor performed his duty, there was a loss in one point for which no talent of mere execu-tion could make amends. The very prejudices of Southey tended to unity of feeling : they were in harmony with each other, and grew out of a strong moral feeling, which is the one sole secret for giving interest to a historical narration, fusing the incoherent details into one body, and carrying the reader fluently along the else monotonous recurrences and unmeaning details of military movements. A fine moral feeling, and a profound sympathy with elementary justice, is that which, in all Southey's historical writings, creates a soul under what else may well be denominated, Miltonically, "the ribs of death."

Now this, and a mind already made up even to obstinacy upon all public questions, were the peculiar qualifications which Southey brought to the task—qualifications not to be bought in any market, not to be compensated by any amount of mere intellectual talent, and almost impossible as the qualifications of a much younger man. As a pecuniary loss, though considerable, Southey was not unable to support it ; for he had a pension from Government before this time, and under the following circumstances :—Charles Wynne, the brother of Sir Watkin, the great autocrat of North Wales—that Charles Wynne who is almost equally well known for his knowledge of Parliamentary usage, which pointed him out to the notice of the House as an eligible person to fill the office of Speaker, and for his unfortunately shrill voice, which chiefly it was that defeated his claim ;* this Charles Wynne had felt himself deeply indebted to Southey's high-toned moral example, and to his wise counsels, during the time when both were students at Oxford, for the fortunate direction given to his own wavering impulses. This sense of obligation he endeavoured to express, by settling a pension upon Southey from his own funds. At length, upon the death of Mr. Pitt, in the beginning of 1806, an opening was made for the Fox and Grenville parties to come into office. Charles Wynne, as a person connected by marriage with the house of Grenville, and united with them in political opinions, shared

---

* Sir Watkin, the elder brother, had a tongue too large for his mouth ; Mr. C. Wynne, the younger, had a shrill voice, which at times rose into a scream. It became, therefore, a natural and current jest, to call the two brothers by the name of a well-known dish—viz., *bubble and squeak*.

in the golden shower ; he also received a place ; and upon
the strength of his improving prospects, he married : upon
which it occurred to Southey, that it was no longer right
to tax the funds of one who was now called upon to support an establishment becoming his rank.   Under that impression, he threw up his pension ; and upon *their* part, as
an acknowledgment of what they considered a delicate and
honourable sacrifice, the Grenvilles placed Southey upon
the national pension list.

What might be the exact colour of Southey's political
creed in this year (1807), it is difficult to say.   The great
revolution in his way of thinking upon such subjects, with
which he has been so often upbraided, as something equal
in delinquency to a deliberate tergiversation or moral apos-
tasy, could not have then taken place ; and of this I am
sure, from the following little anecdote connected with
this visit :—On the day after my own arrival at Greta
Hall, came Wordsworth, following upon my steps from
Penrith.   We dined and passed that evening with Southey.
The next morning, after breakfast, previously to leaving
Keswick, we were sitting in Southey's library ; and he was
discussing with Wordsworth the aspect of public affairs :
for my part I was far too diffident to take any part in
such a conversation, for I had no opinions at all upon
politics, nor any interest in public affairs, further than that
I had a keen sympathy with the national honour, gloried
in the name of Englishman, and had been bred up in a
frenzied horror of Jacobinism.   Not having been old
enough, at the first outbreak of the French Revolution, to
participate (as else, undoubtedly, I should have done) in
the golden hopes of its early dawn, my first youthful introduction to foreign politics had been in seasons and circumstances that taught me to approve of all I heard in

abhorrence of French excesses, and to worship the name of
Pitt ; otherwise, my whole heart had been so steadily
fixed on a different world from the world of our daily ex
perience, that, for some years, I had never looked into a
newspaper ; nor, if I cared something for the movement
made by nations from year to year, did I care one iota for
their movement from week to week.   Still, careless as I
was on these subjects, it sounded as a novelty to me, and
one which I had not dreamed of as a possibility, to hear
men of education and liberal pursuits—men, besides, whom
I regarded as so elevated in mind, and one of them as a
person charmed and consecrated from error—giving utterance to sentiments which seemed absolutely disloyal.   Yet
now I *did* hear—and I heard with an emotion of sorrow,
but a sorrow that instantly gave way to a conviction that
it was myself who lay under a delusion, and simply because

> "From Abelard it came "—

opinions avowed most hostile to the reigning family ; not
personally to them, but generally to a monarchical form of
government.   And that I could not be mistaken in my
impression, that my memory cannot have played me false,
is evident from one relic of the conversation which rested
upon my ear, and has survived to this day—thirty-and-two
years from the time.*   It had been agreed, that no good
was to be hoped for, as respected England, until the royal
family should be expatriated ; and Southey, jestingly, considering to what country they could be exiled, with mutual
benefit for that country and themselves, had supposed the
case—that, with a large allowance of money, such as

---

* Thirty-two years, observe, at the time when these parts were
waitten : but that time was at least fifteen years ago.

might stimulate beneficially the industry of a rising colony,
they should be transported to New South Wales ; which
project amusing his fancy, he had, with the readiness and
facility that characterize his mind, thrown *extempore* into
verse ; speaking off, as an improvisatore, about eight or
ten lines, of which the three last I perfectly remember, and
they were these :—

> " Therefore, old George, our king, we pray
>   Of thee forthwith to extend thy sway
>   Over the great Botanic Bay."

About these three I cannot be wrong ; for I remember
laughing with a sense of something peculiarly droll in the
substitution of the stilted phrase, " the great Botanic Bay,"
for our ordinary week-day name, Botany Bay, so redolent
of thieves and pickpockets.

Southey walked with us that morning for about five
miles on our road towards Grasmere, which brought us
to the southern side of Shoulthwaite Moss, and into the
sweet little Vale of Legberthwaite. And, by the way, he
took leave of us at the gate of a house, one amongst the
very few (five or six in all) just serving to redeem that valley from absolute solitude, which some years afterwards
became, in a slight degree, remarkable to me from two
little incidents by which it connected itself with my personal experiences. One was, perhaps, scarcely worth recording. It was simply this, that Wordsworth and myself having, through a long day's rambling, alternately
walked and ridden with a friend of his who happened to
have a travelling-carriage, and who was on his way to
Keswick, agreed to wait hereabouts until Wordsworth's
friend, in his abundant kindness, should send back his
carriage to take us, on our return to Grasmere, distant
about eight miles. It was a lovely summer evening ; but,

as it had happened that we ate our breakfast early, and
had eaten nothing at all throughout a long summer's day,
we agreed to "sorn" upon the goodman of the house,
whoever he might happen to be, Catholic or Protestant,
Jew, Gentile, or Mahometan, and to take any bone that he
would be pleased to toss to such hungry dogs as ourselves.
Accordingly we repaired to his gate; we knocked, and
forthwith it was opened to us by a man-mountain, who
listened benignantly to our request, and ushered us into a
comfortable parlour. All sorts of refreshments he continued to shower upon us for a space of two hours: it
became evident that our introducer was the master of the
house: we adored him in our thoughts as an earthly providence to hungry wayfarers; and we longed to make his
acquaintance. But for some inexplicable reason, that
must continue to puzzle all future commentators on Wordsworth and his history, our host never made his appearance
Could it be, we thought, that without the formality of
a sign, he, in so solitary a region, more than twenty-five
miles distant from Kendal (the only town worthy of
the name throughout the adjacent country), exercised
the functions of a landlord, and that we ought to pay
him for his most liberal hospitality? Never was such
a dilemma from the foundation of Legberthwaite. To
err, in either direction, was felonious: to go off without
paying, if he *were* an innkeeper, made us swindlers;
to offer payment, if he were not, and supposing that
he had been inundating us with his hospitable bounties,
simply in the character of a natural-born gentleman,
made us the most unfeeling of mercenary ruffians. In
the latter case we might expect a duel; in the former,
of course, the treadmill. We were deliberating on this
sad alternative, and I, for my part, was voting in **favour**

of the treadmill, when the sound of wheels was heard
and in one minute the carriage of Wordsworth's friend
drew up to the farmer's gate.   The crisis had now arrived,
and we perspired considerably ; when in came the frank
Cumberland lass who had been our attendant.   To her
we propounded our difficulty—and lucky it was we did so ;
for she assured us that her master was an *"awful"* man,
and would have "brained" us both if we had insulted him
with the offer of money.   She, however, honoured us by
accepting the price of some female ornament.

I made a memorandum at the time, to ascertain the
peculiar taste of this worthy Cumberland farmer, in order
that I might, at some future opportunity, express my
thanks to him for his courtesy ; but, alas ! for human
resolutions, I have not done so to this moment ; and is it
likely that he, perhaps sixty years old at that time (1813),
is alive at present, twenty-five years removed ?   Well, he
may be ; such a thing is possible, though I think *that*
exceedingly doubtful, considering the next anecdote relating to the same house :—Two, or it may be three, years
after this time, I was walking to Keswick from my own
cottage in Grasmere.   The distance was thirteen miles ;
the time just nine o'clock ; the night a cloudy moonlight,
and intensely cold.   I took the very greatest delight in
these nocturnal walks, through the silent valleys of Cumberland and Westmoreland ; and often at hours far later
than the present.   What I liked in this solitary rambling
was, to trace the course of the evening through its household hieroglyphics, from the windows which I passed or
saw ; to see the blazing fires shining through the windows
of houses, lurking in nooks far apart from neighbours :
sometimes in solitudes that seemed abandoned to the owl,
to catch the sounds of household mirth ; then, some miles

farther, to perceive the time of going to bed ; then the
gradual sinking to silence of the house ; then the drowsy
reign of the cricket ; at intervals, to hear church clocks or
a little solitary chapel bell, under the brows of mighty
hills, proclaiming the hours of the night, and flinging out
their sullen knells over the graves where " the rude fore-
f_thers of the hamlet slept "—where the strength and the
loveliness of Elizabeth's time, or Cromwell's, and through
so many fleeting generations that have succeeded, had long
ago sunk to rest.   Such was the sort of pleasure which I
reaped in my nightly walks ; of which, however, considering the suspicions of lunacy which it has sometimes awoke,
the less I say, perhaps, the better.   Nine o'clock it was—
and deadly cold as ever March night was made by the
keenest of black frosts, and by the bitterest of north winds
—when I drew towards the gate of our huge, hospitable,
and *awful* friend.   A little garden there was before the
house ; and in the centre of this garden was placed an
arm-chair ; upon which arm-chair was sitting composedly
—but I rubbed my eyes, doubting the very evidence of
my own eyesight—*a* or *the* huge man in his shirt-sleeves ;
yes, positively not sunning, but *mooning* himself—apricat-
ing himself in the occasional moonbeams ; and as if simple
star-gazing from a sedentary station were not sufficient on
such a night, absolutely pursuing his astrological studies,
I repeat, in his shirt-sleeves !   Could this be our hospitable friend, the man-mountain ?   Secondly, was it any
man at all ?   Might it not be a scarecrow dressed up
to frighten the birds ?   But from what—to frighten them
from what, at that season of the year ?   Yet, again, it
might be an ancient scarecrow, a superannuated scarecrow, far advanced in years.   But still, why should a
scarecrow, young or old, sit in an arm-chair ?   Suppose *I*

were to ask. Yet, where was the use of asking a scarecrow ? And, if not a scarecrow, where was the safety of
speaking too inquisitively, on his own premises, to the man-
mountain ? The old dilemma of the duel or the treadmill,
if I should intrude upon his grounds at night, occurred to
me ; and I watched the anomalous object in silence for some
minutes. At length the monster (for such at any rate it was,
scarecrow or not scarecrow) solemnly raised his hand to his
face, perhaps taking a pinch of snuff, and thereby settled
one question. But that having been settled, only irritated
my curiosity the more upon a second—viz., what hallucination of the brain was it that could induce a living
man to adopt so very absurd a line of conduct ? Once I
thought of addressing him thus :—Might I presume so far
upon your known courtesy to wayfaring strangers, as to
ask, Is it the Fiend who prompts you to sit in your shirt-
sleeves, as if meditating a *camisade*, or wooing *al fresco*
pleasures on such a night as this ? But, as Dr. Y., on com-
plaining that, whenever he looked out of the window, he
was sure to see Mr. X. lounging about the quadrangle, was
effectually parried by Mr. X. retorting, that, whenever he
lounged in the quadrangle, he was sure to see Dr. Y. looking out of the window ; so did I anticipate a puzzling re-
joinder from the former, with regard to my own motives
for haunting the roads as a nocturnal tramper, without any
rational object that I could make intelligible. I thought
also of the fate which attended the Calendars, and so many
other notorious characters in the " Arabian Nights," for
unseasonable questions, or curiosity too vivacious. And,
upon the whole, I judged it advisable to pursue my
journey in silence, considering the time of night, the
solitary place, and the fancy of our enormous friend for
"braining" those whom he regarded as ugly customers.

And thus it came about that this one house has been loaded in my memory with a double mystery, that too probably never *can* be explained; and I bequeath both mysteries to the twentieth century, as torments that have been prepared for the exercise of their carnal curiosity by the nineteenth.*

Of Southey, meantime, I had learned, upon this brief and hurried visit, so much in confirmation or in extension of my tolerably just preconceptions, with regard to his character and manners, as left me not a very great deal to add, and nothing at all to alter, through the many years which followed of occasional intercourse with his family, and domestic knowledge of his habits. A man of more serene and even temper could not be imagined; nor more uniformly cheerful in his tone of spirits; nor more unaffectedly polite and courteous in his demeanour to strangers; nor more hospitable in his own wrong—I mean by the painful sacrifices, which hospitality entailed upon him, of time, so exceedingly precious. In the still " weightier matters of the law," in cases that involved appeals to conscience and high moral principle, I believe Southey to be as exemplary a man as can ever have lived. Were it to his own instant ruin, I am satisfied that he would do justice and fulfil his duty under any possible difficulties, and through the very strongest temptations to do otherwise. For honour the most delicate, for integrity the firmest, and for generosity within the limits of prudence, Southey cannot well have a superior; and, in the lesser moralities, those which govern the daily habits, and transpire through the manners, he is certainly a better man—that is (with reference to the minor principle concerned), a more *amiable*

---

* "Aux Saumaises futurs préparer des tortures."—*Boileau.*

man—than Wordsworth.   He is less capable, for instance, of usurping an undue share of the conversation ; he is more uniformly disposed to be charitable in his transient collo- quial judgments upon doubtful actions of his neighbours ; more gentle and winning in his condescensions to inferior knowledge or powers of mind ; more willing to suppose it possible that he himself may have fallen into an error ; more tolerant of avowed indifference towards his own writings ; and, finally, if the reader will pardon so violent an anti-climax, much more ready to volunteer his assistance in carrying a lady's reticule or parasol.

As a more *amiable* man (taking that word partly in the French sense, partly also in the deeper English sense), it might be imagined that Southey would be a more eligible companion than Wordsworth.   But this is not so ; and chiefly for three reasons, which more than counterbalance Southey's great amiability : *first,* because the natural re- serve of Southey, which I have mentioned before, makes it peculiarly difficult to place yourself on terms of intimacy with him ; *secondly,* because the range of his conversation is more limited than that of Wordsworth—dealing less with life, and the interests of life—more exclusively with books ; *thirdly,* because the style of his conversation is less flowing and diffusive—less expansive—more apt to clothe itself in a keen, sparkling, aphoristic form ; consequently much sooner and more frequently coming to an abrupt close.   A sententious, epigrammatic form of delivering opinions has a certain effect of *clenching* a subject, which makes it diffi- cult to pursue it without a corresponding smartness of ex- pression, and something of the same antithetic point and equilibration of clauses.   Not that the reader is to suppose in Southey a showy master of rhetoric and colloquial sword- play, seeking to strike and to dazzle by his brilliant hits or

adroit evasions. The very opposite is the truth. He seeks,
indeed, to be effective, not for the sake of display, but as
the readiest means of retreating from display, and the necessity for display; feeling that his station in literature,
and his laurelled honours, make him a mark for the curiosity and interest of the company—that a standing appeal
is constantly turning to him for his opinion—a latent call
always going on for his voice on the question of the moment—he is anxious to comply with this requisition at as
slight a cost as may be of thought and time. His heart is
continually reverting to his wife, viz., his library; and that
he may waste as little effort as possible upon his conver-
sational exercises—that the little he wishes to say may
appear pregnant with much meaning—he finds it advantageous, and, moreover, the style of his mind naturally
prompts him to adopt a trenchant, pungent, aculeated form
of terse, glittering, stenographic sentences—sayings which
have the air of laying down the law without any *locus peni-
tentiæ* or privilege of appeal, but are not meant to do so;
in short, aiming at brevity for the company as well as for
himself, by cutting off all opening for discussion and desul-
tory talk, through the sudden winding up that belongs to a
sententious aphorism. The hearer feels that " the record is
closed;" and he has a sense of this result as having been
accomplished by something like an oracular laying down of
the law *ex cathedra :* but this is an indirect collateral impression from Southey's manner, and far from the one he
meditates or wishes. An oracular manner he does certainly
affect in certain dilemmas of a languishing or loitering conversation; not the peremptoriness, meantime, not the im-
periousness of the oracle, is what he seeks for, but its
brevity, its despatch, its conclusiveness.

Finally, as a fourth reason why Southey is less fitted
K 2

for a genial companion than Wordsworth, his spirits have
been, of late years, in a lower key than those of the
latter. The tone of Southey's animal spirits was never
at any time raised beyond the standard of an ordinary
sympathy; there was in him no tumult, no agitation of
passion: his organic and constitutional sensibilities were
healthy, sound, perhaps strong—but not profound, not
excessive. Cheerful he was, and animated at all times;
but he levied no tributes on the spirits or the feelings
beyond what all people could furnish. One reason why
his bodily temperament never, like that of Wordsworth,
threw him into a state of tumultuous excitement, which
required intense and elaborate conversation to work off
the excessive fervour, was, that, over and above his far less
fervid constitution of mind and body, Southey rarely took
any exercise; he led a life as sedentary, except for the
occasional excursions in summer (extorted from his sense
of kindness and hospitality), as that of a city artisan.
And it was surprising to many people, who did not know
by experience the prodigious effect upon the mere bodily
health of regular and congenial mental labour, that Southey
should be able to maintain health so regular, and cheerfulness so uniformly serene. Cheerful, however, he was, in
those early years of my acquaintance with him; but it was
manifest to a thoughtful observer, that his golden equani-
mity was bound up in a threefold chain—in a conscience
clear of all offence, in the recurring enjoyments from his
honourable industry, and in the gratification of his parental
affections. If in this trinity of chords any one should give
way, at that point (it seemed) would enter the ruin of his
tranquillity. He had a son at that time, Herbert* Southey,

---

* Why he was called Herbert, if my young readers inquire, I must

a child in petticoats when I first knew him, very interesting even then, but annually putting forth fresh blossoms
of unusual promise, that made even indifferent people fear
for the safety of one so finely organized, so delicate in his
sensibilities, and so prematurely accomplished. As to his
father, it became evident that he lived almost in the light
of young Herbert's smiles, and that the very pulses of his
heart played in unison to the sound of his son's laughter.
There was in his manner towards this child, and towards
this only, something that marked an excess of delirious
doating, perfectly unlike the ordinary chastened movements
of Southey's affections ; and something also which indicated
a vague fear about him ; a premature unhappiness, as if
already the inaudible tread of calamity could be divined, as
if already he had lost him ; which feeling, for the latter
years of the boy's life, seemed to poison, for his father, the
blessing of his presence.*

Herbert became, with his growing years, a child of more
and more hope ; but, therefore, the object of more and

---

reply that I do not exactly know ; because I know of reasons too
many by half why he might have been so called. Derwent Coleridge,
the second son of S. T. Coleridge, and first cousin of Herbert Southey,
was so called from the Lake of Keswick, commonly styled Derwentwater, which gave the title of Earl to the noble and the noble-minded
family of the Ratcliffes, who gave up, like heroes and martyrs, their
lives and the finest estates in England for one who was incapable of
appreciating the service. One of the islands on this lake is dedicated
to St. Herbert, and this *might* have given a name to Southey's first-
born child. But it is more probable that he derived that name from
Dr. Herbert, chaplain to the English factory at Lisbon, and uncle to
the laureate.

* Without meaning it, or perceiving it at the time of writing, I
have here expressed the fine sentiment (psychologically so true) of
Shakspere in one of his sonnets—

" And weep to *have* what I so fear to *lose.*

more fearful misgiving. He read and read ; and he became at last

"A very learned youth"—

to borrow a word from his uncle's beautiful poem on the
wild boy, who fell into a heresy, whilst living under the
patronage of a Spanish grandee, and, finally, escaped from
a probable martyrdom, by sailing up a great American
river, wide as any sea, after which he was never heard of
again. The learned youth of the river Greta had an earlier
and more sorrowful close to his career. Possibly from want
of exercise, combined with inordinate exercise of the cerebral
organs, a disease gradually developed itself in the heart. It
was not a mere disorder in the functions, it was a disease
in the structure of the organ, and admitted of no permanent
relief ; consequently of no final hope. He died ; and with
him died for ever the golden hopes, the radiant felicity,
and the internal serenity of the unhappy father. It was
from Southey himself, speaking without external signs of
agitation, calmly, dispassionately, almost coldly, but with
the coldness of a settled misery, that I heard, whilst accom-
panying him through Grasmere on his road homewards to
Keswick, from some visit he had been paying to Wordsworth at Rydal Mount, his final feelings months after the
event, as connected with that loss. For him, in this world,
he said, happiness there could be none ; for that his tenderest affections, the very deepest by many degrees which he
had ever known, were now buried in the grave with his
youthful and too brilliant Herbert.

.   .   .   .

A circumstance which, as much as anything, expounded
to the very eye the characteristic distinctions between
Wordsworth and Southey, and would not suffer a stranger
to forget it for a moment, was the insignificant place

and consideration allowed to the small book-collection of
the former, contrasted with the splendid library of the
latter. The two or three hundred volumes of Wordsworth
occupied a little, homely painted bookcase, fixed into one
of two shallow recesses formed on each side of the fireplace by the projection of the chimney in the little sitting-
room up stairs. They were ill bound, or not bound at
all—in boards, sometimes in tatters ; many were imperfect as to the number of volumes, mutilated as to the
number of pages : sometimes, where it seemed worth while,
the defects being supplied by manuscript ; sometimes not :
in short, everything showed that the books were for use,
and not for show ; and their limited amount showed that
their possessor must have independent sources of enjoyment to fill up the major part of his time. In reality,
when the weather was tolerable, I believe that Wordsworth rarely resorted to his books (unless, perhaps, to
some little pocket edition of a poet which accompanied
him in his rambles), except in the evenings, or after
he had tired himself by walking. On the other hand,
Southey's collection occupied a separate room, the largest,
and every way the most agreeable, in the house ; and this
room was styled, and not ostentatiously (for it really
merited that name), the Library. The house itself—Greta
Hall—stood upon a little eminence (as I have before mentioned), overhanging the river Greta. There was nothing
remarkable in its internal arrangements : in all respects,
it was a very plain, unadorned family dwelling ; large
enough, by a little contrivance, to accommodate two, or,
in some sense, three families, viz., Mr. Southey and *his*
family ; Coleridge and *his ;* together with Mrs. Lovell, who,
when her son was with her, might be said to compose
a third. Mrs. Coleridge, **Mrs.** Southey, and Mrs. Lovell

were sisters ; all having come originally from Bristol ;
and, as the different sets of children in this one house
had each two several aunts, each of the ladies, by turns,
assuming that relation twice over, it was one of Southey's
many amusing jests, to call the hill on which Greta Hall
was placed, the *ant-hill*. Mrs. Lovell was the widow of
Mr. Robert Lovell, who had published a volume of poems,
in conjunction with Southey, somewhere about the year
1797, under the signatures of Bion and Moschus. This
lady, having one only son, did not require any large suite
of rooms ; and the less so, as her son quitted her, at an
early age, to pursue a professional education. The house
had, therefore, been divided (not by absolute partition
into two distinct apartments,* but by an amicable distribution of rooms) between the two families of Coleridge
and Southey ; Coleridge had a separate study, which was
distinguished by nothing except by an organ amongst its
furniture, and by a magnificent view from its window (or
windows), if that could be considered a distinction, in a
situation whose local necessities presented you with magnificent objects in whatever direction you might happen to
turn your eyes.

In the morning, the two families might live apart ; but
they met at dinner, and in a common drawing-room ; and
Southey's library, in both senses of the word, viz., as a
room, or as a collection of books—was placed at the

---

* " *Into two distinct apartments :*"—The word apartment meaning,
in effect, a *com*partment of a house, already includes, in its proper
sense, a suite of rooms ; and it is a mere vulgar error, arising out of
the ambitious usage of lodging-house keepers, to talk of one family or
one establishment occupying apartments, in the plural. The queen's
apartment at St. James's or at Versailles. not the queen's apartments,
is the correct expression.

service of all the ladies alike. However, they did not
intrude upon him, except in cases where they wished for
a larger reception-room, or a more interesting place for
suggesting the topics of conversation. Interesting this
room was, indeed, and in a degree not often rivalled. The
library—the collection of books, I mean, which formed
the most conspicuous part of its furniture within—was in
all senses a good one. The books were chiefly English,
Spanish, and Portuguese ; well selected, being the great
cardinal classics of the three literatures ; fine copies ; and
decorated externally with a reasonable elegance, so as
to make them in harmony with the other embellishments
of the room. This effect was aided by the horizontal
arrangement upon brackets of many rare manuscripts—
Spanish or Portuguese. Made thus gay within, the room
stood in little need of attractions from without. Yet,
even upon the gloomiest day of winter, the landscape
from the different windows was too permanently commanding in its grandeur, too essentially independent of the
seasons, to fail in fascinating the gaze of the coldest
and dullest spectator. The Lake of Derwentwater in
one direction, with its lovely islands—a lake about nine
miles in circuit, and shaped pretty much like a boy's kite ;
the Lake of Bassenthwaite in another ; the mountains of
Newlands shaping themselves as pavilions ; the gorgeous
confusion of Borrowdale just revealing its sublime chaos
through the narrow vista of its gorge ; all these objects lay
in different angles to the front ; whilst the sullen rear, not
visible on this side of the house, was closed by the vast and
towering masses of Skiddaw and Blencathara—mountains
which are rather to be considered as frontier barriers, and
chains of hilly ground, cutting the county of Cumberland
into great chambers and different climates, than as insu-

lated eminences ; so vast is the area which they occupy.
This grand panorama of mountain scenery, so varied, so
extensive, and yet having the delightful feeling about it of
a deep seclusion and dell-like sequestration from the world
—a feeling which, in the midst of so expansive an area
spread out below his windows, could not have been
sustained by any barriers less elevated than Skiddaw or
Blencathara ; this congregation of hill and lake, so wide,
and yet so prison-like, in its separation from all beyond it,
lay for ever under the eyes of Southey.   His position
locally (and in some respects intellectually) reminded one of
Gibbon's.   The little town of Keswick and its adjacent
lake bore something of the same relation to mighty London
that Lausanne and its lake may be thought to bear towards
tumultuous Paris.   Southey, like Gibbon, was a miscella-
neous scholar ; he, like Gibbon, of vast historical research ;
he, like Gibbon, signally industrious, and patient, and elaborate in collecting the materials for his historical works.
Like Gibbon, he had dedicated a life to literature ; like
Gibbon, he had gathered to the shores of a beautiful lake,
remote from great capitals, a large, or at least sufficient
library (in each case, I believe, the library ranged, as to
numerical amount, between seven and ten thousand) ; and,
like Gibbon, he was the most accomplished littérateur
amongst the erudite scholars of his time, and the most of
an erudite scholar amongst the accomplished littérateurs.
After all these points of agreement known, it remains as a
pure advantage on the side of Southey—a mere *lucro
ponatur*—that he was a poet ; brilliant in his descriptive
powers, and fascinating in his narration.   It is remarkable
amongst the series of parallelisms which have been or might
be pursued between two men, that both had the honour
of retreating by deliberate choice from a parliamentary

life :* Gibbon, after some silent and inert experience of that
warfare ; Southey, with a prudent foresight of the ruin to
his health and literary usefulness, won vicariously from the
experience of others.

I took leave of Southey in 1807, at the descent into the
Vale of Legberthwaite, as I have already noticed. One
year afterwards, I became a permanent resident in his
neighbourhood ; and although, on various accounts, my
intercourse with him was at no time very strict, partly from
my reluctance to levy any tax on time so precious and
so fully employed ; partly in consequence of the distance
(thirteen miles) which divided us, I was yet on such terms
for the next ten or eleven years, that I might, in a qualified
sense, call myself his friend.

---

* It illustrated the national sense of Southey's comprehensive
talents, and of his political integrity, that Lord Radnor (the same
who, under the courtesy title of Lord Folkestone, had distinguished
himself for very democratic politics in the House of Commons, and
had even courted the technical designation of *radical*) was the man
who offered to bring in Southey for a borough dependent on *his* influence. Sir Robert Peel, under the same sense of Southey's merits,
had offered him a baronetcy. Both honours were declined on the
same prudential considerations, and with the same perfect disregard
of all temptations from personal vanity.

for a man to appropriate this word inadvertently. I, therefore, greatly *understated* the case against Coleridge, instead of giving to it an undue emphasis. Secondly, in stating it at all, I did so (as at the time I explained) in pure kindness. Well I knew that, from the direction in which English philosophic studies were now travelling, sooner or later these appropriations of Coleridge must be detected ; and I felt that it would break the force of the discovery, as an unmitigated sort of police detection, if first of all it had been announced by one who, in the same breath, was professing an unshaken faith in Coleridge's philosophic power. It could not be argued that one of those who most fervently admired Coleridge, had professed such feelings only because he was ignorant of Coleridge's obligations to others. Here was a man who had actually for himself, unguided and unwarned, discovered these obligations ; and yet, in the very act of making that discovery, this man clung to his original feelings and faith. But thirdly, I must inform the reader, that I was not, nor ever had been, the "friend" of Coleridge in any sense which could have a right to restrain my frankest opinions upon his merits.

I never had lived in such intercourse with Coleridge as to give me an opportunity of becoming his friend. To *him* I owed nothing at all ; but to the public, to the body of his own readers, every writer owes the truth, and especially on a subject so important as that which was then before me.

With respect to the comparatively trivial case of Pythagoras, an author of great distinction in literature and in the Anglican Church has professed himself unable to understand what room there could be for plagiarism in a case where the solution ascribed to Coleridge was amongst the commonplaces of ordinary English academic tuition. Locally this may have been so ; but

---

For I remember to this hour several Latin quotations made by Schelling, and repeated by Coleridge as his own, which neither I nor my too rigorous reviewer had drawn out for public exposure. As regarded myself, it was quite sufficient that I had indicated the grounds, and opened the paths, on which the game must be sought ; that I left the rest of the chase to others, was no subject for blame, but part of my purpose ; and, under the circumstances, very much a matter of necessity.

In taking leave of this affair, I ought to point out a ground of complaint against my reviewer under his present form of expression, which I am sure could not have been designed. It happened that I had forgotten the particular title of Schelling's work ; naturally enough, in a situation where no foreign books could be had, I quoted it under a false one. And this inevitable error of mine on a matter so entirely irrelevant is so described, that the neutral reader might suppose me to have committed against Coleridge the crime of Lauder against Milton—that is, taxing him with plagiarism by referring, not to real works of Schelling, but to pretended works, of which the very titles were forgeries of my own. This, I am sure, my unknown critic never could have meant. The plagiarisms were really there ; more and worse in circumstances than any denounced by myself ; and of all men, the "Blackwood" critic was the most bound to proclaim this ; or else what became of his own clamorous outcry ? Being, therefore, such as I had represented, of what consequence was the special title of the German volume to which these plagiarisms were referred ?

hardly, I conceive, in so large an extent as to make that solution *publici juris*. Yet, however this may be, no help is given to Coleridge ; since, according to Mr. Poole's story, whether the interpretation of the riddle were or were *not* generally diffused, Coleridge claimed it for his own.

Finally—for distance from the press and other inconveniences of unusual pressure oblige me to wind up suddenly—the whole spirit of my record at the time (twenty years ago), and in particular the special allusion to the last Duke of Ancaster's case, as one which ran parallel to Coleridge's, involving the same propensity to appropriate what generally were trifles in the midst of enormous and redundant wealth, survives as an indication of the *animus* with which I approached this subject, starting even from the assumption I was bound to consider myself under the restraints of friendship—which, for the second time let me repeat, I was *not*. In reality, the notes contributed to the Aldine edition of the "Biographia Literaria," by Coleridge's admirable daughter, have placed this whole subject in a new light ; and in doing this, have unavoidably reflected some degree of justification upon myself. Too much so, I understand to be the feeling in some quarters. This lamented lady is thought to have shown partialities in her distributions of praise and blame upon this subject. I will not here enter into that discussion. But, as respects the justification of her father, I regard her mode of argument as unassailable. Filial piety the most tender never was so finely reconciled with candour towards the fiercest of his antagonists. Wherever the plagiarism was undeniable, she has allowed it ; whilst palliating its faultiness by showing the circumstances under which it arose. But she has also opened a new view of other circumstances under which an apparent plagiarism arose that was not real. I myself, for instance, knew cases where Coleridge gave to young ladies a copy of verses, headed thus—"Lines on ——, from the German of Hölty." Other young ladies made transcripts of these lines ; and, caring nothing for the German authorship, naturally fathered them upon Coleridge, the translator. These lines were subsequently circulated as Coleridge's, and as if on Coleridge's own authority. Thus arose many cases of apparent plagiarism. And, lastly, as his daughter most truly reports, if he took—he gave. Continually he fancied other men's thoughts his own ; but such were the confusions of his memory, that continually, and with even graeter liberality, he ascribed his own thoughts to others.